DIRTY WHITE BOY

Tales of Soho

DIRTY WHITE BOY
Tales of Soho

Clayton Littlewood

CLEIS PRESS

Published in the United States by Cleis Press Inc.,
P.O. Box 14697, San Francisco, California 94114.
Printed in the United States.

Cover design: Joe Pearson and Scott Idleman
Woman in doorway photo: © Paul Edmond
Angels photo: © ChrisJepson.com
Sebastian Horsley photo: © Marcio Madeira
Shop photo: © Kate Friend
Text design: Frank Wiedemann
Cleis logo art: Juana Alicia
First Edition.
10 9 8 7 6 5 4 3 2 1

A Note on Language appears on page 281.

Library of Congress Cataloging-in-Publication Data

Littlewood, Clayton.
Dirty White Boy : tales of Soho / Clayton Littlewood. -- 1st ed.
    p. cm.
ISBN 978-1-57344-330-2 (pbk. : alk. paper)
1. Dirty White Boy (Retail store) 2. Gay business enterprises--Social aspects--England--London. 3. Soho (London, England) I. Title.

HD2359.5.G7L57 2008
381'.10866420942132--dc22

                                        2008019377

To the two men in my life—Dale and Jorge

August 7th, 2006: Soho, London

OPEN THE SHOP AT 11 A.M. WE SIT THERE FOR FIVE HOURS before we sell a thing. Then a two-hour whirlwind of activity. Firstly, two South African queens; one in a blue plaid shirt and the other with a "Michael Bolton" hairstyle. I point out the new ICE-B collection and a chic kid-glove leather jacket.

"Hideous! But there again, what do I know about fashion. Do you like this, darling?" says Mr. Plaid as he holds up a floral print dress shirt. Mr. Bolton flutters his eyelashes and the deal is done.

Minutes later, in falls a ruddy-faced man reeking of booze. "I want a lot of clothes—but can you slip in a free T-shirt? What trousers do you have to wear in Vegas? Do you have my size? What about these?" The man obviously has no intention of buying. You learn to spot the fake customers from the real ones quite quickly. "Oh, and I want a big discount. Can you arrange that?"

After 10 minutes of this I can see Jorge is getting annoyed.

"Would you walk into Harrods and ask for a discount before you'd even spent a penny?"

"Don't be mad!" Mr. Discount replies. "Look, I like you. Are you American? I'll spend a lot of money once I sober up. I'm very rich. I own a fairground with a Wurlitzer!"

We close at 8:30. Not making quite enough to pay off last month's rent but enough for a few drinks at Comptons. Drinking outside, we get chatting to a 6'5" tall guy dressed in black with a large silver chain around his neck.

"You and your boyfriend looked very dressed-up at last week's Soho Pride," says Jorge.

Then I remember who they were. One had "SEX" written on his shirt, the other, "PIG." One black, one white. Both in leather. Both with their bums exposed to the world.

"Yes, we were rather, weren't we? Well, I do think it's important to make an effort on the big days, don't you? After all, if you can't dress up on a day like that, when can you?" he says in a very refined voice.

"My name's Clayton," I say, looking up.

"Mine's Clinton," he says, looking down. It turns out that Clinton's a priest at a church in Kings Cross.

"Are there many gay men in your church?"

"Oh, yes, the Bishop is known as Bishop Beryl. And then there's Bishop Wendy. She's in San Francisco at the moment for her annual 'hands-on healing' session."

"What does that involve?" I ask, mystified.

"Well, dear, she loves the sex clubs, so I'll leave it to your imagination!"

August 12th, 2006: A Bad Day for Hats and Cracks

Saturday starts off on the wrong foot.

At 2 P.M. a tall, dark-haired, muscular, tattooed guy and his smaller friend walk into the shop. The muscular one has one of those loud personalities that demand attention. Turns out he's a well-known hooker with his own pay-as-you-view website.

"I can't wait to be in Ibiza next week, cocktail in one hand, snorting coke, wearing these shorts of yours!" he says in a broad Liverpudlian accent. "I'm gonna get me one of these hats too," he says, fingering a white, handmade French import.

His friend has other ideas. "That ain't worth a hundred pounds," he says disapprovingly. "You ain't gonna get that, are you?"

This banter goes on for a while until the short one leaves rather abruptly.

"He thinks he can boss me around, but I'll buy what I fuckin' want with my money!" says Mr. Tattoo. He then proceeds to pull his low-rise jeans down and show me the Celtic tattoo that starts at the top of his bum and descends into his hairy cleft. "Do you think my ass is getting fat?"

Having never seen his ass before to make a comparison, and being keen on keeping in his good books until the sale has gone through, I reply, "No, it looks quite nice from here."

Pleased with himself, he skilfully manoeuvres his buns over the tie display case, pulling his jeans down even further. "Really?" he says, his bum leaving a greasy smear on the glass.

"Of course," I reply, counting out the roll of cash he throws my way in a pay-as-you-view reversal.

Thirty minutes later, his friend walks back in. "He wants his money back! This hat's only worth five pounds!" he says, waving it in my direction.

"I'm sorry that you think that. Unfortunately we can't give refunds. It states on the receipt that you can only exchange the item for a store credit."

"He doesn't want a store credit, he wants his money back!"

This goes on for about five minutes. I'm not going to back down. We need every penny to survive. "Look, I happen to know that your friend did want the hat! It was you who didn't want him to have it. Why didn't your friend come in and ask for his money back if he was that disappointed?"

He spins round and stomps out. Did I handle that well? I sit there on the display case, pondering.

"It's called buyer's remorse," says Jorge later. "Someone will buy an item and they quickly regret it. Whether you refund them depends on the scenario."

"But did I do the right thing?"

"Well, you made the decision that you thought was right at the time."

I'm not so sure. Business is slow all day. On a Saturday too. Supposedly our best day of the week. It feels like I put a shopping curse on the day.

Falling off to sleep that night, I imagine Mr. Tattoo pulling down his jeans seductively on his pay-as-you-view site, revealing his golden Ibiza-tanned buns with "Don't Shop at Dirty White Boy!" stencilled across them.

August 16th, 2006: Daddy's Asian Boy

By 4:30 P.M. we haven't taken a penny. By 9 P.M. we are up to a thousand. Thank God for prostitution! Whenever a Sugar Daddy comes in with a chicken, we know the till will ring. We must have had half of QX in since February.

Today's big spender is a Daddy, in his eighties, shopping for his Asian boy. The boy is tall and slim, with a lisp. He tries on the Costume National low-rise jeans from Paris, Iceberg "hand-sewn" T-shirts, and Armand Basi polos. But after an hour Daddy decides that boy looks better in the Gianfranco Ferre white embroidered dress shirt, so a sale is made.

Half an hour later, boy returns with an Asian accomplice.

"Can I swap shirt for something else? I took shirt to please friend but it not my style." So everything has to be unpacked all over again.

It still amazes me how the line "Your ass looks good in that" can turn the tide. Some queens simper and coo. Some give a haughty look. Some pretend they haven't heard a thing. But most end up buying. Boy goes into overdrive on hearing the "ass" line, turning into a Chinese Naomi, parading up and down the aisles, although his accomplice has other ideas.

"We want big discount!"

I explain that almost 75 percent of the Spring/Summer items are half price, but Boy 2 wants a discount on a discount.

"Look" I say, slightly firmly, but still with a hint of flirtatiousness to keep their eyes batting, "to get the items you want you'd only need to add a bit of cash to the total. After all, Daddy bought the first one." They settle on a credit note.

"We be back—we like it here!" they say in unison as they sashay out of the shop.

August 17th, 2006: I'm a Bear!

Old Compton Street is closed to traffic from 6 P.M. to 8 P.M. because of a bomb scare in Comptons. Apparently a queen left her Gucci handbag in the toilet.

As we drink outside, two customers, Abdullah from Abu Dhabi, who's twisted his ankle spinning round at XXL and landing on a bear (you'd have thought it would be a soft landing), and what sounds like "Brohallah" from Lebanon, join us.

"We don't have a real gay scene in Abu Dhabi," says the bearded Abdullah. "I didn't even realise what a bear was until last night, and then I find out I am one!"

August 18th, 2006: 24/7 at Costa

From the early hours until very late at night, amongst the tourists, the waifs, and strays, there are distinct groups of people seated outside Costa coffee shop, on the corner of Old Compton Street and Dean Street.

In the morning it's the financially solvent gay man, living local, "working from home," flicking through the *Independent* or surfing the net. iPod, Nokia, BlackBerry, Dell. Voicemail. Always connected. Never sleeps. Watching the markets. Grande cappuccino and a low-fat blueberry muffin.

By 3 P.M. the hookers arrive. A combination of Brazilians and, er, more...Brazilians. It's not unusual to see a gaggle of them nursing the same latte for two-three hours, watching for prey below the red-lit coffee sign. Like a mini Amsterdam; their heads move from right to left and left to right, like leering Wimbledon spectators in slow motion. Thus Old Compton Street repeats itself every few decades for a new gay generation.

The clothes shop at the end of the street, Swank, was in the 1930s/40s known as the Black Cat. It was in this coffee shop, immortalised in *The Naked Civil Servant*, that Quentin Crisp and Bermondsey Lizzie sipped at their tea for hours on end while discussing the trade in Dean Street. I'm sure the hookers at Costa have similar discussions today.

At 6 P.M. the middle-management "business gays" arrive; tattoos and piercings hidden beneath Boss shirts. Manbags a-go-go. It's just a medium frappuccino to go with the "dress-down Friday" chinos. Only 30 minutes to spare before Body Pump at 3rd Space. No time to chat, darling. Love you too. Air kisses. See you at Barcode!

The drunken hen night and "We love the gays" girls' brigade attack the street from 10 P.M. By 11 P.M., having already downed one too many Smirnoff Ices, they're ready to detox at Costa over a "cuppa." We've closed the shop by then, so my analysis of this particular species is limited, but I am able to report that there is usually one left standing, clutching a Camp Attack GAY flyer, singing along to a Will Young cover, wrapped around the nearby lamppost into the earlier hours.

When I peer out the window the next morning, apart

from the beer deliveries for the Admiral Duncan, all is quiet again and Soho manages to grab a few minutes of valuable shut-eye.

August 22nd, 2006: Theft

Why are the gangs who steal from the shop always black? After six months of being in business my political correctness is rapidly evaporating.

Since we've opened we've had two gang attacks, one big credit card fraud, and last week two expensive items went missing after three black queens had been in. Unfortunately they managed to pick a moment when Jorge was downstairs and I was swamped upstairs. Jorge, who can spot a missing item at 50 paces, noticed immediately that two Ferre shirts were missing. I blamed myself. I had a suspicion that something untoward was happening. One of the queens had gone into the changing room and I wasn't sure how many items he'd taken.

They operate in groups. Two will distract you while one is stealing. In this instance the one in the changing room removed the security tags and dumped the tags on the chair. He even had the audacity to ask me on his way out to save two items for him that he would collect later.

It's hard to describe how you feel after. Stupid, gullible, angry. We've been working seven days a week for six months to try and make this shop work. We've sunk in every penny we've had. It's affected our relationship, health, and social life. God knows when we'll be in a position to take a holiday. As we sometimes sleep at the premises, it's like waiting inside your home, around the clock, to be robbed. It can get really stressful.

Yesterday Jorge was outside the shop having a cigarette and I noticed a fracas developing outside. One of the queens had minced past yelling a "Hey, girl!" number at him. Well, he wished he hadn't. I jumped up from behind the desk and we both screamed at him.

"You or your friends ever set foot round here again, we'll break your fucking legs, you Goddamn piece of fucking shit!" (Or words to that effect.)

Screaming definitely helped. We do have a police panic button, and a metal pole behind the desk as a next step. Let's hope it never comes to that...

August 23rd, 2006: Flirting and Friendship

Sometimes customers can mistake friendliness for friendship, which, if not kept in check, can involve a customer chatting away for 30 minutes without spending a penny. You quickly learn how to overcome this so that the wad of cash still ends up in your greasy palm. Here's what we do...

The first method is to try and manoeuvre the conversation back to clothes (and away from their fluctuating weight, boyfriend's infidelity, favourite piercing, etc.). This is a skilled art. The conversation must be steered very gently so it doesn't have the feel of a hard sell. It's no good saying "This Costume National black polo would look great with your dark jeans" as they tearfully recount the hymn from their cat's recent funeral. A more subtle approach is required. I would suggest bowing your head very slightly, starting the conversation along the lines of "Allow me to take your mind off your loss..." while holding up a First Collection cashmere knit.

The second approach is to try and slowly extract yourself from the conversation. Again, this is easier said than done. Trying to wind down a customer on Day 3 of their 14-day holiday in Maspalomas Beach is difficult. From a customer's point of view, however, they feel that they've gained a friend. This is good. In my case, if they don't buy, you can end up feeling like you've prostituted yourself for 30 minutes.

As I steam-press the shirts this morning and the condensation begins to smother the windows, it crosses my mind that I'd probably have to flirt less, and the shop would be far more profitable, if we transformed it into a gay sauna.

Undressing could be more profitable than dressing. Hmmm. I wonder where we could get hold of designer cum towels?

August 23rd, 2006: Rant

There's an overweight Pakistani man, dyed hair, in his fifties, who's come into the shop five times now to ask if we would like to sell our lease. Apparently he has two supermarkets in the West End already.

Now, our location has a history of businesses opening and closing very quickly. In the early 20th century it was the location for a succession of grocery shops. In the 80s there were a succession of clothes shops and peep show booths. In the 90s, it was the bar Minty's, owned by scene queen Minty, and the previous business was our landlady's, selling underwear (until she fell foul with Westminster Council after they found she was also selling dildoes and poppers in the basement). We even had a middle-aged gentleman in the shop last week walking round looking at everything but the clothes. When I asked if I could help him, he told me he used to dine in our shop when he was a boy and it was a very well-known Italian restaurant, frequented by Charlie Chaplin.

So I can understand someone thinking that our shop may soon be up for grabs, as businesses just don't seem to last very long here. In fact, we could be the next to go. We're late with the VAT bill, a month behind with the rent; designers are queuing up to be paid. The list goes on. And now, on top of everything else, we have this vulture circling.

To make matters worse, whenever he comes in, the shop is empty. So he walks in with this huge smile on his face, as if to say *You won't be here much longer, guys, just sign here when you're ready*. Well, he left with his tail between his legs this morning. "Get the fuck outta here! We've got your details!" said Jorge, pointing at the door.

Mr. 7-Eleven gave us a sickly smile, looked around as though sizing up the walls for vegetable shelving, and left. There is no way we'll hand the lease over to him, whatever happens.

August 24th, 2006: Monster Cock

"Hey, honey! I've gotta get myself something pretty to wear. I've been wearing this tired old top for four hours now and my new man's coming to meet me here. Quick, what you got?"

Chico is a very colourful, Afro-Caribbean American, based in London. Decked out in Gucci, D&G, Prada. You name it, he flaunts it. And he's become one of our regular customers.

Over the past few months I've got to know quite a lot about Chico. Turns out he was once a Diana Ross impersonator who married rich, but his boyfriend died. Thus he was left with a large amount of money, two properties, and a broken heart. The perfect aphrodisiac for a QX hooker.

The first time Chico came in the shop, he brought Mukhtar. Mukhtar, whose photo had been splattered over the centrefold of our gay weekly magazine QX the previous month, had become the talk of the town, primarily because of his 9-by-8-inch "monster cock."

Now, normally, when the QX hookers describe themselves in 9-inch terms you know the measuring stick has probably started at the lower end of their stretched ball bag. In Mustapha's case stretching wasn't required, as the shape of the cock suggested some kind of surgical enhancement. So much so that what was left resembled a throbbing Bride of Wildenstein.

Strangely enough, last week we were also visited by two other well-known London sex acts, a "self-fister" and a "self-sucker."

Now, we do have a shop policy of asking anyone who comes into the shop with coffee to leave the cup on the side table. Similarly, if a customer is eating, we ask them not to handle the clothes, as a slight grease stain on an expensive shirt can mean we're out of pocket big time. So when Self-fister came in I was tempted to ask him to please wash his hands before handling the clothing, as tomato-skin stains on the cashmere knits can be a bugger to remove. Self-fister was accompanied by an older gentleman who looked like Daddy, but could have just as well have been his full-time manicurist. Anyway, I digress.

So for a month Mukhtar was Chico's escort, and whenever Chico and Mukhtar came in, Chico would buy Mukhtar a little "token." Over the course of a month these tokens came to quite an amount, and as we got to know each other more, with each hooker who came along, I started to feel sorry for Chico.

"Girl, this is the one! I haven't felt like this for so long!"

One night in the Village, though, Chico broke down and cried on my shoulder. He cried about the last six months spent with his dying boyfriend; how he'd nursed him to the bitter end; the family harrowing him for their share of the will; and how he still has so much love left to give. I wanted to tell him what was on my mind about the hookers, but it didn't seem right to spoil the moment.

August 25th, 2006: Directions

If I could have a fiver for every person who's asked me for directions. Standing in the shop doorway for any length of time is like waving a red flag at a bull. Literally one after the other. Every Tom, Dick, and Harry bombarding you with questions.

"I'm looking for LVPO!" "Do you know where the Prince Edward Theatre is?" "Can you tell me where Soho House/Bar/Hotel is?" Even "Where's Soho?" (I point to the floor) and "Where are the hookers?" (I point to the brothel above).

To anyone watching me from a distance, I must look

like an air traffic control man with Tourette's (in a designer uniform).

For the most part I don't mind helping out, as you do get to meet a varied cross section of lost souls. But after six months of acting like a walking information booth, to relieve the boredom, I have started to play with my audience.

"Do you know where Chinatown is?"

"Yes, thank you!"

It's quite easy to take this even further. As they stumble forward, like something from *Dawn of the Dead*, mumbling the desired location, I wait until they hit the two-foot barrier, then try and get in there first. "Do you know the way to Big Ben?" I shout. In a few cases they are so thrown off track that they do a double take, turn right round, and stumble off.

Mind you, I'm sometimes thrown off guard myself and have to admit defeat, bow my head, and apologise. If any readers have the answers to this week's most bizarre questions, please let me know: "Do you know a shop where I can buy juggling equipment, I mean the mini batons, not the balls?" Or "Can you tell me where there is an Egyptian restaurant round here that also sells chips?" Finally, yesterday's: "I'm looking for a local book shop that has a section on Victorian clockmaking."

August 28th, 2006: The Pale Man

QX recently ran a feature on the "faces of Soho." Drag queens, DJs, club owners, cabaret acts, promoters, party hosts. Anyone who's anyone in "gay glitterati" land.

The Box, a gay bar off Seven Dials, currently has a piece of artwork stretching the whole length of the bar showing all these Soho celebrities. Yet you'll rarely see any of these faces on a day-to-day basis. The movers and shakers who bring a touch of glamour to Soho's nightlife are usually just here for a night. They flit in, create some fabulous party, then fly off again with their records, makeup, and glitzy outfits.

The real faces of Soho are never featured. You won't see them in the documentaries on Soho that seem to pop up on our televisions with increasing regularity. Yet they are the lifeblood of the village. They are the underclass, the true eccentrics, the waifs and strays the party crowd passes by as they make their way to the Shadow Lounge.

There's the old woman with the waist-length beaded hair and striking makeup who strides down the street with a "Don't fuck with me" look on her face.

The failed actor with the blond quiff always wearing the same light-brown leather jacket, waiting for his one big chance.

The old homeless man, dressed as a barefoot geisha girl.

There's Danny and David outside our shop, taking punters to the lap-dancing club, or to the girls upstairs.

And then there's the Pale Man.

I see the Pale Man every day. He walks, with his head down, past the shop on the Dean Street side, then down Old Compton Street, around the block, again and again.

Sometimes he's one of the first on the street. Sometimes he's the last. I follow his movements every day, but he never sees me. He never looks up. Always the same route. Always the same expression on his face. Pensive. Anxious. Mumbling. His face is very lined and he looks like he's in his late 50s (although he could well be 10 years younger).

When I first saw him, in February, he had colour. But over the past few months he's become very pale. Now he's almost translucent. His pace is much slower too. Half stumbling. Like the final stages of a death march.

Last week he'd had his dry grey/brown hair cut very short at the sides. This surprised me, as I realized he must be aware of his appearance. Maybe it was a last stab at making himself presentable. Not that anyone notices him on Old Compton Street.

I watch the crowds as the Pale Man passes. Either they

don't see him or they pretend not to. Maybe he's a ghost. I feel sad when I see him. I have a feeling he won't be walking this street for much longer.

August 29ᵗʰ, 2006: Boys from Burnley

One of the first lessons Jorge taught me about selling clothes is the difficulty of selling to someone while they're shopping with their friend. He explained that if the shopper is good-looking and the non-shopping friend is bit of a dog, the chances of a sale are virtually nonexistent. Whatever Mr. Good-looking puts on, Mr. Ugly Friend will invariably put down.

"Oh, no, you can't wear that. Brown doesn't suit you." "Oh, God! You look awful in that!" "That hat makes you look like a thug."

When a situation like this arises, there are a couple of ways of dealing with it. The first is to gradually befriend Mr. Ugly Friend, perhaps by mildly flirting, to make him feel less the outsider.

The second option is to manoeuvre the conversation against Mr. Ugly Friend. This is a tricky one, as you are in danger of Mr. Good-looking playing Sir Lancelot and them both walking out.

I decide to go with the first option.

"I don't know how anyone can spend two hundred pounds on a pair of jeans. I get mine from T.K.Maxx. Two pairs for twenty quid." At this, Mr. Ugly Friend spins round and shows me his prize jeans, striking a variety of poses, his ass reminding me of an old-school geography wall chart depicting Canada.

"Where are you from?" I ask.

"We're from Burnley," he replies, sounding like Ena Sharples. "I love it down 'ere but I miss the food. My favourite is pie, peas, and gravy. You can't get that in London so we 'ave Steak Diane instead. But I always bring black puddings down with me in case we meet people." I imagine him handing them out on the dance floor in G.A.Y.

He looks at Jorge. "Look at those muscles. I could get mine like that if I wanted." He flexes one of his arms. "I go to the gym once a week. It's called the Saint Peters Centre. It's near the church," he says, as if I was a local resident.

At that point, Mr. Good-looking walks over wearing a hat, and this time the feedback is far more complimentary, and a sale is made.

"Now, that one suits you better. Buy that one. It hides your receding forehead!"

August 30th, 2006: Exhibitionism

As Quentin Crisp once said, "Exhibitionism is a drug. You get hooked!" And the exhibitionism Quentin described in himself, parading up and down Old Compton Street, is still very much alive today.

Sitting on my chair, watching the crowds pass by the window, I realise that the exhibitionism displayed outside is also prevalent in our shop, in the dressing rooms.

The dressing rooms hold a fascination for exhibitionists. Maybe it's the mirrors inside, or the half-exposed curtain, the reminder of furtive schoolboy glances in swimming pool changing rooms. Whatever the reason, a customer in the cubicle for more than 10 minutes trying on swimwear usually signifies a "cock showing."

Jorge had the shop in the US for 15 years, and he's seen 'em all! All sizes, all nationalities, hairy, shaved, cut, uncut, pierced, pink, low or high hung. You name it—he's had it flashed at him. In a typical scenario a guy will spend a few minutes in the dressing room, "getting himself ready." Then he steps out, in a revealing piece of swimwear, asking for fashion advice.

Now, when you buy clothes from Dirty White Boy, we are different from the majority of clothes shops in that Jorge provides style advice. This may range from the colours you should wear for your skin tone to wearing something that is "age appropriate." But when someone is standing in front of you semi-naked, bursting at the seams, their helmet popping up and their Prince Albert sparkling away, you get the feeling it's not just the hem they want adjusted.

I've quickly learnt to differentiate between the gay and straight exhibitionists. The straight ones stick to flashing the upper body. With the gay ones, it's all about the willy.

I like the straight ones the best. If it wasn't so sexy it would be comical. They stand in front of the mirror, curtain drawn back, topless, admiring themselves from every angle, a hint of a look in your direction, as they try on a pair of shoes. And you know they know they are being watched.

It's exhibitionism at its safest. There are no boundaries crossed. It doesn't go any further and everyone gets something from it. In fact we may incorporate it into the new Dirty White Boy strap line. "Dirty White Boy, where you can shop 'til you flop!"

September 2nd, 2006: Memories

Saturday morning. Two gentlemen walk past the shop doorway. One looks like he's in his sixties and the other in his nineties.

The older man walks slowly, with an old-fashioned walking stick, the type you see in old British black-and-white heritage films. He looks dishevelled, but stylishly so. I try not to stare at the nasty bruise on his nose, the result of a bad fall or an operation, I guess. Then he stops and looks up at me, accusingly, on the doorstep.

"I've been coming here for sixty years. I've seen it all!" he says. His friend nods in agreement. "It's all changed. You see that shop down there?" He points his walking stick at the "open all hours" supermarket on the corner of Old Compton Street and Frith Street. "Used to be a fish restaurant. You see this street?" He waves his stick round with surprising speed in the direction of the Oxford Street end of Dean Street, just missing my face by a fraction. "Used to be a Jewish synagogue down there. You know the Jews? Persecuted in Yorkshire as far back as the eleventh century. They were moneylenders. Cromwell. He brought them over. He killed Charles. Just like him from Wuthering Heights. Bronte. Heathcliff. He did it too. I've seen them all. I was 'ere in the thirties. You should have seen the men then. All swishing. We was all persecuted back then."

I try to follow his train of thought as he moves from subject to subject. He stares straight at me and I can feel his friend's eyes watching me too.

"It'll all change again when you're my age. You'll see. You'll see," he admonishes me. "It never stays the same," he says, his voice starting to tremble.

Then he stops, for a few seconds, as if pondering the next sentence. "I'll be dead soon. After ninety-three years I'll finally be dead."

I lower my head, as it seems the appropriate thing to do, and I wonder if he is suffering from something terminal that he isn't coping with.

"Thank fuck for that!" he chortles, and off they go.

September 3rd, 2006: A Giant Stiletto

Sunday morning is my favourite day of the week on Old Compton Street. The street is like a ghost town. Usually just one or two joggers or the odd straggler from a club, tottering home. Bizarrely, this is when the police are most out in force. They walk past the shop with nothing to do except look professionally grim.

This Sunday is slightly different. As I peer through the window display on the Dean Street side, just outside the Soho bookshop, a man head-to-foot in black latex lies spread-eagled on the floor, his arms and legs flayed out and upwards as though he is skydiving.

On a typical Saturday night this would be quite a common phenomenon and hardly worth mentioning. But it's Sunday morning. What makes this occasion different is that Latex Man is struggling, like a fish out of water, due to a 10-foot red stiletto heel crushing him from above. He looks like a human cigarette being stamped out. As he squirms beneath it, a photographer bends down and clicks away from either side.

What is going on? Is it an art student's final dissertation about the stresses of life and how we are all crushed from above? Is it an advertisement targeted at women with elephantiasis? Or maybe the 10-foot stiletto has dropped from the sky onto Latex Man as he made his way home from a local fetish club and the photographer just happened to be in the right place at the right time.

This being Old Compton Street, the few people who walk by hardly give the scene a second glance. In fact, even I carry on with opening the shop. And when I look out again a few minutes later, the giant stiletto, the Latex Man, and the photographer have all gone, whisked away by their savvy marketing team or by confused ambulance staff, no doubt.

September 7th, 2006: The NVCs

When celebrities come into the shop, they behave in different ways depending on how well known they are.

The well-known ones don't engage in conversation. People like Graham Norton and Peter Stringfellow walk in, confident of their stardom. It's an unspoken rule. They don't talk. We don't talk back. No eye contact. Everyone knows their place. And, hopefully, if you've deferred for long enough, Mr. Stringfellow will buy another see-through 100 percent silk black extra-large thong.

When a Non Visible Celebrity like a screenwriter, director,

or American B movie actor comes in, they act very differently. They're aware that you probably have no idea who they are and they therefore feel compelled to put that right, providing you with a potted history of the trials and tribulations of their life leading right up to their current project.

This is interesting to listen to, but a bit strange. It's very unlikely that I would inform the checkout girl at Tescos how many "A" grades I achieved at Broadoak Comprehensive in 1974. Firstly because she'd think I was mad but also because I wouldn't want her to become so absorbed in the conversation that she'd inadvertently double-scan my crème caramel 4-pack puddings.

Why the NVC needs me to recognise their greatness is mystifying. Could it be the NVC is surrounded by so many VCs that they're trying to make their non-visible status more visible? Maybe, as they're still on the cusp of being known, they inhabit a kind of celebrity limbo land where nonentities are still worth talking to.

Whatever the reason, when the NVC tells you that he has just finished filming the murder of his wife's lesbian lover for next month's episode of *Emmerdale,* there's really not much you can say except "That's really nice!" or "Oh, I love a good murder." In most cases what you want to do is stare blankly and say, "I'm sorry, I never watch *Emmerdale,* as a soap set in a muddy field holds no interest for me." But of course you can't. It may jeopardise the sale. So, you're led down this fake path of gushing to make the NVC feel good.

As I stand by the shop doorway contemplating the conversion of stardom from non-visible to visible, I am brought back down to Earth rather quickly by a reminder of the route a lot of actors probably have to take to become visible.

Looking all of 16 and dressed in a sky-blue shell suit, the latest pimp on the street saunters over.

"Wan' a woman upstairs?" he says with an Italian twang,

eyebrows raised toward the brothel above.

"No, thanks," I reply. "Nice of you to ask, but I'm gay."

He looks at me for a second, switching his sales technique in an instant. "That's okay! I'm bisexual. How 'bout a ten-quid blow job instead?"

September 9th, 2006: A Big Flood

Barcode is empty. We've been here for an hour, drinking, musing over the day's events.

Yesterday we had a huge argument, an argument that'd been brewing for two days, and the atmosphere between us is still not quite back to normal. It feels like a first date, and at 1 A.M. we make our way home, heady from the amount of drink we've consumed in such a short period.

As we open the door to the shop, I hear the sound of running water in the basement. We look at each other. Oh no! Another leak from the brothel upstairs. The fifth in as many months. Only this is no ordinary leak. Water is gushing down the stairway, down the walls, through the light fittings, big puddles of dirty brown water everywhere.

We sober up rapidly. Buckets, pans, sweeping the big pools of water into the drain.

"I'm going up to the brothel!" I shout above the noise, leaving Jorge to move jackets, clothes, and boxes into the far corner of the basement that seems to have escaped the torrent.

I race up the side door on the Dean Street side, the door with the yellow neon "Model" sign. By the time I reach the first-floor landing I can see what the problem is. The madam is standing on the balcony watching one of her pimps trying to push a broken water pipe back into its original position, water spraying all over the place, the pipe waving around like an aggressive snake.

"What the hell's going on?" I scream. "Our shop's flooded out!"

"I'm sorry, luv. The plumber's on his way. It just snapped!"

As she says "snapped," the lights suddenly go out, and through the darkness voices cry out, "Hey I'm only halfway through!" "Turn the fuckin' lights back on!" "Get off my face!"

As I make my way back downstairs, the fire alarm suddenly wails into action and Jorge, stripped down to his jockstrap, tries manically to rescue furniture and merchandise. After a while the noise of the alarm becomes too overwhelming and we call the Fire Brigade.

So to the small crowds passing down Old Compton Street at 2:30 A.M. this morning who witnessed three uniformed firemen, a muscular guy dressed in a black jockstrap, a handful of prostitutes in various states of undress, punters in a variety of outfits ranging from schoolboys to nurses, I apologise for disturbing your night.

September 10th, 2006: Chico's Big Date

"Hey, honey! Chico's here!"

Sunday afternoon, and in waltzes Chico dripping in D&G, Gucci, and Ferre Black Label.

Whenever Chico bursts into the shop the atmosphere turns into a camp extravaganza, and any straight customers shopping at the time peer through the clothes racks with a mixture of fear and fascination.

"So which shop did you go to?" I ask, peering into the plastic shopping bag.

"The sex one!" he replies with a grin.

He isn't wrong. When he opens up the bag, coiled up at the bottom like a sleeping boa constrictor lies the biggest dildo I've ever seen.

"I only bought it 'cos it was in the sale. I can't usually take them that big but it was winking at me on the shelf, saying, Chico! Buy me! Buy me!"

"What about the other boxes?"

"Well, I bought six altogether," he says, without a care in the world.

"Six?"

"Well, honey I've got a hot date coming over at eight and you know I've just gotta have all the essentials. So every hour I'll go up a size and colour until we get to Big Joey!"

As he goes to leave I notice the label at the back of his jumper hanging out, so I tuck it back in.

"Oh, honey! Leave the Gucci hanging out! You know what a shallow bitch I am!" He laughs, and off he goes to the Sheraton for another date with a *QX* centrefold.

September 15ᵗʰ, 2006: Queen Judy

Not everyone who visits Dirty White Boy is a customer. The majority of people who come in are just "visitors." These visitors can range from the casual browser, wiling away a few minutes between appointments, to thieves, who descend in small gay gangs, throwing attitude in the hope that they will distract you, to the local eccentrics, who think of any shop in Soho as their home.

From Quentin Crisp in the 30s to Francis Bacon in the 60s, Soho has always attracted eccentrics. These are the real faces of Soho, and Queen Judy is one of them.

When Queen Judy enters it's with a combination of a skip and a run. The estranged straight brother of local club promoter Jeremy Joseph, Queen Judy could be the exotic love child of Grayson Perry and Zandra Rhodes. A mass of garishly luminous colours, like a Jackson Pollock painting lying in a pool of vomit, multi-coloured ponchos and leggings, floor-length scarves in the summer, over-large sunglasses, and a bright-pink trilby balanced precariously on a mop of unkempt hair. For the past six months my conversation with Queen Judy has remained the same, and every time he enters he acts as if it's the first time we've ever spoken.

"Do you sell pink trousers? Oh please! Please! I just have to have pink trousers!" he says as he hands me a pink business card bearing the name "Queen Judy."

I politely take it, pretend to examine it again; then open the desk drawer and add it to the 10 I already have.

"I'm Queen Judy. I've got a pink hat but I need pink trousers. Can you help? I'll pay! But in instalments if that's okay."

Each time I explain to Queen Judy that our clothes are ordered six months in advance and the designers aren't showing pink in their collections for next Spring/Summer, his face drops and he looks like he's about to cry.

"I have to have more pink clothes soon!" he pleads.

Then, last week, Jorge came to the rescue. "We do have one pair of pink trousers coming in from Thierry Mugler. But they won't be here until early next year."

Queen Judy's face lit up. "Oh my God! Please save them for me. Here, take my business card!" Then he skipped out the door with a beaming smile, singing, "I've got my pink trousers! I've got my pink trousers!" and leaving a handful of bemused passersby in his wake.

September 18th, 2006: I Am Invisible

I'm sitting by the window, the smell of the pastries from Patisserie Valerie wafting through the air, sipping a grande mocha, flicking casually through the latest *Vanity Fair*. The only sounds, the romantic trundling of the delivery trucks as they creep slowly up the street unloading their delicacies, and the madam from the brothel above leaning out the window shouting to a drunk, "Get outta my fuckin' doorway or I'll rip your bollocks off!"

I look up from my magazine as two tall, well-dressed men walk into the shop and make their way to the jeans section.

"Good morning, guys!"

They don't respond and carry on their conversation.

"...so I logged on to Gaydar last night under my fake profile to catch him out and I messaged him and I said, 'Do you fancy a fuck?' And he wrote back, like in 30 seconds, and he said, 'Sure, come over, I'm versatile but I'd flip for you.' And you know what really hurt?" The taller of the two turns to face his friend, holding a pair of Iceberg jeans against his legs. "Just last night he told me his piles were playing up!"

It's strange, but when you work in a shop you're deemed invisible by a majority of the buying public, so much so that when you do speak, "Excuse me, guys, if I can help you at all do let me know," the question is usually met with a mixture of disdain or a look as if I was something smelly they'd just stepped in.

By lunchtime it's happened again. This time a small, effeminate Asian guy in his twenties and a much larger, much older, bearded gentlemen. The Asian guy trails his fingers along the clothes rails until he stops at the most expensive shirt we have, by Roberto Cavalli.

"Daddy, please, can I have a new shirt? Cupcake wants a shirt. Pleasy! Weasy!"

"Cupcake's being a naughty boy and you know what happens when you're naughty, don't you?" says Daddy, looking down sternly.

At this, Cupcake bends over and starts to lightly spank his own bottom with his delicate hand. "I get spanky wankys."

This scenario then moves a step further as Daddy Waddy starts to lightly spank Cupcake's bottom with his bulging leather wallet. Sitting behind the desk, I realise that unless I interrupt very quickly Daddy Waddy's belt will soon be off and Cupcake will be having a Cantonese ejaculation all over the cashmere polos.

"Can I help you with a size at all, gentlemen?"

Again they both look round in horror and stare at me as though the potted plant had just come to life.

Then, just before closing time, a middle-aged lesbian couple comes in. The Levi's circa Castro Street 1973, matching fleeces, and deck shoes indicate that a big sale may not be imminent.

So I sit quietly in my chair and listen carefully as "Kath" explains to "Joyce" that the abnormal, odorous discharge from which she is suffering is in fact bacterial vaginosis, which can be effectively treated by a botanical alternative medicine formulation containing a blend of 15 all-natural herbal extracts, of which, strangely enough, she has a month's supply in her bag.

September 18th, 2006: Energising Britain's Prostitutes

I watch the madam from the brothel upstairs cross the street six or seven times a day.

We've been open since February, and in that time she must've put on two stone. What started as a dainty step has literally become a stomp. A big lady already, she now sways while she stomps, like the Titanic on its maiden voyage, majestic but menacing, sailing down the street, her bottle-blonde mane swishing from side to side, her face set into a hard grimace. And when she returns it's always with the same shopping: Wotsits (they look like the cheese-flavoured ones although they could well be Barbeque Beef) and bottles and bottles of Lucozade.

When the Lucozade first started to arrive I hardly paid any attention. But as the days turned to months, with her trips taking longer and longer as she combs the late-night supermarkets, I couldn't help but notice how much of the stuff was being consumed. Always returning with one bottle under each arm, which, when she walks toward you, coupled with her very large breasts, gives the impression that there are four nuclear warheads aimed in your direction.

Six months later, after what seems like a tanker truck of the stuff has made its way upstairs, I start to wonder what they are doing with all that Lucozade.

Is it a fetish that's passed me by? Do the punters writhe underneath a fountain of it like an energy-flavoured golden shower? Or perhaps the clue is in the Lucozade strap line? "Aids recovery." Recovery for who? The clients? Surely the "girls" wouldn't want the clients to recover that quickly. So maybe it's for the "girls" themselves. Although "aiding recovery" conjures up nasty visions of overworked orifices.

Intrigued, I go to the Lucozade website and find that Lucozade can help maintain concentration, focus, and alertness, and is being promoted along with their "Energising Britain" campaign.

How marvellous. So there you have it. After being first produced in 1927 by a Newcastle chemist as a source of energy for those who were sick, Lucozade is now enabling the prostitutes of Soho to stay focussed into the early hours.

September 18th, 2006: The Flyer Boys
Thank God for the Flyer Boys.

When life gets tough and stressful I look out the shop doorway and watch the Flyer Boys at play. Whatever the weather, whatever the time, the Flyer Boys parade the street, handing out their glossy advertisements for Ultimate, Beyond, Area, Salon, G.A.Y. Club Bar, and "Late."

Always happy, always sparkling in glitter and makeup, pecs toned to perfection, tanned and fabulous; flirting, laughing, and gossiping. They don't mind if you don't take their flyer. They don't mind if you don't come to their club. They're just happy to light up the street and give us carnival, 24 hours a day, 365 days a year, bringing their Rio to Soho.

I wish I'd started my London life as a Flyer Boy. Maybe life would've stayed one big party. When I die I want to come back as a Flyer Boy.

September 19th, 2006: The Girls Above Pop Down

Sue, the madam from the brothel upstairs, comes into the shop with her smaller but equally busty girlfriend, Maggie.

Sue frightens me. When we first moved in, I had to run upstairs because her hand basin was leaking into the shop, and while I was there she offered me a free blow job. I thanked her but quickly made my way out. Since then she's eyed me with suspicion, like a dinner party hostess who's noticed you didn't eat the crème brûlée.

I'm warming to Maggie, though. I suppose in cinematic parlance she'd be known as the "tart with a heart," the kind who pops up as an extra on the banisters in *Bad Girls*. After apologising profusely for the leak the previous Saturday— "It was probably a frustrated punter head-butting the open pipe work"—she turns the conversation to our jeans.

Now, sizing is a problem in European retail. UK sizing differs from Italian, which differs from French and Spanish, and this problem is compounded by the almost universal human folly of downgrading your own sizing when an assistant asks for your size.

So when Maggie says she wants to buy Sue a pair of jeans, I look over at Sue, whose expression reminds me of an East German Olympic shot-putter on her final throw, and my immediate reaction is to put my hand in my pocket and pinch my right testicle, which I do in times of stress.

"Sue's a thirty-eight!" says Maggie, casually.

I take a deep breath and edge over toward the stretch denim. This is going to be difficult. If Sue is admitting to being a 38, then she is really a 42. But what's a 42 in Italian? Plus 16?

As these figures go through my mind I can feel Sue staring back defiantly. Stalling for time, I start to rummage through the layers of jeans, fiddling with buttons.

Fortunately, help is at hand. Maggie's mobile goes off just as Sue is fingering a pair of 36s.

"Sue, it's Brian. Can we do him in five minutes?"

"Who's Brian?"

"You know! Brian with the clothes pegs and the veg."

"I ain't going to the market now. Tell 'im to bring his own!"

As I refold the denim, it crosses my mind that, like Toto, I'm not in Kansas anymore.

September 20th, 2006: The Pied Piper of Old Compton Street

I wish I could be one of those people who say, "I don't give money to beggars," but something kicks in when I'm approached and I just hand over whatever change I have. Only, now, it's becoming too much. The doorway to our shop is fast becoming a stop-off point for all the "lost" of London, and I've become their Pied Piper.

There's the guy who sells the *Big Issue*, the homeless people's magazine, chatting away amiably, boasting about his latest convictions. But as the evening descends, he becomes drunk and threatens to set our shop on fire.

There're the pimps, Danny and David, out from early afternoon to the early hours, dragging unsuspecting prey to the girls upstairs.

There're the drug pushers, plying their trade when the sun sets, like vampires, flying off down the street once they've bled their customers dry.

And then there are the homeless.

I hand over money and old clothes to the homeless, and they return with friends. It's like trying to throw breadcrumbs to a solitary pigeon in Trafalgar Square. So I hand over more clothes and they start eyeing the ones in shop. But I'm going to have to back off soon because we're starting to attract more homeless than customers. They're friendly but with an edge—an edge that can gradually wear you down.

Sometimes I wish they'd all just go and find another

pitch—I feel I've done my bit. But then contrast this: here I am trying to sell more and more expensive designer clothes to people who don't really need any more, and trying to stop myself giving away old clothes that I don't want to those who don't have any and really need them.

September 20th, 2006: A Wet Leg

Looking out the window onto Dean Street this evening, I saw a well-suited businessman pissing against the wall, the pool of urine snaking between his legs, down the street, toward two blonde women in short skirts and high heels chatting nearby.

Unbeknownst to the women, the river of piss started to form a "piss moat" around their stilettos. I felt like Tippi Hedren in *The Birds*, in the scene where she's hiding inside the grocery store, watching helplessly as a fallen petrol pump spills its load toward a man getting out of his car about to light a cigarette.

While I contemplated doing a Raleigh, along came two policemen who tapped the man on the shoulder. The man, being considerably worse for wear, turned round, and unable to stop in mid-flow, continued pissing down the leg of one of the policemen, reminding me of the cover of a porn DVD I'd seen advertised in Clone Zone quite recently.

September 21st, 2006: Walking Home

I'm walking up Moor Street, nearly home.

My pace quickens as I pass Ed's Diner on the corner. I'm more aware of my surroundings now, looking up at the architecture above the shops.

I turn left onto Old Compton Street, my mood lifting as I hit the street. The atmosphere beckons, and for a brief moment I'm transported back, following in the footsteps of all those who've walked this street over the centuries: Casanova, Verlaine and Rimbaud, Quentin Crisp, Francis Bacon.

Now on I'm on the south side of the street, passing the "Tudor" pub, the Three Greyhounds. Over Greek Street I walk, alongside Café Bohème and Bar Sol Ona, tuk-tuks lined up outside the Prince Edward as the evening performance comes to an end. The crowd flooding the street. Young and old. All nationalities and sexualities, backgrounds and classes. The business crowd, fashion folk, media luvvies, bemused tourists, chavs and lads, hen nights and stag nights, drag kings and queens, gay and straight couples, the *Big Issue* sellers and the homeless.

The noise of the honking taxis mixes with the music from the bars as the Flyer Boys jostle with the Essex lads who raise their glasses, saluting their teams on the video screen in Bar Soho. Drunk, high, and excited. A melting pot of London life, thrown together on one street. Like a modern-day Hogarth painting.

Now I'm dodging the messenger bikes as I cross Frith Street; past Aware and its colourful Versace underwear, Amalfi, and Pulcinella diners with their set menus and bread baskets.

The crowds surge past, a rich tapestry of immigrants. I feel like Shara Nelson in the *Unfinished Sympathy* video. This is the only street of its kind in London. Straight and gay mixing comfortably. A merging of sexualities. A microcosm of what's going on in society. And there—there's my home.

The *QX* centrefolds spill onto the street outside Costa, gossiping, flirting, and texting, and in the distance the Comptons crowd block the traffic while the bouncer tries to steer them in. Paradiso Boudoir, "a 'fantasy' boutique for men and women," is on my left, and my home, Dirty White Boy, just opposite; the pimps, and the dealers, hustling and arguing, outside the door.

I put the key in the lock, open the door, step inside. Home.

September 22nd, 2006: Ben

I stand outside the shop and watch the weekend crowds hurry by. Ben, the teenage pimp and hustler, is a few feet away. He swaggers over.

"How you doin', mate?" He looks up at me. Cocky and streetwise.

"I'm good," I reply casually, not forgetting the £10 blow job he offered me only last week.

"You work here, don't you?"

I nod.

"You ever get any trouble?" he says.

Here we go. "Nothing we can't handle," I reply without looking at him.

"Well, if you ever get any trouble, just let me know. I've been working here for five years. I'll look after things for you."

Oh, so now its protection money he's after. I turn to face him. "That's nice of you to offer, Ben. But I think we can handle it."

I step back into the shop. Sit down. Watch as he leans back against the shop window, inches away from my face. I can see the dirt on the back of his sky-blue jacket (did he sleep rough last night?), his cheap track pants and trainers; his inquisitive, fox-like face, with the hint of a moustache and patchy, week-old stubble on his otherwise flawless skin. He surveys his pitch. He'd suck your cock while fingering your wallet and probably knife you too, if you caught him.

A middle-aged, well-dressed black guy walks by and nods at him. Just a slight beckoning that no one would notice ordinarily. Ben hesitates. I can read his face. He's tense, considering the offer. Does he follow or risk losing his pitch? He digs his forefinger into his cuticles. The nails are dirty and bitten. What will he do? His head moves back and forth, biding for time.

I follow his eyes. Now he's noticed a cute young blond

boy crossing Dean Street. Their eyes lock. The blond boy looks back. Easier prey. Ben makes a move toward him. The Artful Dodger pursuing his Oliver. They talk. Ben takes a step closer and I can see the blond boy laugh, slightly nervously, not looking at Ben directly. Ben confident and direct, standing taller, making the most of his short frame.

As they talk I imagine their lives together, and their whole story maps out in my head... Will Ben's life improve through this chance meeting? Will he leave the streets? Will they support each other through their teens, into adulthood? Through illness? Become life partners?

Or will Ben cheat on him, steal from him, drugs, bringing down? I imagine the blond boy trying again and again to get Ben on the straight and narrow, until one day he gives up and Ben returns to the only home he ever knew. I see it all.

I want to tell Ben not to fuck this up. But I can't. And by the time I reach the shop doorway they've already gone.

September 23rd, 2006: A Royal Visit

I first saw her in Comptons. I was standing outside on the street drinking and by chance I turned round to look inside. She was staring straight at me. With her Indian features, large nose, and brunette bob, she looked like a dark-skinned Barbra Streisand. She smiled, blew me a kiss, and pulled down her black slinky top, pressing her trannie breasts against the window, her protruding nipples resembling 1950s electric light switches.

Weeks would go by before I'd see her again, and when I did, she'd either be stepping seductively out of a taxi accompanied by an older gentleman, or negotiating some kind of deal outside the brothel, flicking her hair constantly from side to side. It crossed my mind that she probably worked upstairs on a part-time basis: "temping," as it were.

This Saturday afternoon, she comes into the shop with a reluctant, bespectacled businessman.

"Carmine, I don't need another shirt!" the man slurs, as Carmine pulls him into the shop by both hands.

"Believe me, darling, you do," says Carmine. "If you think I'm going round another bar with your crazy ass looking like that, then—look at this!" she purrs as she sashays down the aisle, reaching for a Sonia Rykiel striped button-down. "Now go and try this on and stop moaning," she says, pushing the man toward the dressing rooms.

As the businessman slinks off, a small man accompanied by an Amazonian, reddish-brown-haired woman walks in. This is a role reversal, the man skipping round the shop manically, picking clothes off the hangers, while the taller lady sits down on the chair next to me, nodding or shaking her head whenever the man returns with a garment. Her face looks vaguely familiar, and as I pretend to fold clothes I watch her, while Carmine parades around the store as if on a catwalk, swishing past the smaller man on each circle of the trouser rack. Where have I seen this lady before? Then it hits me.

"Excuse me!" I say, clearing my throat. "I hope you don't mind me asking, but have you appeared on the stage recently?"

She smiles back and says, "Yes, I have."

"Were you in *Mary Stuart*?" I ask, incredulously.

"Yes," she says with a twinkle in her eye.

"You were in the Schiller play!" I say, almost accusingly. "You, you were Mary, Queen of Scots. I... I... I saw you at the Apollo!"

I can't get the words out fast enough. This is the Tony-Award-winning, Oscar-nominated Janet McTeer. *A Doll's House*, *Tumbleweeds*, *Carrington*, the lady's a genius.

"Can I just say, you were fantastic! It was the best play I've ever seen in my life!" I gush.

She smiles again and thanks me.

"Jorge, remember the play we saw?" I shout across to

Jorge, who is dressing the businessman.

"Oh my God, it's you! You played the Queen. You were amazing!" says Jorge.

I look at him and arch an eyebrow, remembering him whispering in my ear early into the second act, "Can we leave when she gets her head chopped off?"

At this point, Carmine, no doubt feeling a bit upstaged, bends over the desk, balancing precariously on her Westwood heels.

"He'll take these!" she says, draping three shirts over the counter with one hand while drumming her bloodred nails on the glass with the other.

Still reeling from meeting the Queen of Scotland, I'm unable to concentrate fully on the Queen of Old Compton Street. I look over at the actress. "Can I ask your name?"

What am I saying? I know her name. Janet McTeer.

"Janet," she says quietly.

"Did you say Janet?" I ask, trying to keep the conversation going, struggling for things to say.

"Yes," she says again, nodding her head.

What is wrong with me? Of course she said "Janet." Why wouldn't she? Oh please, God, I think, let me think of something intelligent to say. But, as so often happens to commoners in the presence of royalty, I revert to being a frightened mouse, my voice coming out in squeaks.

Janet is looking at me strangely now, as is Carmine, and I now have two queens staring right at me. This is how Princess Di must have felt when popping over for tea at Buck Palace. So, not sure whether to fold the shirts or reach for an autograph pad, I reach inside my pocket instead and pinch my right testicle.

Moments later, the spell is broken. An older, bearded Muslim man with a black, tightly bound turban marches right up to the counter, stands between the two queens, and, without so much as a bow, says in a very loud voice, and without a care in the world, "Where can I find a gay bath-house with a dark room around here?"

September 27th, 2006: A Bad Dream

I wake up and look at my watch. 4:38 A.M. Visions, scenarios, characters, disturbing my sleep, giving me a headache. I have to keep writing. I don't know how long Jorge and I will be here; business is so unpredictable. Weeks? Months? I need to document it all, because this moment is important. I don't know why. It's like I've got a "biological blog" ticking away inside me.

I knock back two Tylenol with a swig of water and tiptoe upstairs, looking out onto Old Compton Street. Not a soul around. The first time I've seen the street totally empty. Just the distant wailing of a police siren and the far-off echo of laughter or crying, I can't tell which. Ghosts from the medieval plague pits and pest houses of Marshall Street, forever trapped beneath us, in grounds never consecrated.

I sit in my chair by the window, thinking about a recurring dream I've been having. I dreamt that Jorge and I were dead, in Heaven somewhere, being chased by a sniper; and the more we were shot the more it brought us back to life, until we were both reborn.

It's usually Jorge who has the bad dreams. He's often "visited" by dead family members, or the numerous friends he lost in the 80s. Sometimes they talk to him, and, years ago, he'd phone the mothers of some of these friends and pass on the messages. I lie next to him when he has these dreams and stroke his face, whispering in his ear that everything will be okay. He grabs my hand unconsciously while he sleeps and calms down.

I look at my watch again. It's past 5 A.M. The tablets are starting to kick in; my headache is fading away, gently, to the back of my head. I stand up slowly and take one last look at the street.

It looks so peaceful now. It sees so much life, but even Old Compton Street needs to rejuvenate; taking stock of what happened the previous day before embarking on the next.

September 27th, 2006: The Little Match Girl

I sit by the shop window looking out. It's like one big magnifying glass, focusing in on the minutiae, drawing me into lives other people don't notice, or do, but choose not to; the drunks, the street people, the hookers, the pimps and pushers.

There's a small girl outside the shop doorway as I write this, about 16. She's like Hans Christian Andersen's *The Little Match Girl*. Brown, unkempt hair pulled to one side and held in place by a clip. She's wearing a blue shapeless top, way too big for her, and cheap tracksuit bottoms.

I watch as she approaches men passing by. I can't hear what she's saying but they shake their head as she follows them. A few brush her off, not with force, but with a wave of their hand, or their body language, visibly recoiling.

Just as Blair delivers his "long goodbye" speech, promising another nine months to complete his reform agenda, I watch a scene play out in front of me that is almost Dickensian in its sadness.

I walk to the shop doorway, knowing she'll approach me. She does.

"You want a lady, mister?" she says. I notice that her face is without makeup. She looks like she's slept rough.

"No, thank you," I reply, smiling back.

"It's free to look. It doesn't cost a thing to look."

I shake my head.

She looks directly at me. "You gay?"

"Yes, I am."

She shrugs and turns to walk off.

"Wait! Do you work upstairs?" I ask, trying to draw her back into conversation.

"I don't sell my body. I wouldn't sell my body for no one," she fires back aggressively.

"I'm sorry. I didn't realise. I know the girls upstairs, that's all. We know each other. I just thought you were..." I try to backtrack, realising I've offended her.

"Look, I work for them, but I'm the pimp." At this, her face changes: smug, as if being a pimp elevates her status.

"How much do you get for taking a man upstairs?"

"Don't ask me no questions, mister, and I'll tell you no lies." She moves back, like she's afraid, like I'm her abuser, and repeats the line again, this time only half looking at me, watching the crowds. "Just don't ask me those type of questions again, mister, and I'll tell you no lies."

I watch her for a while but she keeps a wide berth; circling as far around me as she can. So I go back to my seat, wondering if she has a mother, if she has a family, if she has friends, where she'll end up.

September 27th, 2006: My Sex Life

My sex life with my partner is like a roller coaster, and, strangely, it only hits me today that there is a direct correlation between the amount of sex we have and the shop's takings.

Working on our quarterly VAT returns, I am able to plot on a graph the following: when more money comes in, there's less stress and more sex; when there's less money coming in, more stress and less sex. Simple, really, but I feel like Sir Isaac Newton on discovering the Universal Law of Gravitation. It is a real "Eureka" moment.

I'm not sure I should submit my findings to HM Revenue and Customs along with my revenue balance sheets, but it's a simple formula which I think should be at least taught in schools. Forget Pythagoras, kids need to be taught the Ejaculation Equation in their maths classes.

In our case, when the shop takings are good, we role-play

like Oscar nominees, getting through more cum towels than Chariots. When takings are down, it's a case of finishing yourself off.

I'm sure there's an MBA Business Psychology dissertation exam question lurking in there somewhere: *Projected Orgasms vs Retail Index Ratios: Discuss.*

September 28th, 2006: The Chinese Delegation

As I hoist up the metal grates to the shop this morning, on the Dean Street side, I am confronted with rather a bizarre sight: six Chinese businessmen lined up outside the doorway to the brothel. This being 11:30 A.M., the brothel is still closed, the girls getting some very valuable shut-eye.

Unperturbed, the businessmen stand silently, in identical suits, like a row of penguins, briefcases on the ground between their feet. As I sweep up round them I notice that even the few passersby hardly give the scene a second glance. Unless your eyes ventured to the yellow neon "Model" sign above, it'd be logical to think that the men were just queuing at a local bank or post office.

Intrigued, I brush outside for a good 15 minutes (14½ minutes longer than usual). But eventually, as the tarmac starts to wear down, I venture back inside. There I busy myself by dusting round the window ledge like a nosy neighbour peering through grimy net curtains.

At 11:55, the men must sense movement up above, as they pick up their briefcases and gather in a group, gesticulating and talking animatedly.

My mind is awash with thoughts about what they're saying. "Who's brought the Delay Spray?" "Does anyone have a small tissue?" "Is it customary to tip?"

What is the reason for this early-morning episode? Is this the start of the Chinese "peaceful economic expansion" that we've all read about, the girls being one of the first beneficiaries? Or maybe the waitress at the Golden Dragon was a bit heavy-handed with the shark fin in the soup last night.

Whatever the reason, five minutes later the madam from upstairs hollers down the stairway, "Okay, boys! Three at a time!" And, as if they've drawn straws, without a word, three of the businessmen, briefcases tucked under their arms, march up; leaving the other three to form an orderly queue outside again.

Fifteen minutes later, as if they'd synchronised bodily functions, the first three troop down and the rear guard take up the firing line. By 12:30 it is all over, the six of them laughing and joking and patting each other on the back as they head off back down Dean Street toward Chinatown for a revitalising pot of green tea.

September 29th, 2006: Strong Legs

A middle-aged man with matted hair, dressed in khaki shorts, socks up to his knees, and an old string vest, marches into the shop, plonking himself in front of Jorge, who is sitting behind the counter.

"I've got very strong legs and I'm the same age as Felicity Kendal!" he barks.

"That's nice," says Jorge nervously, beckoning me over with his eyes.

"My legs are very, very strong. Like two young oak trees," he shouts, his face getting redder and redder, like a kettle coming to the boil. "But I'm working on my arms as well. Do you want to know how I'm making them stronger?"

"Umm, yes."

"I half fill two buckets with water and I stand in the garden with a bucket in each hand, lowering and raising the buckets, up and down, up and down," he says, demonstrating, in case we don't quite understand the complexity of the movement. "Once I can lift two full buckets of water, do you know what I'm going to do next?" He slams his hand down on the counter, causing Jorge to jump up in his seat. "I'm going see if I can hold a Singer sewing machine above my head with one hand!"

And with that, he turns round and marches right back out.

October 2nd, 2006: A Soho Survey

9 P.M., we've just closed the shop. The stress of the day finally coming to an end. So I sit down and start completing a survey targeted at local residents and shop owners as part of Ken Livingstone's proposed "Clean up Soho" campaign.

Please use the space below to add any further recommendations you may have.

Oh goody. So I start my list.

Dear Ken,

Can we please just have one night a month dedicated to "Dagenham hen nights," as Old Compton Street is fast becoming their safari park. You'll be locking us up in enclosures next. "Quick, Sharon—get your camera! Look at that bear licking his baby cub!" P.S., The odd good-looking stag night we can cope with.

Thank you for providing eight policeman every Sunday morning to cope with the three people on the street. However, I think the two policemen you provide on a Saturday night may need a bit of support.

I am just getting to the bit about pedestrianising the street, perhaps with the odd Henry Moore sculpture and a few fountains, when the wail of police sirens fills the street. Two police cars career over toward the shop, policemen flying out the doors like bats from a belfry.

I run to the window on the Old Compton Street side just as a man is being wrestled to the ground by the policemen, a gun still in his hand. An obviously frightened man stands nearby. "He was going to shoot me in the head!" he screams.

I make a mental note for the survey: Forget more police. Please provide UN backing.

As the police cars speed off and the hen nights resume their drunken rendition of Will Young's *Evergreen*, I look over to the main door.

Inches away from my face, a woman in her sixties stares at me through the glass. Her face is truly frightening, like a Francis Bacon picture dropped in a puddle. In one hand she holds a pint glass of beer which slops over her clothes as she sways, her face contorted into a grotesque version of a smile. I notice the spaces in her mouth where teeth once found an unhappy home. What is left looks like a bombed-out Stonehenge.

"I'm the devil and I'm going to fuck your brains out!" she rasps, reminding me of a chat-up line first used on me when I was 19, on my first visit to Heaven in the 1980s.

I leave her standing there and return to my survey. I make another note for Ken: "If the budget stretches, a psychiatrist on each street corner would help!"

October 2nd, 2006: Clothes That Must Never Leave

I'm staring at the clothes on the racks and shelves.

New collections are coming in every day. Fall/Winter replacing Spring/Summer. New stock for old. Although a few items have been here for two seasons or more.

There's the brown Blue Marlin track top, the Rykiel multi-coloured knit, the Man Save the Queen shirt. I first saw these clothes when I was visiting Jorge in Provincetown, before he moved the shop here.

I don't want them to ever sell. They're stability. A constant reminder. They've become friends. I want them to stay in the shop forever.

There are some things in my life I don't want to let go of, that sometimes I feel I'm close to losing. Another 30 years of my life ahead of me without them being there, arm's length away. I can't bear the thought of that. Growing old without them, after everything we've been through. Only meeting them again in my dreams. How will I cope when that happens?

October 2nd, 2006: King Size

We've just started to stock black L'Homme Invisible underwear with "King Size" written in big, bold, white lettering over the baggy crotch. Dressed on a shop mannequin and stuffed at the front like a Gaydar pic, they're one of the first things that catch your eye on the way in. Interestingly, they provoke quite different reactions.

Gay men are drawn toward them, trance-like, arms outstretched, like zombies in *Dawn of the Dead*.

Straight men tend to take a quick peek, nervously looking round the shop to make sure no one's watching.

And women head straight to the rack, rubbing the front of the garment between their fingers, as if hoping the genie will pop out of the bottle.

What conclusion can we draw from this anthropological study? Gay men love big cock, straight men are scared of it unless it's dangling between their own legs, and women like a good feel before they sample the goods? Who knows. What I can report is that Old Compton Street doesn't appear to be a heavily endowed location, as the smalls and mediums have all sold out, whereas we still have plenty of larges and XLs left in stock.

October 9th, 2006: Opera on Wheels

Flicking through the centre pages of *QX* this morning, trying to match the cock pix with the Brazilians sitting outside Costa, I hear the distant sound of opera in the air.

Now, I wasn't blessed with the opera gene, but I do recognize what sounds like *La Traviata*, the virile voice soaring majestically down the street, getting louder and louder. Expecting a black limo to cruise slowly past, music blaring from the sunroof, I am surprised to see instead that the voice is emanating from a small, frail-looking, middle-aged man in a wheelchair.

With one arm he operates the remote control and with the other he gesticulates dramatically, his arm rising up and down with the passion of the song.

"*Lunge da lei per me non v'ha diletto,*" he sings at the top of his voice, steering himself around the tuk-tuks, headed directly for the shop.

Moments later he is inside, the wheelchair climbing the step, as he climbs the melody with equal ease. As the shop is empty, he is able to manoeuvre himself around without a problem, the purr of the electronic wheelchair providing the background to the emotional song.

"Can I help you? I ask quietly, waiting for a break in the song.

"*Ed or contenta in questi ameni luogi tutto scorda per me,*" he sings back, smiling, while he whizzes around the aisles.

"If you need a hand with any of the sizes, just let me know."

"*De' miei bollenti spiriti il giovanile ardore ella temprò col placido sorriso dell' amor!*" His voice reverberates around the room as he reaches for a hat.

Suddenly he stops. Mid-sentence, it seems (the end of Act 3?). He places the hat firmly on his head, looks toward me, and throws one hand back, as if ready to burst back into song. But although his mouth is open, no words come out. What is he waiting for? A duet? He nods at me.

I nod back. "The hat really suits you!"

Then, as if my finger has pressed the Play button, the man's face bursts into a smile and his wonderful voice fills the shop once again.

"Dal dì che disse: vivere io voglio a te fedel, dell'universo immemore io vivo quasi in ciel."

He throws the cash my way, spins his chair round, and with what sounds like the rising crescendo of the final chorus, he sails away, one arm stretched before him, singing his song of love and loss, back down the street, like a mighty, victorious warrior.

October 9th, 2006: The Rose

Last week, as I was opening the grates to the shop on the Dean Street side, I noticed that someone had left a single red rose wrapped in cellophane wedged inside the crack of the side door. Figuring its owner would walk by soon and retrieve it; I gently picked the rose out of the door and laid it carefully on the ground.

A week went by. This morning, standing in my usual spot, I spy the rose again, this time at the front of the shop. It is still wrapped up in the cellophane, but by now the rose has turned yellow and is completely flattened, as if it's been run over.

The road sweepers are out every afternoon in their little "Moonraker" vans sucking up everything in sight, so I can't work out how the rose could have reappeared. Is it a sign? Does its return have some kind of spiritual significance?

As I stare intently at the dead flower, pondering the message that He Above is trying to send my way, a little wire-haired terrier trots over, takes one sniff, cocks its little leg up, and pisses all over it.

October 10th, 2006: The End of Summer

Old Compton Street is changing. Summer is officially over and the sun is now an infrequent visitor. The wild colours of the street have become muted in the past couple of weeks. The street is still busy, the party atmosphere still clings with hope to the brisker air, but there're subtle changes taking place.

The Flyer Boys are losing their sparkle. Covered up for the first time. The body paint's been packed away. The tans, more bottle than sun. Less animated than they were only weeks before, they hand out their calling cards with less of a purpose. Not the career it once was.

The drag queens, like exotic birds that fly to warmer climes to roost, their grand entrances are not so common now. When they do land, they ruffle their feathers and it's off with the sequined backless tops and its all about couture-cut sleeves and full-length cocktail skirts.

Even the weather-defying, cap-sleeved muscle boys are hiding their buffed bodies behind looser-fitting Abercrombie sweatshirts. Their underdeveloped legs, encased in big break G-Star once again. Their pecs, hibernating after a long active summer of pumping and partying.

For the "girls" above the shop, it's also time to wind down. They've had an exhausting summer of pumping too; 25 a day at 15 minutes a go, working two weeks on, two weeks off.

With less sex tourism, the pimps take to haggling between themselves, pushing each other around, resorting to small-time drug deals, stored in big, baggy hoodies.

Inside the shop the last of the Spring/Summer sale clothing heads out the door, the bargain hunters retreat with glee, and we unpack Fall/Winter. Boxes full of Costume National, wool gabardine winter coats and Gianfranco Ferre, leather motocross jackets. The finest clothes for the finest wallets.

Like an old soul in front of a gas fire, Old Compton Street prepares for winter.

October 11th, 2006: Wednesday Night, 11:55 P.M. to 1:20 A.M.

11:55 P.M.

I'm sitting inside the shop by the window. It's dark. No one can see in. I'm alone. All the lights are off except

45

the dimly lit spotlights. Car headlights zig-zag, throwing shadows across the floor.

There's movement outside, people walking, groups, but no one can see me. It's quiet. The noise from outside slightly muffled behind the glass. I'm looking and watching. Sitting in my little red chair. Peering out. Like a voyeur. My computer's on. I'm poised. Ready. About to start typing. Here goes…

Two men walk past. One, Mediterranean-looking; wearing a blue-and-white-striped top, supporting a guy wearing a dark overcoat and a backpack. The man with the backpack crashes against the grates.

"Mark, fuckin' pull yourself together. You drink too much, man. You got to get a fuckin' grip. Just tell her it's over. Tell her you don't want her anymore," the Mediterranean man pleads.

Mark's legs suddenly give way and he falls to the ground. His friend pulls him to his feet, struggling to keep him there. They make their way slowly down Dean Street, Mark lurching from side to side.

I go downstairs and make a sandwich, eat it quickly, and go back upstairs to the keyboard.

12:30 A.M.

Two men. One with dreadlocks poking through his baseball cap. He's wearing a white tracksuit and he's smoking. The other's a skinhead, in a black jacket, standing right outside the window. They look into the shop, at the Cavalli display. The only lights in the shop are directed on the mannequin. They don't see me, inches away.

"What I did, right, was kick the bars in. First we got a crowbar and wrenched 'em loose. Then we kicked the fuckin' glass between," says the one with the cap, demonstrating with his foot.

The grates rattle.

"Then we just grabbed the shit. No one fuckin' came. Sold it to me mates."

The skinhead smiles in approval.

12:55 A.M.

Two men driving tuk-tuks park right outside next to each other. One's wearing an orange T-shirt, blue shorts, and a cap. The other, jeans and grey jacket. They look Eastern European. They sit there, chatting, laughing, and sharing food from a wrapped package.

1:00 A.M.

I see Danny outside. One of the pimps. He looks in the window. Sees me. Puts his thumbs up. Smiles. I wave back. He turns back to the street.

"Ladies! Ladies!" He motions to three men walking past. Two look in their twenties, the third, shaved head, in his forties. They stop. Danny walks over. "You want some ladies? No charge to look. If you don't like what you see there's no charge."

"They fit?" says the shaved-haired man. "I don't want no fat bird!"

A tall black man wearing a crombie, brogues, and a shirt and tie walks across Dean Street toward the group. "What they looking for, Danny?"

"We want fit birds, mate. Not fat! Fit! And they gotta have big tits," says the shaved-haired man.

"Come with me, guys. These girls are really fit. I'm tellin' you."

The tall man beckons the three men to the door to the brothel, just behind where I'm typing. I hear them stomp up the stairs. One comes back down less than a minute later. He walks away, looking back over his shoulder every few minutes.

1:10 A.M.

I'm getting tired now. The typing becoming heavier. Harder to concentrate, to focus outside.

Two teenagers. The hint of a goatee on each. They stand six inches away from me. One turns toward me and still doesn't see me. He digs deep into his pocket and pulls out a wad of plastic with a brown lump inside. He picks a piece off and gives it to his friend. Suddenly he looks right at me. We hold each other's gaze. He shrugs and turns away.

1:20 A.M.

There are seven men outside the window. They're in a group, talking, as if hatching a plan. One throws a punch at another. Like he's sparring with a punching bag. I can't make out if it's real or not. It's not. But it still looks threatening.

Every now and again the group look over. In my direction? It is in my direction. They're discussing what to do. I feel like I've been foiled. This doesn't look good. I'm going to post this and close down the computer now before something bad happens.

October 12th, 2006: Healing the World
Moses comes in this morning.

In his mid-twenties, dressed in a green baggy cardigan, with blue baggy jeans; his hair, wild, brown, pre-Raphaelite kiss curls framing his face, accentuating his chestnut oval eyes.

"I haven't seen you for such a long time. I've been thinking about you," he says, his voice soft, his accent northern Spanish. "The day is beautiful. I manifest beauty wherever I walk."

He reaches into his bag and pulls out a small blue bottle of essential oil from Neals Yard, applying a few drops to his wrists, reaching over and applying a few to mine.

"Rub it on your forehead, face, chin, and all the way down. It's geranium oil," he says quietly. "I'm going to Crystal Palace tonight. You must come. Amma Chi will be there. There'll be thousands of people. She'll be clearing the karma of humanity, channelling and chanting, manifesting beauty. We pray, sing songs, and heal the world of violence," he says, his voice becoming more and more excited, his brown eyes widening. "Some people have been there for three days already, without eating or sleeping. I did it once and nearly died. It's a very ancient mantra, older than the Bible, six thousand words repeated over and over. It's pure love. We'll all be wearing white robes."

I nod, trying to wipe the oil off on a tissue beneath the counter.

"Then Amma manifests flowers, petals from her hands, and oil. It smells of roses and sandalwood. I'll bring some in for you. My present to you. It's all about love and harmony. It's very emotional. We sit there for hours and cry for the love of the world."

Twenty minutes later, in comes Moses's boyfriend, sporting a huge black eye.

"How did you get that?" I ask, wincing, as it looks really painful.

"Oh this?" he says, feeling his swollen face. "I had a really rough sex session with Moses last night. He hit me a bit too hard. It was fun, though. I'm just off to Clone Zone now to get us some fisting gloves for the weekend."

October 14th, 2006: In the Event of My Death

We are having a little local difficulty with gangsters. I won't go into details, for obvious reasons, but should my blogs one day come to a complete stop ("Thank God!" I hear you say) and my headless torso is found floating in the Thames, please note the following:

1. The bloated appearance of my torso is actually due to water retention, as I am only two donuts a day away from a six-pack.

2. The bloated appearance of my penis is, however, natural.

3. Any clothes attached to my torso are designer, and (if we are still trading) are only available at Dirty White Boy,

where we provide free alterations on all our clothing and they're ready in 24 hours.

4. To save time during the autopsy, you will find the residue of the following chemicals in my body; "E," "K," and a very small amount of "C," although most of it will be over two years old (not used since I took my wedding vows).

5. My undercarriage is shaved, and this is not a sign of West African black magic.

For recognition purposes, please bear in mind:

1. I do not have any tattoos (although I once had a henna tattoo in the 90s and was almost extradited from Miami when the tattooed guy I slept with woke up the next day to find black inky flakes all over his body).

2. I have an open pore on my back which occasionally fills up. My ex-boyfriend always insisted it was the size of a pothole, although I would dispute this, as it always took him a good twenty minutes to find it before he could have a good squeeze.

Should my head bob to the surface a week later, I would like to point out that:

1. For a dental match, all teeth are my own.

2. Any wrinkles are due to the water exposure, as I have been using Nivea day and night since first seeing the Nanette Newman ad in the 70s.

3. The salt–and-pepper "Barbara Bush" hair colour (more salt, I admit) is not due to pollution but is, unfortunately, natural.

In the event of my death, could my MySpace friends advise my boyfriend, Jorge, and my ex-boyfriend, Dale, that although I do not have any money to leave a proper will, I do have 360 points on my Tesco Clubcard, which should provide them with a month's worth of Crunchy Nut Cornflakes. Plus, I have 15,000 Virgin airmiles, which should get one of them a flight to Alicante (one way).

P.S. Could you also please tell Jorge he is never to remarry, or if he does the bitch has to be over the age of 43 so I'll always be the Princess Di.

October 14th, 2006: Me? Gay?
A well-dressed, well-groomed gentleman, spectacles hanging on a long gold chain around his neck, comes into the shop.

"I'm looking for a floral-patterned, pink silk flowing shirt. But it has to have very big red roses all over it. Do you have one?" he says, as he flicks through the racks of shirts, disinterestedly.

"We have one here," I reply, smiling, holding up a Gianfranco Ferre First Collection shirt which matches his requirements exactly.

"Oh no!" he says, in mock horror. "That's far too gay!"

October 15th, 2006: Thong Man
Thong Man calls every few weeks to check if we've received the latest L'Homme Invisible underwear range from Paris.

An ex–art lecturer, in his seventies, with rather a large paunch and short tufts of black hair, Thong Man is a real connoisseur. Although I'm the seller and he's the customer, the tables are well and truly turned whenever he breezes in.

He's always very polite, waiting patiently until I've got a free moment before our "class" begins. Then he takes a few pairs of undies off the racks and he talks me through the lining, the cut of the pouch, the "snug factor" for each testicle, the feel of the silk against the foreskin; talking about the Mini Boxer, the Boxer Muscle, the Slip, the Mini Slip, the Thong, with the same kind of enthusiasm that Sir David Attenborough uses when sifting through six-foot ant mounds.

It would be easy to dismiss Thong Man as a bit of a pervert, but it doesn't come across that way, as he treats each piece of underwear as though it's a work of art. I'm sure he must've been a great lecturer and I treat him like one, sitting behind the counter, hanging on to his every word like the teacher's pet.

Sometimes he brings his own thongs in with him, and when he does he holds them up to the light, pointing out the intricate weaving used on each hem, on each fold. Then, when the class is over, he neatly refolds his thongs, carefully placing them back in his bag, lovingly, like he's tucking a baby in bed. I imagine him at home each night, walking through his walk-in wardrobe, like Imelda Marcos, gliding his fingers feverishly along racks and racks of underwear, sorted by colour, by fabric, by season.

Strangely, Thong Man is one of the few customers with a genuine interest and appreciation in our clothes. One day he may even buy some from us. Until then, I'll continue with my classes, as I feel as if I'm being groomed by Thong Man, in preparation for the day that the "underwear baton" is passed my way.

October 16th, 2006: The Cuban Closet

Jorge's mother has been staying for the last few days. Eighty-six years old. This is the first time she has left Miami since arriving there in the 60s, having left Cuba with her two small children just before Castro came to power.

The Cuban culture, coupled with her age, means that Jorge's homosexuality, although tolerated, is not discussed. Thus the day before her arrival, Jorge carried out a frantic "de-gay" of our flat, while I sat and watched disapprovingly, spouting "I'm so glad I'm out" and "You're a traitor to the cause" mantras.

Out went the gay rags, the Oscar Wilde and Mapplethorpe biographies (the picture of the bullwhip up his ass being a slight giveaway) and last month's *Vanity Fair* (Tom Cruise on the front cover). All my Clarins eye creams, moisturizers, and Aveda hair products were hidden, magically replaced with Imperial Leather soap and Head & Shoulders shampoo. Condoms, lube, cock rings were banished from their "quick-access areas," and family photos dusted down and arranged carefully in their place. Ninety-five percent of my film collection was "bin-bagged" (including my Beverly Callard Work Out video); even the Lalique ornament depicting two lovebirds found a new nest underneath the spare bedding. It felt like we'd been ransacked by Straight Eye for the Queer Guy and I'd woken up married to Jim Davidson.

As our shop is on the gayest street in the UK, what Jorge hadn't quite worked out was how he was going to manoeuvre his wheelchair-bound mother around the neighbourhood. Although it was relatively easy to bin-bag my entire Bette Davis DVD collection, two tattooed bears would prove more of a challenge.

The first day he took her out, he pushed her along Old Compton Street, on the opposite side to the Admiral Duncan, before crisscrossing the street again as he passed Comptons.

This toing and froing obviously added time to each journey, and his mother asked at one point whether Old Compton Street was the longest street in London. By the second day she thought that this mode of travelling was in fact a British custom and, like Pavlov's dog, she began repositioning herself in her wheelchair, ready for a quick detour, every time she spotted a rainbow flag.

Putting love before principle, I decided to help by strategically walking on the inside of the street as we passed Clone Zone, skilfully timing my step so that I completely blocked out the "free porn DVD with every new dildo" window display.

We are now on the last day, and I think, for all Jorge's efforts, his mother has twigged. She keeps asking Jorge why he has a "strange haircut" like all the other "strange people," and she's asked him four times already when I'm going to take the gifts she'd brought me back to my own home.

The closet bubble finally burst tonight. Unable to contain himself anymore, Jorge shouted back at her, "Clay's not taking the gifts home. They're staying here. Okay?" It all went very quiet and I have a feeling it's going to be a very long drive to the airport tomorrow...

October 19th, 2006: Let the Complication Fade

The shop's takings continue to plummet ever downwards. Like a runaway steam train, the last of the wood thrown onto dying embers. "Ladies and Gentlemen, this train will not be stopping at the next station due to spiralling debts on the track."

I step outside and stand by the Dean Street window. The shop weighs heavy. I need a break from this place. To fly away. Let the complication fade. Long distance. Fade away. "Nobody really knows what they're doing; we're all getting by on a wing and a prayer."

I look across at Costa, the evening crowds chatting happily, then down at my fingernails, at the dirt underneath. I dig my bottom teeth under the nail of my right forefinger. It leaves a bitter taste as I swallow. The tension subsides, just for a moment. I glance to my left.

There's Ben, Dean Street's Artful Dodger, in his sky-blue tracksuit and cheap trainers, unshaven face, standing feet away; distressed, like he's been crying, which isn't like him. He's normally such a confident, cocky street kid.

He holds my gaze for a second, then turns his head, eyes to the ground. His cheek looks red, his eyes watery. Me in the school playground.

"Ben! You okay?" I call across. "Are you in some kind of trouble?"

I take a step toward him. He takes one back.

"I don't need no help. Just leave me alone."

Stalemate.

So I move back a step. Back to my own problems, the weight of my world. And he, he moves back to his.

October 22nd, 2006: What the Eye Doesn't See

"What we got to do is hit a shop that takes loads of money. It's no good with these ones round here," says one of the men outside the shop.

As they discuss their impending crime, a small, cheaply dressed girl walks over, her hair scraped back severely from her forehead and held in place in a tight ponytail. "Any of you want business?"

"Fuck off, you drugged-up slag!" sneers one of the men. "Who'd want a crack whore like you?"

As I watch this scene play out in front of my window, I notice, just across the road, outside Soho Books, a film crew setting up cameras, lighting equipment, and chairs. Intrigued, I decide to see what is happening.

Dodging the group of men outside who are discussing the timing of their next gang attack as casually, and as vocally, as if arranging what time they'd all meet at the pub later, I walk over to the film crew. "Hello," I say cheerfully, addressing the person who appears to be the director. "I work just across the road. What're you filming today?"

"Hello," he replies gruffly, without even looking in my direction. "Pop video."

"Oh, that sounds interesting. What's it about?" I say, trying to keep the conversation going.

At this, he turns round, sighs, and with a haughty look on his face peers at me from the top of his glasses as if I were a naughty schoolboy who'd just stepped into the headmaster's office. "It's a concept we're filming here. If you know what we mean by that," he says, condescendingly.

"Yes, I've come across that term," I reply, determined to remain cheerful, despite suddenly wanting to take his glasses off, snap them in half, tread on them, and walk off.

"Well, with the help of these actors over here," he says, sighing again and pointing to a group of college kids sipping coffee nearby, "we're going to use crime as the concept and create a criminal environment here that most people don't even notice when they come to Soho. It's around you everyday, you know, and you've probably never even seen it."

Bored with our conversation, he turns round to face his film crew. "Right! Get the actors ready," he shouts at his team. "And can someone please get rid of those people over there?" he says, pointing at the gang of thieves and the prostitute standing nearby.

October 23rd, 2006: The New Recruits

Monday evening, a huge hullabaloo going on outside the shop. Sue and Maggie, the girls from the brothel above, are pacing up and down Dean Street, talking into their mobiles, like City Traders in red stilettos.

Every few minutes Maggie gives me a little wave and blows me a kiss, while Sue, the madam, the larger of the two, screams into her phone, "Where are they? They were meant to be here by now!" She clutches the phone as if it's a hand grenade, and the look on her face suggests that she's about to pull the pin any second.

What's going on? Late condom delivery? An Asian block booking cancelled at the last minute? Intrigued, I reach for the Pledge and dust the windowsill frantically, my nose leaving greasy smears on the glass.

Just as I'm at the point of Pledging the paint away, a van screeches along Old Compton Street and parks on the corner of Dean Street. By now I'm desperate to find out what's going on and totally ignoring the customers in the shop.

"This look good on me?" says a camp Thai boy standing behind me trying on an Armand Basi skullcap.

"Yes, your bum looks great in that," I say, eyes fixed firmly on the street.

Suddenly the van doors are pulled back and out step six pretty girls laden with bags and suitcases. Spanish, Italian, Eastern European. They look really excited to be here. Like convent girls on their first school outing. They look around, laugh, joke, and shake their dreamy "Julia Roberts in *Pretty Woman*" hair.

Sue and Maggie rush to greet them, and the new arrivals politely kiss them three times on each cheek. Not quite getting the Mediterranean custom, Sue moves her head in the wrong direction and ends up getting kissed three times on the nose.

As I watch transfixed, wondering if the newcomers know what lies in store, two of them look in my direction. Realising I've been caught gawping, I turn back round a bit too quickly, knocking the camp Thai boy to the floor. As he falls, he grabs my arm, and I land right on top of him, pinning him to the floor.

"Oh! You so big... What good service. I shop here again!"

October 26th, 2006: My Love Affair
Whenever I leave Soho it's just like saying goodbye to a lover.

As I walk down Old Compton Street and head down Moor Street, past the Palace Theatre, the atmosphere starts to change. Memories of drunken sex sessions gradually disappear. I start to miss his voice, his touch, what we have in common. Lying in his arms, I miss that freedom to be myself. And yet, when we're together again, I'm anxious. I question what brought us together in the first place, how long we're going to last, who sleeps in our bed when I leave.

This place pulls me backwards and forwards. One minute, it's the greatest love of my life, and the next, a love affair that's coated in sadness wherever I turn.

I think of my friend Chico, who nursed his partner to the bitter end. When it was over he was left with too much love to give and a lot of money left to spend. He handed out both to every *QX* hooker in town. One of them came into the shop on Saturday and told me that Chico won't be coming back. He's been locked up in prison for raping a guy. Three guys testified against him. There's just no way. He's seven stone, totally passive. Couldn't rape a fly. It was a setup.

I see another friend. One of the most beautiful boys to arrive in London two years ago. Lean, defined, Nordic features. Now, his eyes have lost their sparkle; his face, sunken; his teeth, shattered after collapsing on "G"; his body, lost. Blown his money. Blown his looks. Blown his brain.

Last night, as I walked past the cash machine on Dean Street, I saw a beautiful young girl with thick, red hair cascading around her shoulders, sitting on the ground, wrapped in a blanket, in the rain, begging. Something about her beauty made me feel very sad; I was about to cry.

My love affair with this place is playing with my mind, toying with my affections. It's a loving and a destructive relationship in equal measure which feeds into my writing. If I don't leave soon, someone's going to get hurt. But I can't leave yet. Not just yet.

October 27th, 2006: An Unusual Start to the Day

As I lightly dust the crotch of the naked shop mannequin this morning, in walks Duane, fresh from his porn audition in Spain. Tall, lean, handsome, Duane fulfils all the necessary requirements for the Kristen Bjorn productions.

"How did it go?" I ask, trying to decide whether a quick spray of Windowlene would add a nice gloss to the left-hanging nut.

"I got the job," he says, watching me buff. "Apparently I did really well. Fucked three guys and shot the furthest. It was weird, though. Sort of like auditioning for *X Fucktor*."

We chat for a while, Duane describing the positions he adopted, me telling him how many thongs I've sold, when in walks Clinton, the leather-clad priest.

"Hello, dear," says Clinton. "How's life in the wacky world of retail?"

"Okay," I reply. "Meet my friend Duane."

As I continue polishing, their conversation moves quickly from the best way to wear a studded cock ring to orgy etiquette. ("Is it polite to fuck the host in front of his boyfriend?" "Would you help yourself to a cucumber from the fridge?")

By now I've studiously buffed both balls and am working my way up to the penis, rubbing away frantically like a hooker on coke, when in walks Sue, the madam from the brothel above.

"Hello, luv. Have you got any metal cutters? We've got a guy chained to the bed upstairs and we've lost the key!"

October 28th, 2006: The Flipping Fireman

I am standing outside the shop as a woman is about to take a picture of our shop sign, Dirty White Boy. For some reason the sign's as popular with tourists as the Changing of the Guard. Spotting a potential sale, I move in quickly.

"Why not buy a T-shirt with the logo on instead?" I say, rubbing my grubby fingers behind my back.

"That's a good idea!" says the "chavette," and in she steps.

"Oh, this is perfect." She holds up a blue T-shirt with the logo emblazoned all over it. "I'm buying it for an ex-boyfriend. He thinks he's straight, but he's definitely not."

"What makes you think he's not?" I ask, edging her toward the till.

"Honey! Do you want me to spell it out?" says Miss Chavette.

"Yes, please," I reply, feeling a blog coming on.

"Listen, sugar. When your boyfriend flips you over every night so you're choking on the pillow, with no foreplay, then you get an inkling. You know what I'm sayin'?"

"Oh, well," I say, folding the T-shirt. "We've all been there."

"Actually, do you mind if I go for the extra large?" Miss Chavette asks, changing the subject, her face turning a bit sour. "He's a fireman and he's got a very big build."

"A fireman?" I drool. "Does he have the outfit and everything?"

"Oh, yeah! He's really high up. He's even got a big band round his helmet!"

November 4ᵗʰ, 2006: Thank God for Soho's Straight Men

They swagger into the shop, all big and butch, with a "Right, mate!" after mistaking my salivating cruise for a friendly gesture. Usually fresh from digging up some grotty road, the smell of tarmac in their tousled hair, with big workman's muscles.

"I'll take three of those, one in each colour," they'll say, pointing to the £200 Zegna shirts.

"You should really try them on first," I reply, as my feverish hands inch toward their wad of hard-earned cash. But it's always, "Nah, it'll be fine, mate, and you don't need to bother with the fancy wrapping." And I watch, mortified, as they stuff the best shirts we have into their Army and Navy mountaineering backpacks.

Then we have Soho's gay customers.

With them it's all about the grand entrance. Usually fresh from the gym, where they've spent 20 minutes doing their chests (never legs) and 45 minutes in the sauna.

"Hello, can I help you?" I say. They either studiously ignore me or look at me as if I'm the Gaydar date who doesn't quite match the pic. Then, after eyeing up our stock of 23 of the most famous designers in the world, they'll throw some waspish retort over like, "I don't see Prada" or "I can't *do* charcoal grey."

If I do manage to win them over, there are still a number of hurdles I have to smilingly leap across before a sale is imminent, although I do find it's usually best to just keep on nodding when asked, "Do you think my bum looks good in these shoes?" or "Will the taupe on this collar match my jeans/sofa/shih tzu?"

Mind you, even flattery doesn't always work, as I found on Saturday when attempting to get Nigel from Aberdeen to part with his beautician's wages. Sporting the kind of fake tan that would make Dale Winton pull a face and a voice that sounded like somebody was pulling very hard on his testicles, he didn't mince his words when I tried to help him with a shirt.

"This isn't my size and even if it was I really hate it, it's too young for me," he says, as he puts his Girls Aloud crop-top T-shirt back on.

Last, but not least, we have the lesbian customers.

They'll stomp in with their Birkenstocks and fleeces, head straight to the sale rack, and flick through the extra-large jeans. There's none of this "Does my bum look good in this?" It's more about "Can I get my bum in this?"

But what I love about the lesbian shopper is there's no attitude, no pretentiousness, and to them it doesn't matter if it's last year's collection because, quite rightly, it's just a pair of jeans. Maybe we should open another shop just for them: Dirty White Dyke!

November 5th, 2006: Cultural Differences
On Sunday afternoon, a rather large American bursts into the shop and marches up to the counter. "I bought these Levi's last year in Texas for thirty dollars!" he barks, looking down and admiring his overly tight, 1970s-style jeans.

As I peer over the counter, I can't help but notice that his willy is squashed so tightly against his right thigh that I imagine the poor thing to be on the verge of death.

"Well, you certainly have an eye for a bargain," I reply, wondering if it requires the kiss of life.

"I do!" he shouts back. "That's why I'm not buying anything here!" With that, he marches right back out.

Minutes later, in comes a Chinese gentleman with a briefcase under his arm. He tiptoes up to the counter, places his briefcase on the floor by his side, clears his throat, and announces, "I got very big damp problem!"

"Oh dear," I say sympathetically. "Have you tried drinking less tea?"

"You no understand. My tiles fall off in bathroom. One hit me on head when I take shower."

I am a bit stumped at this and wait patiently for him to elaborate; he doesn't. So I give him a kind of raised eyebrow, half smile, as if to say, "Tiles! Who'd have them?"

No response.

Then he suddenly blurts out, "No money for clothes! I need to buy tile." He picks up his bag, turns round, and tiptoes back out again.

November 7th, 2006: Twin Towns?

Standing in the shop doorway this evening, I am suddenly accosted by three cameramen and a wire-haired interviewer.

"Hi!" says Wire Hair enthusiastically in a broad Welsh accent. "We'd like to ask you some questions. Is that okay?"

Before I have a chance to check my teeth for spinach, he is off.

"We're filming a documentary, comparing my hometown in Wales with Soho, because we think there're probably some similarities. So. First question. Are you single?"

"No, I'm married."

"And where's your wife at the moment?" he asks, ticking

a box on his survey.

"He's sitting in the shop" I reply, pointing to Jorge.

"He?" says Wire Hair, looking up from his survey. The cameramen takes a step closer, filming me from all angles as if I am an exotic flower in a David Attenborough *Life on Earth* special.

"Yes, he!" I repeat, suddenly feeling the urge to pout like Posh.

"So. You're. A. Married. Gay. Man," he says, placing emphasis on every word like a teacher delivering a How to Speak English class.

"Yes. I. Am," I say. I notice that he is now drawing a separate little box on his survey.

This banter goes on for a while. I explain how Jorge and I were married in Massachusetts, and under the Civil Partnership Act he was able to come into the country as my partner. By now I can see Wire Hair is getting a bit exasperated, wishing he'd found an easier target.

"Okay. Now I don't suppose there's a lot of crime here? Not right in the heart of London?" he says smugly, thinking this would be an easier question.

"Well," I say, clearing my throat as if getting ready for an Oscar speech. "In the past month we've had three gang attacks, credit card fraud, someone waving a gun at the shop, and every night the local *Big Issue* seller threatens to burn our shop down."

Wire Hair scribbles away frantically, ticking boxes left, right, and centre.

"Then, two Sundays ago, there was a rape on Dean Street in broad daylight, and a murder the month before on Frith Street."

By now he's run out of boxes and is staring at me with his mouth open, pen held in midair.

"Then there's the pimps and the drug dealers, they're usually here by eight. What else? Oh yes! We've got a brothel above. But that's not crime as such because I think the council are paid to ignore it."

Meanwhile, the cameramen whiz their hefty cameras toward Dean Street, Old Compton Street, the brothel, back to me again, as if filming some kind of mad James Bond car chase. Wire Hair looks back and forth, as though about to get mugged at any second.

"Quick question," I say. "Any similarities between Soho and Tyddewi so far?"

November 8th, 2006: Introducing...GAGs

I think by now we all know what is meant by the word *chav*. Pick up *Heat* magazine and you'll no doubt be inundated with articles about a very close relation, the "WAG." Well, for any cultural anthropologists out there, I would like to introduce you to another equally strange phenomenon. Ladies and gentlemen, let's hear it for "gay Asians and their granddaddies," or GAGs.

Although the *Penguin English Dictionary*'s definition of a *gag* has its use here—"something thrust into the mouth to keep it open"—let's think of the GAG as a gay couple: one being a camp Asian man and the other being an extremely older European gentleman. But are GAGs a new phenomenon? Are GAGs the new chavs?

Well, actually, no. GAGs are no strangers to these shores; there have been sightings in the urban areas of London for many a year. However, their appearance does seem to be on the increase, and retail chains are quickly waking up to the fact that there is a new market out there, as Granddaddy can often be found dishing out huge wads of his pension to buy the gay Asian a pretty, sparkly top. Indeed, it is thought that M&S's sudden rise in profits is in fact due to the GAGs flocking to their women's wear diamanté winter collection.

So, what is the reason behind this sudden increase?

Is global warming to blame? Gay Asians flocking to this country to seek refuge from rising sea levels and tsunamis and, once here, British granddaddies are simply "doing a Madonna"? In other words, is Asia the new gay Malawi?

It's still unclear. What I can report is that Dirty White Boy very much appreciates this new grouping and we would like to point out that our new, super-duper small, glittery, crop-top T-shirts are now in stock!

November 12th, 2006: Letting Go

It's been happening so slowly I didn't realize anything was amiss.

A few days ago I was looking round the shop and it suddenly hit me: where once these shelves were full, brimming with beautiful clothes, now they're half empty, gathering dust. I've been so caught up in everything else going on I didn't really notice. But one by one, all those lovely clothes, wrapped up so neatly, have been sold, ready for someone else to try on. They've been slipping through our fingers and we never thought to try and hold on to them—replaced with something equally beautiful, I know, but not quite the same. And now it's too late to get them back, those clothes we once shared at the beginning, those clothes that made us both so excited, the first time we met.

November 20th, 2006: The Gay Rainbow

It poured with rain this afternoon from one o'clock to three o'clock. Old Compton Street went from "hustle and bustle" to "let's take shelter." Big dirty puddles and big dirty umbrellas; muscle queens rushing around, shrieking, protecting their hair. A colony of ants under attack.

When it stopped, I stood on the doorstep of the shop and looked down Old Compton Street. At the end of the street, high above, a rainbow appeared, linking the north side and the south side. Like a gay-rainbow-coloured gateway leading to paradise.

I imagined Him Above looking down, saying, "Fuck Westminster Council for not allowing gay businesses to have a rainbow flag above their premises. I know! I'll give them one of their own!"

November 22nd, 2006: The 8½-inch Cock

Last week, I was typing away by the window, very late at night, watching the evening's entertainment outside—police arresting pimps, crackheads dancing in the street—when I noticed a grey-haired man in a duffle coat walking up and down, peering in at me. After his third lap, I was starting to get a bit nervous, thinking perhaps Dennis Nielsen had been paroled. So I shut down my laptop and, rather than going home, went downstairs to sleep.

Fast-forward to a few minutes ago. I'm standing on the doorstep and a guy with a grey goatee and Nana Mouskouri glasses walks up to me, stopping inches from my face.

"Do you remember me?" he says, licking his top lip and breathing what smells like Batchelors Cuppa Soup (Oxtail flavour) in my face.

"Erm, no I don't think so..." I reply, noticing he is fiddling with something in his pocket which doesn't look like a wallet.

"You were watching me the other night. I wanted to come in but there were too many people around," he whispers.

Then the penny drops. "Oh, I remember," I say, taking a step back.

"I've got eight and a half inches down here," he says, grabbing the crotch on his brown nylon stay-press trousers and moving a step closer. "How about we take a wander into your dressing room and I'll show what I can do with it?"

"Well, I think we both know what you can do with it," I squeak, like a virgin on her wedding night. "Look, I appreciate the offer, but I have a boyfriend." I run back into the shop clutching my behind.

What is it about this shop and the dressing rooms? We seem to be attracting all sorts lately looking for a bit of "how's your father?"

To give you another example, this weekend we had a straight guy take the L'Homme Invisible underwear into the dressing room. After a few minutes, and much puffing and panting, he pulled back the curtains dramatically, as if about to sing a show tune, and said, "What do you think, mate?"

Now don't get me wrong, straight men are good eye candy, but the genital reality doesn't quite work for me. I can't be doing with yards of pubic hair. Tickle my tonsils by all means, but I ain't blowing a yukka.

So for all you customers out there—if you want to come in and flash your willy, please do—but please note that, for the foreseeable future, staff are under strict instructions to look but not touch.

November 24th, 2006: Another Leak

Chuckling to myself in bed while reading Rupert Smith's *Service Wash*, I suddenly hear a "drip...drip...drip..." noise coming from the stairway.

"What's that?" I whisper to Jorge, who is snoring beside me. "Jorge! Can you hear that noise?"

"You're dreaming," he says, dreaming.

"I'm not. I'm wide awake. There's something in the room, I swear!"

Drip, drip, drip, drip.

Then it hits me. The dripping noise is in fact—a drip.

"Oh God! The brothel's leaking again!"

This is the seventh leak this year from the "girls" above. So after prodding Jorge in the back (with my finger) and getting no response, I jump out of bed, put my trackies on, look down at the outline of my protruding willy, take the trackies off and put my underpants on first, and then run up the stairway and out onto Dean Street.

Although it is late, the street is still buzzing. The pimps, Danny and David, are scouting around, and a couple of "girls" who use the side street to do their "business" are standing against the shop window, applying makeup.

"Hey, Clay," shouts Danny as I rush through the side door to the brothel above. "I can get you blow job discount if you want one!"

By the time I climb the stairway to the first-floor flat it is quite dark, the only light streaming from underneath the flat door. Hearing voices and what sounds, bizarrely, like Madonna's "Like a Virgin" playing in the background, I knock hard three times.

"Sue! Maggie! Let me in! We've got a leak in the basement!"

No response.

I shout again. This time, someone shouts back, "Come in!" I turn the handle, fling the door open, and burst into the room, only to stop dead in my tracks when I realise what I thought was someone shouting "Come in" is in fact the muffled sound of someone shouting, "I'm coming!"

It takes a few seconds before I realise where the voice is coming from, as all I can see initially is Sue at one end of the bed, squatting down, and Maggie halfway down the bed, both of them bobbing up and down, naked—Sue's long blonde hair flying round like a bleached Kate Bush and Maggie's breasts jangling like coconuts in a hurricane.

Now, as these girls are on the large size, it is only between bounces that I can make out that there's a long, thin, pale man being pulverised underneath, his face buried deep inside Sue's bush and his willy being pulled out of all proportion by Maggie's crack canyon.

"I'm coming!" he screams (although what comes out is more of a bush tickling: "I'm-m-m-m chumming!").

"What is it, Clay? Can't you see we're busy?" Sue puffs, bouncing up and down as if on a merry-go-round.

"I've come about the leak. I think your sink's overflowing again!"

"Maggie," says Sue, keeping her rhythm perfectly on the man's face, as if it was some kind of Olympic event. "Did you leave that tap on?"

"Not me," Maggie replies, cupping her breasts and looking in my direction.

"I'm-m-m-m chhhu-u-m-m-m-m-m-ing!" screams the pale man underneath, his legs banging up and down like he's having some kind of epileptic fit.

"Do you mind if I just check?"

"No, go ahead, love, but make it quick, we'll need to use that sink in a minute to clean off."

So I step into the shower room and, sure enough, the sink is overflowing, a pool of water spreading across the floor.

Five minutes later I am back in the basement, tiptoeing across the room and creeping back into bed.

"Bad dream?" Jorge grunts, half asleep.

"You could say that," I whisper back, as I drift off.

November 27th, 2006: Dangerous Liaisons

I sit behind the counter every day and talk politely to each customer who comes in. Just everyday chitchat, really—the weather, the clothes, the clubs, always making sure that the customer feels at ease. I'm professional, right down to my fingertips.

Every now and again, however, a rude customer will come in and put this professionalism to the test. When this happens, I'm chomping at the bit to answer them back. But, instead, I take a deep breath and repeat the mantra "The customer is always right," thereby restoring peace and harmony.

But sometimes, when the rudeness gets a bit too much, a

transformation takes place. My number one crop turns into a blonde, swept-back bouffant. Pearls appear in my ears. My face is powdered white, with big rouge cheeks, and I go from Clayton, shop owner, to Glenn Close in *Dangerous Liaisons*. Then I'll follow the rude customer around the shop, batting away their bitchy asides with equally waspish retorts of my own—but instead of whispering them behind a big ostrich-feather fan, mine go on in my head. They're just as deadly but, as I need their grubby cash, the gob stays shut. Here's what happens…

"Good morning. How are you today? It's a lovely day, isn't it?"

"I want to try that T-shirt on in the window!"

(Why not use the dressing room?) "Of course, sir!" I take the T-shirt down off the hanger and hand it to the customer.

"Is this the price?" he sneers.

(No, it's the size of my willy in centimetres!) "That's correct, sir!"

"Forty-six? Is that pounds?"

(No—yen!) "Yes, forty-six pounds. That is correct. They are hand-glittered and sparkled and we have them imported from the US."

"I don't care about that! Do you have my size?"

(Triple XL?) "Yes, we do. If you'd like to step this way and start with this size I can get you a bigger one if you need it."

Customer comes back out of the dressing room wearing said garment. "I don't like it!"

(Time for flattery.) "Well, it's a great colour for you."

"Well, I suppose it works with these trousers."

(And it matches your orange face.) "And the orange on the sleeve matches your Mediterranean complexion."

"You think so?"

(Oh, dear… Please don't look at me like that.) "You'll be fighting them off in this street."

"Okay. I'll take it!"

I think you get where I'm coming from. So the next time you step into Dirty White Boy demanding attention and throwing clothes at me like I'm the underpaid PA in *The Devil Wears Prada*, remember: Glenn Close. Before *Dangerous Liaisons* she did *Fatal Attraction*, and we all know what happened to the bunny, now, don't we?

November 27th, 2006: How to Lose a Sale
An American walks in, browses around the rails, lays a shirt on the counter, and says, "I'd like to take this shirt, please."

"Certainly, sir," I reply. "I'll wrap it for you."

"No need to do anything too fancy," he says. "By the way, what are the best gay clubs around here?"

Thinking I am being very funny, I summon up my "Derek" impression from *The Catherine Tate Show* and say, "I beg your pardon?"

"Which are the best gay clubs in the area? Which gay club do you go to?" he says.

"Which gay clubs do I go to? Gay clubs? Me, dear? Gay, dear? No, dear. How very dare you!"

He looks at me a bit strangely, but I carry on regardless. "I've been working in this shop for twenty-five years and never have I been accused of parking the bike up the dirt track. How very dare you!"

He runs out of the shop.

November 29th, 2006: Black Tufts vs. Miss Leather-clad
Sitting behind the counter today, keeping myself busy by breathing and staring into space, I suddenly become aware of a commotion outside—so I immediately spring into action and start dusting frantically around the windowsill.

After a few minutes, a small crowd has gathered (to watch the commotion, not my dusting).

"Get your hands off me!" a leather-clad woman says, struggling with her handbag.

"Someone help me! She's got my money!" shouts a middle-aged Pakistani man sporting a bright red Pringle jumper and the last remaining tufts of dyed black hair above each ear.

This palaver goes on for a few minutes, backwards and forwards, like a handbag tug-of-war, until the crowd, realising it is just another hooker/client fight, gradually disperses. Not me. I decide to do a Sir Lancelot number and subtly dust my way to the doorway.

"Hey! You!" says Black Tufts. "Please help me! She's got my money!" He pulls the handbag toward the shop.

"Oi! Mate! Tell 'im! I ain't got his bloody money!" shouts Miss Leather-clad, jerking the bag back.

By now the "fight" is starting to get more aggressive, and before I know what is happening they are pulling, fighting, and scratching their way inside the shop doorway.

"Please—can you both stop? Not in here!" I say, waving my duster in their direction.

"I want my money! You stole my wallet!"

"I didn't steal your wallet. You got your bleedin' blow job and it cost you. That's all!"

Smack! Pop! Kerpow! The "gruesome twosome" are getting close to knocking down my Punto Blanco underwear display. So, realising a waving duster isn't really having the desired effect, I decide to take firmer action.

"Listen!" I shout. "LISTEN!" They stop, Black Tufts still holding the handbag and Miss Leather-clad pulling on the Pringle. "You can't just come in here fighting. I'm trying to run a business here!"

"Well, she's got my money!"

"No, I ain't!"

"Stop it! Both of you! Have you got his money?" I say, turning to face Miss Leather-clad.

"No! I've got his thirty pounds, that's all! Do you think I'd blow that for free?" she snarls.

She has a point. I turn to face Black Tufts. "Did you know your blow job would be thirty pounds?" I say, sounding like Judge Judy.

"Yes—but she took my wallet as well!" says Black Tufts, loosening his grip on the handbag.

Then, as quick as a flash, Miss Leather-clad gives the bag a violent jerk and runs out of the shop, the tattoo of her stilettos echoing behind.

"That was your fault!" shouts Black Tufts. "You were probably in on this together—you're probably her pimp!" And with that, he speeds off down Old Compton Street in hot pursuit.

November 29th, 2006: Brother Martin

As I chat outside the shop with David, one of the pimps, a stocky bear with a shaved head and a long brown beard, dressed in a grey cloak, walks over.

"Hello, guys."

"Are you a buddha?" says David to the bear.

"No, I'm a Franciscan monk. My name's Brother Martin," he replies in a strong American accent, shaking our hands.

Yeah, right! I think. What comes out is "You're really a monk and you live in a monastery?" Which, on reflection, is a bit of a stupid question.

"Yes. In Canning Town. Although I'm originally from Nebraska, I actually started off as a friar in the South Bronx. Here, take one of these." He hands me a green slip of paper and a pendant of the Virgin Mary on a blue string.

"Umm, I'm sorry to sound ignorant, but what do I do with this?" I say, staring at the blank piece of paper.

"Oh, I am sorry! Here, take another." He hands me another piece, on which is written *Before I formed you in the womb I knew you. —Jeremiah 1:5.*

"Well, thank you, Brother Martin. Umm, are you just passing through or have you deliberately chosen this spot?"

"I'm here to talk to anyone who needs my help."

"Well, you're going to have a busy night of it here," I say, looking round at the pimps, hookers, trannies, and gay men cruising past.

By now I am warming to Brother Martin, and, dare I say this and not be struck down from Above, I'm starting to find him bearishly sexy. I look at the pendant in my hand. "We sell something similar in the shop," I say. "Would you like to see?"

As we walk in I can see Jorge's eyes widening, as if to say, *God, who have you brought in now?*

"Oh, yes. What a beautiful collection you have. Escapularios. They originated in Elsford when the Virgin Mary appeared to St. Simon," the monk whispers quietly, looking down at the jewellery in the display case. "But they really need to be blessed by a priest."

"You can't do that?"

"No, but I can say a prayer for you and your shop while I'm here. What's the name of your shop?"

Oh, dear. "Ummm, Dirty White Boy?" I squeak, waiting for a bolt of lighting to strike me down at any second.

"Well, even Jesus was a dirty Israeli at one time," he says, which I take to mean that the washing facilities weren't quite up to scratch.

Then Brother Martin takes our hands and prays. "Our Father. Please watch over these two men who have been so friendly to me. Help them achieve their dreams. May Dirty White Boy be a successful business…"

When he's finished praying for our souls, he raises his head and his eyes catch sight of the crucifix around Jorge's neck.

"It's Cuban gold," says Jorge. "My father gave it to me."

Brother Martin takes a step closer. "Oh, yes. Beautiful. He's really suffering on that one," he says with relish.

"Anyway, I must go and help people outside. Can I stop by next time?"

"Of course!" we reply in unison.

He takes one last look around the shop, makes the sign of the cross, smiles at us, and cheerfully disappears back down Old Compton Street.

December 1st, 2006: Homophobia on Old Compton Street

There's a scene in the groundbreaking 1970s television production *The Naked Civil Servant* in which Quentin Crisp is sitting in the Black Cat having coffee with his friends. Suddenly the door bursts open and they're attacked by a gang of homophobic yobs (or "roughs," as they're called in the film). The scene is set in the late 1930s or early 40s.

Nearly 70 years later, it's disappointing to think that homophobia is still very much prevalent on the same street, just a few doors down from Quentin's old haunt.

Sitting in the shop tonight with my partner, Jorge, we are suddenly faced with three drunken louts screaming homophobic abuse, pulling clothes off the racks, and starting to get violent. We manage to get them out of the shop and press the police panic button.

Fifteen minutes later, the police arrive. Emotions are running high. After we lecture the police on the need for more of a police presence in the evenings and less on a Sunday morning when the streets are empty, they take all the details of the incident. Then, some great news comes through the police radio—they've caught the three yobs!

Apparently, once they left our shop they made their way to the Escape Bar on Berwick Street and caused a similar disturbance there. Unfortunately for the yobs there were three gay plainclothes policeman drinking in the bar at the time. So a few minutes later the yobs were in a police van and carted off to Regent Street police station.

This of course means that, if we want the case to go to

court, Jorge and I have to make statements. So we spend two hours in the police station, until sometime after midnight. The case will definitely go to court, as it's a premeditated hate crime and the courts take this kind of crime seriously, apparently.

I have to say the police were fantastic. Although I moaned to them about the lack of a presence, when you do see them they are always very helpful. In this instance, the young policeman we dealt with was very gay-friendly, assuring me that we would never see these guys again except in court.

I can deal with the gang attacks, the mafia landlady, the constant leaks from the brothel above, the pimps, hookers, and drug dealers outside the shop—all the problems that come with trying to run a shop in Soho—but I ain't taking homophobia. I'll press charges and I'll look the yobs in the face in court as I'm doing it. Hopefully they'll be banged away for a month at least and end up in a cell with a big butch Daddy lifer looking for a prison bitch to bounce on his knee. That should expand their "horizons" somewhat...

December 5th, 2006: I Must Remember Not to Blog This
Today I receive an email from a total stranger.

"Hi! I've been reading your blogs for some time now and what I've noticed is they're all about sex—transsexual hookers, HIV, big cocks, rent boys, pimps, catching crabs..."

Hmmm...I think, staring at the crotch of the shop mannequin, he has a point. I email back: "I confess. You're absolutely right. Please let me know if you feel I've left anything out."

I live in Soho—what does he expect me to write about? Britain's submarine-based Trident defence system?

As I sit there pondering launching myself as some kind of "cyber Erica Jong," something whizzes past the Old

Compton Street window. I tear my eyes away from the crotch and press my nose against the shop window just in time to see a motorised four-poster double bed, complete with blankets, pillows, and three guys snuggled up inside, ravishing each other, as it speeds by.

The guys appeared to be having a ball (or two) and what is strange is that the bed didn't seem to have a driver (though there seemed to be a lot of fiddling for the "stick"). This being Old Compton Street, no one paid any attention...

What is the meaning behind this "porta-orgy"? Some kind of wacky marketing campaign advertising John Lewis's new "bouncy beds" range, perhaps? Chariots opening a deluxe VIP dark room maybe? Or have Westminster City Council rents become so high that the brothels are simply being forced onto the streets?

Whatever the reason, my first thought is, No, I mustn't blog this—don't want to come across as "sex obsessed." So I sit back down on my perch and am concentrating on picking my teeth with a bent paper clip when in walk three Brazilian escorts heading straight for the underwear section.

As they browse through the undies, I pick up *QX* and flick to the hooker section to look at their willies.

After a few minutes of texting, chattering, and swapping K bottles, "Marcelo, 25, new to London, text numbers ignored" walks over with the L'Homme Invisible underwear in his hand.

I quickly look down at his *QX* pic underneath the counter. "You'll need a medium."

He is followed by "Brazilian hunk, all colours, versatile/top, Earls Court" holding a black thong.

I look down again. "I'd go for a large."

Finally, over strolls "Steve, 9" x 5½" cock, dungeon, duo available" with a see-through slip. (Steve?)

"We don't have your size."

Underwear in hand, the three troop merrily over to Costa

to get the best seat, just in time for the lunchtime trade. Now, I must remember not to blog this...

December 7th, 2006: The Gay Gym—Rules and Regulations

Soho Athletic is a gay gym situated on Macklin Street, just off Drury Lane.

Now for all you non-gays, gay gyms have strict codes and conventions that must be adhered to at all times. They aren't documented in the gym handbook, but these are unspoken rules that if not followed will result in your membership being instantly revoked.

Rule 1: Avoid eye contact.

If your eyes happen to linger for too long on the hairy thigh of a muscle bear, you will receive a dirty look, whether Muscle Bear likes you or not. That is the rule and Muscle Bear is Lord of the Gym.

Rule 2: The Brazilian contingent "own" the gym during the day.

If you are partial to beach bodies, dark eyes, dark skin, and have oodles of cash, the best time to go is between 2 P.M. and 6 P.M. Please note that Brazilians arrive in "packs." Don't be put off by this, as most are only there to cruise the sauna (see Rule 4).

Rule 3: Equipment.

You are allowed a maximum of three sets on a machine. Any more than that and Miss "I've Gotta Be Back at the Office in 10 Minutes and I Still Haven't Done Abs" will give you a withering look, a "tut-tut," and start tapping her heels like she's auditioning for *Chicago*.

Rule 4: Sauna.

Rule 2 states that the saunas are used by the Brazilian contingent between 2 P.M. and 6 P.M. Exceptions are made for those with a Black Amex.

Please note that quick glances are now allowed—that is,

you will notice that the dirty look you received in the gym just minutes before has now transformed into a lecherous leer as you delicately adjust your towel.

N.B. When making your way to the dressing area, if you happen to pass the sauna and see arms and hands moving in rapid succession—please note, this is not some crazy new dance craze.

Rule 5: Showers.

The golden rule for showers (as opposed to the golden shower rule) is that those with a big willy face outwards and those who require a bit of "soaping" face inwards.

You will notice that the Lord of the Gym is not quite so fearsome now, and the puny chav who was, only seconds ago, bottom of the food chain has now risen (literally) to the top.

N.B. Please also note that Muscle Bear has now miraculously reciprocated your gaze. He is now up for it.

Rule 6: Getting dressed.

For those for whom soaping didn't help it is customary to put your underwear back on very quickly. Those with big willies take the longest to get dressed, and the underwear is the last item to be put back on, even after shoes, socks, and coat.

Rule 7: Leaving.

The rule here is: Whatever just took place in the sauna/shower—don't expect to finish the encounter with a candlelit meal. On leaving the changing room area, the person you were exchanging love tussles with only seconds before now has the right to stare right through you (unless he's Brazilian, of course, and he's clocked your wallet).

Signed

The Management

December 10th, 2006: Acts 1 and 2

It takes me a second to place his face. You know that feeling when you see someone and you know you've met before but you just can't recall when and where? Then it hits me.

My first thought, and don't ask me why, is to hide. I move quickly to the back of the shop, pretending to re-arrange clothes, mentally preparing a surprised "Oh my God—how nice to see you again" speech while I watch him between the racks, nervously, music drifting in and out.

"But no one says a word/I felt I should apologise/For what I hadn't heard…"

He hasn't aged well. The once handsome face is now very lined; the brown, thick, luxurious head of hair, almost gone. But there is no mistaking it is him—the stance, the quizzical, almost puzzled look on his face as he stares at the clothes.

I feel apprehensive. My first lover on one side of the shop, my new one on the other. Neither aware of the other; neither aware that this moment is even taking place or what it signifies. Like two different worlds colliding, my teens and my forties. The first world innocent, when sex was carefree, new, but hidden and illegal; the second world, slightly jaded, the sex, dangerous, but the life "open," with a partnership recognised and legalised.

"A silence filled the room/Awkward as an elephant/In the crowded court of your love/I was now a supplicant…"

It is unsettling having these two worlds in the same room; this clash playing out in front of me, worlds that would never meet ordinarily—but, at the same time, part of the same whole. For some reason, again don't ask me why, I don't speak up, can't speak up and unite the two.

"And as clumsy as I felt/At stumbling on this theft/To save further embarrassment/I made my excuses and left…"

Five minutes pass. Then he leaves. Like a ghost, leaving me disorientated and unable to concentrate, my mind going back and forward in time, wondering what it all meant, wondering what might have been, wondering what the third act would bring.

December 16th, 2006: Santa's Christmas Pressie

Standing in the shop doorway, watching the Christmas shoppers rush by, I see a tuk-tuk career across the street, stopping just outside the shop. Out step three men in full-length red robes with white trims and long, white, flowing beards, all three looking a bit worse for wear.

"Look, Mummy!" says a little girl with blonde pigtails standing nearby, pulling on her mum's coat. "Three Santas! I thought there was only one."

"Well, darling, Santa can't possibly carry all those presents on his own, you know. He needs a bit of help to get to reach all the little boys and girls around the world," her mother reassures her.

Satisfied with the answer, the little girl looks up at the three Santas with a big smile on her face and takes a step toward them.

"Happy Christmas, Santa," she squeaks, grinning away, waving her little gloved hand.

Suddenly, the smallest Santa takes a deep breath, makes a huge retching noise, and projectile-vomits what appears to be Heinz Spaghetti Hoops all over little girl's shoes, socks, and legs.

"Oops!" says Santa, wiping the hoops off his beard. "Bit too much sherry in the Christmas pud!"

December 19th, 2006: Sniff! Sniff!

A well-dressed gentleman with slicked-back hair, wearing a long, dark wool gabardine coat, walks into the shop and tries on a very expensive Zegna silk shirt.

"I'll take it!" he says snootily, throwing it down on the counter. "And I'll wear it now."

After he pays, Jorge, as is customary, folds and wraps his

old shirt up, and as he does so he feels something in the top pocket. "Excuse me, sir. You've left your glasses in here," he says, pulling them out and handing them back.

The gentleman takes them from him without a word and Jorge continues folding the shirt carefully. Then he feels a bulge in the other pocket.

"I think you've left something else in here," says Jorge, reaching inside. Out comes a silver coke bottle and a matching straw.

"That's medicinal!" says the gentleman in a haughty voice, grabbing his drugs and bags, leaving abruptly, and wide-eyed.

December 29th, 2006: The "Girls Upstairs"—A Christmas Special

"Hi, Clay! How was your Christmas?" says Sue, as she stubs a cigarette out under the heel of her Nike trainer.

"Good! We had Christmas with my family. Lots of food and drink. But now it's back to Sell! Sell! Sell! How was yours?"

"Oh, you don't want to hear what we got up to!" she says, laughing.

"Sue, you know I do. Come on! Spill the beans," I reply, getting my "blog brain" back in gear.

She takes a packet of Benson and Hedges from her Tescos carrier bag, pulls a lighter out from her left bra strap, and proceeds to smoke as she talks, her breasts bouncing up and down like albino children on a trampoline.

"Did you see all those guys on the street dressed up as Father Christmas?" she says, blowing a smoke ring in my direction.

"I did."

"Well, we 'ad one upstairs."

"A Santa?"

"Yeah. Fully dressed. On Christmas Eve."

"What did he want you to do?"

"Just sit on his knee while he sang Christmas carols."

"How long did he stay?"

" 'Bout an hour," Sue replies. "Then he gave us a kiss and said, 'Thank you, children. I've gotta go now—Rudolph's waiting.' He even left a half-eaten mince pie on the table!"

December 29ᵗʰ, 2006: Hand Man

There's a man who comes into the shop every month or so. "Tall" is probably the only redeeming feature. He's the type of man you could have as a neighbour for years, find out he's a serial killer, and when the press ask you to describe him, you'd just stare blankly back, shrug, and say, "I can't. He was just…normal."

But there is something that sets this man apart, one feature about him that's unique. It's something he carries with him wherever he goes. A hand. A mannequin's hand, to be exact, and he holds it just like you would a lover's.

It's strange, but although he's been coming in for months, I can describe the hand more than I can the man who carries it, placing it tenderly on the counter while he browses the clothes racks. It's a greyish silver, with chipped fingernails revealing brownish fibreglass underneath, and it looks old, like from the 60s, the fingers pointing outwards like a camp ballerina, or the poses models would pull in my mum's old clothes catalogues.

While Hand Man looks round, I imagine what became of the rest of the mannequin. Does it sit ghoulishly in his basement, dressed in his dead mother's clothes, rocking slowly backwards and forwards in an old wooden chair? Or is it dressed like a hooker, lying in bed, waiting, with clean panties and freshly applied makeup? Or maybe it's "male" and it's lying on its front in a leather harness with a fur-lined orifice.

Whatever the answer, Hand Man offers no explanation,

and I never ask. He flicks through the clothes, his hand on the counter, looking back every so often to check it's still there, and I smile back, wondering who will be the first to break the spell, wondering who will be the first to admit that something's not quite right.

December 31st, 2006: Pretty. Pretty.

It's rained for most of the day today. Buckets and buckets: people running up and down the street, holding on to their cheap, colourful brollies, pulling up coat collars or stepping into the shop, not to shop, just to seek shelter.

One of these non-shoppers is an American, sandy-coloured hair, bearded, the type of look that could be viewed as "bear" on this street, but casual elsewhere, although he doesn't appear to be gay, his hair too unkempt.

I first notice him examining a belt, holding it at each end and extending it, marvelling at its texture. I watch him closely. It's as if he's been blind from birth and suddenly been given the power of sight. His eyes are enlarged, amazed.

"It's unbelievable," he says.

Now I'm all for accessorizing, but the passion he puts into the words makes it sound like he's just found the Holy Grail of the belt world.

"Unbelievable," he repeats, this time in almost a whisper.

Then he places the belt carefully back on the rack and turns to face me, taking slow steps forward, looking at me strangely, as if I was a pot of gold coins and he was ready to stuff his pockets.

Over the past few months I've learnt how to deal with the slightly deranged customers: go into super-calm mode, with no sudden movements or raising of the voice. But this is a bit different. He's inching toward me like a zombie. So I inch back. It's like a bizarre mating ritual.

By now the shop is full, Jorge serving customers, but

when I look around no one is paying any attention to our mating ritual and, for some reason, my throat has suddenly gone dry and I've lost the power of speech. This is getting a bit freaky.

Then, just as I run out of floor space for inching backward, as I'm perched at the edge of the stairway, like that final scene in Thelma and Louise, his eyes spot something in the display case—the Calvin Klein sunglasses—and he moves toward them.

"S-o-o-o-o pretty," he says, bending down to look. And there he stays for a full 10 minutes, just looking. I take a deep breath and inch my way back from the stairway precipice.

"Do you want to see them?"

"Oh, yesssssss," he replies, with a mouthful of esses, like Gollum.

I reach into the display case, him staring at me, without blinking, still in his crouched position, and I place the glasses on the counter.

"They were eighty-four pounds, but they're half price now—so yours for forty-two."

"Pretty glasses," he says, looking at me, his head just peeping above the counter.

"Aren't they," I reply. "Want to try them on?"

"Pretty glasses," he whispers back.

"Yes. Pretty glasses."

Then he fishes around in his pocket, puts something on the floor, stands up, still staring at me, mouths "pretty glasses," and slowly walks backwards, out of the shop.

At this point Jorge walks over, unaware of what has just occurred. "Did he like the glasses?"

"Um. Yes, I think he did."

"Oh, look what he's left on the floor," says Jorge, bending down. "It's a solid gold ring."

"Umm," I say, looking at the ring, wondering what it all means. "Very…pretty."

January 2nd, 2007: The Show Must Go On

2007 starts badly. I open the doors to the shop and invite in, with welcome arms, our first customer of the new year, a bailiff. And, just like Dracula, once you invite them in over the threshold, you're doomed.

Let me explain.

We've had numerous leaks from the brothel upstairs (due to the "girls" washing their "bits" in the sink and leaving the tap running), and our solicitor advised us to stop paying rent until the problem is sorted out. But what we weren't told was to expect a call from the heavy mob—big, beefy, East End hard men, straight out of *Lock, Stock and Two Smoking Barrels*.

Digging deep, and using all my recent experience from serving snotty French queens and drug-fucked rent boys, I go into charm overdrive. After a few edgy moments we agree that £3K might persuade the mob to leave—for the time being. So Jorge troops off to the bank and I'm left with the chief Hard Man. The atmosphere, tense. How to engage him in conversation? This is going to be difficult (though made easier by the fact that he looks like a handsome Kray twin). I decide to go for the "tell me about your life" angle.

"Would you like a coffee?"

"Sure," replies Hard Man.

"So your job must get pretty scary at times," I say, passing him a coffee overdosed with enough sugar to kill an American schoolkid.

"Oh, yeah. Been shot at. Knifed. Bottled. Seen some sights, too. Had to take possession of a sauna in Farringdon not long ago. Clipboard in me hand, wandering round the rooms, while guys were banging away on all fours!"

"Wow—that sounds...er, a bit much for a guy like you to have to do."

"Nah. I'm used to it. Just me job, innit," he sniffs.

"So, do you know our landlady?" I ask, taking a seat nearby.

"Oh yeah. Well, they're a celebrity family, innit—everyone knows 'em. Mind you, they ain't the worst landlords round here. I've done a few places in Soho. The Queen owns a lot round here. She don't mess around. You don't pay your rent with 'er, you're out the next day. She's the toughest," he says, wincing as he sips his coffee.

"Really? She looks so nice on the stamp!" No response. "So...er...what does your wife think about you doing this job?" I say, trying a different tack.

"Left the wife. Got a new partner. She don't care what I do. She just wants kids of her own."

"Oh, okay. So you're planning for children?"

"Don't really want any more, mate. Already got five. Had the 'snip' a few years ago and I'm not sure if it's reversible—it's been so long. Plus I 'ad complications with the first one."

"Really?" I say, taking a quick peep at his package while he scratches his goatee.

"Oh, yeah. Doctor put real stitches inside me bollocks instead of dissolvable ones. Me balls got infected and they swelled up like Buster Gonad. I should've sued. They ended up having to sew 'em to me thighs."

"They sewed your balls to your thighs?" I ask, incredulously.

"Yeah—to stop 'em flapping about."

I was a bit stumped at this. "Umm...so what would happen to our goods if you took them?"

"Auction, mate. They'd sell 'em off. Cheap as chips."

A vision of an auctioneer holding up my personal effects to a room full of men and women, as they peer over their spectacles, fills my head. "Ladies and Gentlemen. How much for this silver cock ring? Fairly good condition. Do I hear ten pounds to start us off?"

Seconds later, Jorge walks back in with an envelope of cash and pays Hard Man, who leaves, promising to be back within five days if the rest of the rent isn't paid.

At this point a customer walks into the shop to tell me he's just read an article of mine in the *London Paper*. But instead of being happy, I'm near to tears. I'm not really listening. What does it mean now? With no shop, Jorge would retreat back to his own country, I'd lose everything. My relationship, my job, my possessions, everything. I'd even lose MySpace. This shop is my muse—everything I write stems from here.

But, who knows what may happen. We won't go down without a fight. We may be able to negotiate. Life is a roller coaster. Our doors are still open and, as the saying goes, the show must go on.

January 9th, 2007: A Runny Nose

I get a release from writing. When something big happens in my life I write it down. Always have. Suitcases full of diaries, papers, meaningless scribbles, private moments, song lyrics—they're all there, as a reminder, memories to revisit at some point. Maybe I never will—but it's comforting to know that I can.

There was a time in my life when I thought the only time I could write was when something big happened. I realise now that's not quite true. But the events of the past week have dried me up completely.

When everything you have is about to be snatched away your emotions go into overdrive. Eat your heart out, Elton— if it's diva mood swings and drama-queen tantrums you want, look no further. But...after much toing and froing, we eventually sealed a deal with the landlady. For the moment at least, Dirty White Boy is back in business!

So I take my usual seat by the window, breathing deeply, trying to reunite with my calm cells, reflecting on the past week's events, when in walks a customer who threatens to upset the harmony.

"I need a top! And I need it now!" says a Mediterranean-looking gentleman, bursting into the shop with a runny nose and "age inappropriate" jeans.

"Allow me to show you a few items," I reply calmly, levitating toward the Zegna knitwear.

"Yes. Yes. Quick. I'm very busy."

At this, Mr. Runny Nose literally runs toward the clothes rails. "I want to try this. This. And this!" he says, pointing in three directions at once. "And this! Do you have this in my size? What about this? What other colours do you have in this? What's a French size 44?"

By now Runny Nose is running round the clothes aisles like a Super Market Sweep contestant on crack, and on each lap I attempt to hand him a selection of outfits. Then his mobile phone rings.

"My phone!" he says, reaching into his leather manbag as he sweeps past the final furlong.

"Hello! Yes. I am. In London. Happy New Year to you too. Yes. Hurry. I'm shopping. Is that cool? Okay. Be back tomorrow."

He throws the phone back into his bag. "Don't know who that was!" he says as he sails past. "Now, where was I? Oh, yes. Clothes. Now, what I'm really looking for is a white shirt to go with my..."

And he continues talking all the way out of the shop, leaving without so much as a nod, a smile, or a wave goodbye—probably forgetting moments later that he'd even been in in the first place!

January 11th, 2007: A Chance Meeting

Every now and again I meet someone on this street who makes being here worthwhile. Today was one of those days...

A little old lady looks in my direction as she passes slowly by. She's bent down by age. She's wearing a black, glossy fur coat and a matching hat. She looks at me closely and smiles, sweetly. Maybe sweetly is the wrong word. It's more like she's smiling "knowingly." That's it; knowingly, as if we've met before.

She stops. Her smile is slightly crooked, as if she's lost her teeth; her features, hard, mannish, but welcoming at the same time. I smile back politely and notice the red blouse under her fur and a necklace with a single pearl dangling between her still firm bosom.

"It's cold tonight, isn't it?" I say, trying to engage her in conversation.

She takes a step closer. I can see her clearly now. Only it's not a woman. She's a he. Her face is devoid of makeup and her skin is soft, almost translucent and closely shaven, with no visible stubble, although I'd still place her in her eighties.

I stretch out my hand. "My name's Clayton."

She extends her index finger and we "shake." I'm wondering why she did that. Is her hand deformed?

"My name's Michele."

Her voice is deep and croaky. Not like a smoker's croak but a croak that comes with old age; no hiding her gender. And the name, it doesn't quite fit—I was expecting something more exotic.

"Are you from around here?" I ask, smiling.

"No. Not here… Lancaster Gate."

"Going anywhere nice?"

"Just off to buy a book. On Egyptian magic. About Queen Isis."

"Really? Is that a hobby?"

"You could say that. I'm a witch. I suppose… I suppose you'd call me a pagan witch. A pagan, anyway."

I'm at a loss now what to say but want to keep talking,

want to know more about her. She looks me in the eye, still smiling. A second passes but it feels longer, as if a further connection is waiting to be made.

"Have you been coming to Soho for a long time?" I ask.

"Oh yes. Since I was sixteen."

"It must have been very different back then. What was it like? Did you go out here?" I'm eager now. So many questions. I want to hear everything. I'm tempted to ask her if I can get my little black book from inside the shop and make notes—but at the same time I don't want to interrupt the flow.

"Oh I was always out here on this street. It was very different. So exciting." She looks round, as if remembering. "I used to go to the Golden Lion mainly," and she points across the street to the pub on Dean Street. "Ronnie Kray was in there all the time. I knew him quite well. Nielsen was there too, you know. He had a mental disorder."

"Did you…" A question is burning inside me but I don't want to offend her by bringing up events that may be before her time. "Did you…um…ever see Quentin Crisp on this street?"

"Of course," she replies, her eyes twinkling mischievously. "He was a friend of mine."

"You met Quentin Crisp? You knew him?" I'm staring at her in awe now.

"Yes. He used to invite me over to his flat. He stayed in Chelsea a lot. His flat was in Beaufort Street. A room at the front."

"Oh, yes, I know it." I think about the number of times I've sat outside that flat, staring up at the window.

"He used to invite me over for Welsh rarebit. He would say, 'You must come over for Welsh rarebit and a game of chess.' He'd speak just like that. Very elegantly. And he was very good at chess. He'd always beat me. Lovely man. When did he die? Six? Seven years ago?"

"Yes. About that. Where did you first meet him?" My words are tumbling out of me now.

"In a coffee shop."

"On this street?" Thinking she will say the Black Cat.

"No. The As You Like It. On Monmouth Street. He was always in there."

I'm looking over my shoulder now. The shop's busy. Jorge struggling to serve customers. I look back at Michele, then back to the shop. "Michele. I have to go back inside. I work here."

"Oh, really. Have you ever been in the Compton Arms?"

"You mean Comptons?"

"Yes. The men are very strong in there. Big arms." She attempts to flex her arm through her black fur coat. "I used to go in there years ago. In that bar in Earls Court too! I went up to a strong man in there many years ago and he said, 'Oh no! You're too young for me.' His arms were so strong."

"Michele, I'm sorry. I have to go."

"Oh, okay. Perhaps we'll meet again, Clayton."

"I hope so. I finish at nine every night. Maybe we can have coffee one night if you're passing."

She smiles eagerly. It crosses my mind that she thinks this may be a date.

"That would be nice. I go to Costa," she says, looking over at the coffee shop opposite. "But I sit downstairs to avoid the crowds."

"Okay. Goodbye, Michele. It's been very nice to meet you."

I extend my hand again and she extends her index finger. We attempt another "shake."

"Goodbye." Her eyes, still sparkling, her face beaming.

"Goodbye, Michele."

I watch from the window, quickly scribbling everything

down in my little black book as she adjusts her fur hat and sets off again, slowly, slowly, back down Old Compton Street.

January 11th, 2007: Old Compton Street, January 2007
Our first January on Old Compton Street. The air is brisk and biting. The crowds, usually swarming across the street, all gone. Soho is cold and empty, like a village past its prime, its heyday long since over.

The pimps and dealers huddle close together outside the shop, no longer competing for the best spot. It's as if they've called a truce and joined forces to get through the next few months. The punters are few and far between now. So they stamp their feet to keep warm, crack jokes, and, should a lone businessman walk past, they go in for the kill like a pack of wolves.

But they're not the only ones affected. If the pimps are struggling the whole food chain suffers. The "girls" upstairs, usually out and about on errands, are nowhere to be seen. I hear the odd punter stomping up the stairway, but the noise is now noticeable, whereas only a month or two ago it was so frequent it blended in. The few punters they do have are there for longer, too; the girls lavishing them with full service, charging half the normal rate, time no longer an issue.

Even the *Big Issue* sellers and the homeless are noticeable by their absence; they've retreated to Leicester Square and Piccadilly tube stations, following the crowds to try and eke out the semblance of an existence.

The Flyer Boys, once so hyper and alive, now hand out their adverts with little interest and shrug if you don't respond—their clothes less bold, their smiles less inviting. With no drag queens to back them up, they feel exposed. There'll be no more drag queens on this street for a while now. Their catwalk is closed. Their audience all but disappeared. Rare birds nest in warmer climes.

This is the season when the coffee shops thrive. Customers

sip on their mochas and cappuccinos to keep warm, sitting firmly inside, guarding their seats, flicking through newspapers, every now and again looking up to peer through the window to watch stragglers traverse the street.

For the rest of us it's all about getting by on a wing and a prayer. EuroPride, Soho Pride, the World Cup win in Little Italy, distant memories. So we try to entice customers into the shop with big red "sale" signs; the Fall/Winter collections ready to be snapped up by the shrewd shopper before Spring/Summer hits the racks in February. But the dice are firmly stacked in the shoppers' favour, and they know it. They haggle over pounds and we back down with gritted teeth. It's a brothel down here too.

What will the New Year bring? The gay bars watch nervously and wait, anticipating the fickle trend of gay custom to venture south of the river, remembering the move once made in the 80s from dimly lit bars in Earls Court. The straight businesses watch too, ready to pounce and reclaim their turf.

The next couple of months will be tough on this street. It's a cutthroat village that takes no prisoners. Only the strong will survive.

January 14th, 2007: Russian Rent

"Clay, when you've been in a co-dependency relationship for many years, especially as a caregiver, you tend to blend into the background," says my MySpace therapist friend, David Parker, over dinner. "This explains why you've always written privately, in diary form."

I pick at my tapas, wondering how he could've deciphered me so quickly, probing to hear more but wanting to change the subject at the same time.

"Now you're in a new relationship, your writing is reflecting this new life—and consequently, you're making your writing public for the first time."

As David goes to the loo, I reflect on what he's just said, which has brought me, strangely, close to tears.

The next day, sitting in the shop, I'm still mulling this over when in walks two of Jorge's Cuban friends, the Royal Ballet star Carlos Acosta and his friend, Ruswel Pineiro. The three of them talk about how they escaped from Cuba and about their new life here in London.

Ruswel's first novel, *Havana: Between the Sky and Heaven*, touches on prostitution, pimps, drugs—subjects that ensure he can never go back to Cuba for fear of being arrested. This makes me think again. I write about exactly the same subjects as Ruswel. Thank God my only fear is bad grammar.

By now my head is reeling from all this writing analysis. So I reach into the top drawer of the desk, pull out my little black book, and doodle away, drawing strange phallically shaped snakes, waiting for a subject to materialise.

Moments later, two people walk in. I say "hello." They both ignore me. Don't even look at me. I immediately get a sense that I'm not going to like these people, but I decide to write about them anyway, as it seems preferable to just sitting here drawing snake cocks. So I press my writing finger firmly to the page and metamorphose into a gay A. A. Gill.

Okay, so here we go. One is in his fifties, balding, squat, overweight, with a tight black raincoat. His skin is white, painfully so, with big, black circles around his eyes. He looks like an albino sea lion.

The other is a tall, blond, square-jawed boy in his twenties. He reminds me of one of those Abercrombie models that lie seductively on their Mies van der Rohe daybed narcissistically stroking their six-packs. All pout, pec, and waiting to be fingered. The two couldn't be more different.

I'm watching them carefully—but, at the same time, averting my eyes, should they notice me. The older man looks over. He sees me writing.

I say "hello" again, and I'm ignored, AGAIN!

The blond boy flicks through the shirt rails, nonchalantly, like he's seen it all before. I want to slap her. The older man is standing behind him, watching him intently. It crosses my mind that he'll be even closer behind him later on. Money buys beauty.

They're talking very quietly. Sound Russian. Every minute or so the boy hands the man a shirt without even looking in his direction. It's all very *The Devil Wears Prada*.

The man brings each shirt to the counter, asking for the boy's size. He smiles. But it's not a pleasant smile. It's a smug smile. One that says, *I know you know I'm paying for him—but I don't care.* I smile back. A smile that says, *I know nothing.*

Then the two make their way to the dressing room. The boy hasn't once looked in my direction. He's either embarrassed or isn't even aware of my existence. Not sure which. They've taken three shirts and four pairs of trousers. I offer to help, but the man guards the dressing-room door as if Mariah Carey's in there. He's looking at me coldly now.

Every few minutes the boy's elegant hand reaches out, returning garments, like a designer striptease. The older man hands me back the clothes.

"He likes this. He doesn't like this."

Luckily there's more of what he likes than what he doesn't. Minutes later, they've decided. The boy's selected two shirts, two trousers. I fold them neatly, glancing up to look at the boy. He does everything possible not to look at me. I sense his embarrassment.

Then the man hands the shopping bags to the boy with a sickly smile. A smile that says, *Okay, bitch! Daddy's bought your little trinkets, now get back to the hotel and get that ass lubed up.*

Just as they're about to leave, the boy looks at me for the first time. Our eyes lock. For a second. I feel for him. I smile. A smile that says, *Close your eyes and think of Russell Crowe.* He doesn't respond. They make their way to the doorway.

"Goodbye. Have a safe trip back," I say.

They don't answer—but, as I have their cash, I'm not really bothered now.

I sit back down, finish writing in my little black book, and think, God this isn't even worth blogging. Then I think, Oh, what the hell—I've spent 10 minutes on it and I can hardly upload my snake cock pictures now, can I?

January 19ᵗʰ, 2007: A Strange Question

I'm sitting here by the window, drawing in my little black book again, when in walks a woman with long blonde hair.

"Hello," she says, a slightly puzzled look on her face. "Now, I know you're a gay shop, but do you know the direction to Leicester Square?"

I look at her for a second before answering. "Hello," I reply. "Now, I know you're straight, but can you tell me the time?"

She stares at me, her mouth open, then spins round on her heels and walks straight back out.

January 19ᵗʰ, 2007: A Wing and a Prayer

So I pick up my little black book again and carry on doodling, listening to the pimps outside. "Ladies. Ladies. Upstairs. It's free to look." Or my current favourite: "Spandex, Y-fronts, cats and dogs and mice."

While I ponder the meaning of the last one, two big black women with garish makeup bounce into the shop. Just as I think they're about to launch into "It's Raining Men," one of them speaks.

"I read your columns in the paper, man," says the larger of the two, a big beaming smile on her face, her breasts practically wrapping themselves around my neck.

"Thank you. I hope you like them," I reply, leaning back to breathe.

"You write about round 'ere, don'cha?"

"I try."

"Don't say anything bad 'bout us girls, will ya? This is where we work. We need the money." Her smile reveals a sparkling diamond stuck on one of her teeth. Her friend stands behind her, shaking her hair from side to side, as if testing its staying power during a windstorm.

"Of course not. I wouldn't do that," I reassure them. "You're what make's this place special. There's no Soho without you girls."

"Thanks, man. We love you guys here. We love you being on this street."

"That's very nice of you to say."

"Have you got any money? We need some money for fags."

So I reach into the till and hand the girls some change, wanting to believe that what they say is for real and not just a ploy. After all, we're all in it together on this street, all trying to eke out a living, all trying to get by on a wing and a prayer.

January 19th, 2007: A Night of Transsexual Singers and Spanking

We close the shop at 9 P.M. every night, and once the door's locked I pull up my chair and tap, tap, tap away at my keyboard, trying to describe life outside the window, trying to find something beautiful amongst the squalor.

Last night I was doing just that when, lo and behold— something popped right up in front of me. I peered out into the darkness to get a closer look and could just make out a flash of blonde hair, a blur of something red, and a pair of ruby lips mouthing, "Hi!"

So I jump up from my seat, run to the door, pull up the

grates, and find a beautiful woman with a "Purdy-style" blonde bob. She's dressed in a red cowboy shirt adorned with gold brocade, tight black trousers, a rhinestone-studded belt with silver hanging chains, and black, dominatrix-style leather boots. It's my MySpace friend Frances, the transsexual singer/songwriter and sex therapist.

"Hi! You must be Clayton!"

"Frances! How nice to meet you in the 'real' world. Come on in!"

Minutes later we're sitting round a table, Frances telling me about her life, her five children, her affairs, and her "transformation."

"I've had the upstairs done but not the down," she says, without batting an eyelid. "I've never been a 'Woe is me!' transsexual. I've always been happy. But one day I just woke up and thought, Why not try it? So I did, and you know what? I'm still happy!"

We talk with ease, as if we've met before, her life flowing from her lips and me pumping her with questions. As she talks, I rest my elbows on the table, chin in hand, and marvel at her smooth silky skin, perfect makeup, blonde "sun kissed" hair slightly parted to one side, and her dainty fingers laden down with sparkly, square rings.

"Right! Let's go to the Colony," she suddenly announces, jumping up.

The Colony Room (also known as "Muriel's" after Muriel Belcher, the former proprietor) is just across the road, the entrance through a small, *Alice in Wonderland*–type doorway. It opened in 1948, and one of its first members was the artist Francis Bacon. Since Bacon's day the place still attracts artists such as Damien Hirst, Sarah Lucas, and Tracey Emin.

I've always wanted to go to the Colony Club but was too afraid to walk up the stairs in case someone bellowed down, "Get out of here! You're a nobody!"

As we cross the street and walk up the winding staircase, my mind races back to everything I've ever read about this place—how the room is as notorious for its decor as for its clientele, how the walls are a vomit-green colour. It is all true.

Sitting inside the Colony is like having a drink in your hippie brother's bad–acid-trip-painted bedroom, studenty-looking goths sprawled across decaying sofas, chatting intellectually about the meaning of art and the end of post-modernism.

Then you notice the art and the black-and-white photos displayed haphazardly around the room, like being in an art museum basement, all cobwebs and lost treasures.

I sit on the bar stool, my neck swivelling round like a barn owl, while Frances chats with the barman/owner, Michael, a middle-aged man, slightly bent over, either from age or constantly serving. After three head spins my eyes land on a large, ruddy-faced old man at the edge of the bar.

"Hi, I'm Clayton."

"I'm Peter. From Janus."

"Oh, Janus! The sex shop. That's the up-market one on Old Compton Street, isn't it?"

"We like to think of ourselves as that, yes," he says, smiling back. "Although it's a bit different inside."

"Why's that?"

"Well, we specialise in spanking and CP."

"Wow. I didn't realise there was such a demand."

"You'd be surprised. I've been there for thirty-five years," says Peter, sipping on his beer. "And spanking's never been so popular. You'll have to come in one day for a tour. We've had to add extra rows of videos to cope with the demand."

"Sounds like Blockbuster."

"Buttbuster would be a better description."

As if on cue, Frances returns. "Right. Let's go the French House. I'm starved. And I need to eat soon. I'm on stage tonight in Vauxhall."

"What will you sing?"

" 'American Pie,' a few Johnny Cash songs, then a few of my own thrown in."

In bed later, I dream strange visions of spanking and canes, with country and western songs sung by transsexual beauty queens. When I wake up, my first thought is, God, it really happened. Now, how can I put all this in a blog...

January 22nd, 2007: The Return of Thong Man

This morning Thong Man returned.

Now regular readers will probably recall that Thong Man is my underwear teacher. An ex-art lecturer, in his seventies, Thong Man is the Imelda Marcos of the underwear world, and he's made it his mission in life to visit the shop every now and again, never to buy, but to educate me on everything from the cut, the fabric, the history, to "what can be done about stubborn stains in the laundry."

"Stubborn stains," he says, with a slight "tut-tut" and a raised eyebrow, as though I was somehow to blame for all the partially wiped bums of this world. "Clayton, no matter how stubborn the stain, you must never boil-wash a silk tanga."

Now, I'm the first to admit, I'm an underwear philistine. Although we sell an extensive range, I know very little. As long as it's clean and doesn't have a Minnie Mouse face on the front, I'll wear it.

In fact, my only previous experience in this field was as a kid, secretly browsing through my mum's Gratton catalogue while she was at Bingo, flicking excitedly to the jockstrap section and experimenting with my ejaculation techniques. (I once came three times before I hit the thermals!)

But, under Thong Man's tutelage, that's all changing. I now have a rudimentary knowledge.

Did you know, for instance, that it was in the 1960s, that decade of generational conflicts and student revolts, that male underwear first went through a radical change? Apparently, it was in that decade that underpants became smaller and the waistband dipped dangerously low for the first time.

This paved the way for the flamboyant seventies, when checks, stripes, and even flowered cotton briefs were all the rage. Oh, dear. To think it was that period that had my schoolboy willy's pulse racing.

However, it was in the 1980s that underwear went through its most innovative period, one of the main reasons being the growing self-confidence of the gay pride movement. I could go on, but will leave it there before you think I've turned into some kind of "Tom Cruise Scientology knicker fanatic."

So should you ever come into my shop and are flicking through the briefs, don't be alarmed if you see my hand moving back and forth under the counter. I'm not reliving my schoolboy fantasies at your expense but simply flicking through an underwear book that Thong Man presented me with today.

"Clayton, with this book under the counter you will have an encyclopaedic knowledge of underwear at your fingertips and you'll be able to answer every question that will ever crop up!"

January 23rd, 2007: Filthy Rich

I know what you're thinking—that I'm sitting behind the counter, with my little black book open, doodling away, that someone's about to walk into the shop and I'm going to describe them; throw in a bit of humour, a bit of innuendo, end with a little joke; 500 words to titillate you while you wile away the afternoon. And you know what? You'd be right! Although the guy that's just walked in, I don't think there's going to be much humour with this one. Let's see...

You know, its funny how I can sum these people up, but

you can after a while—like this guy, he just reeks money. But he won't spend a thing. I've seen his type before. Let me just get the descriptive bit out of the way first.

He's in his fifties. Hair slicked back. Greying at the sides. Distinguished. Wearing one of those wax trench coats—I forget what they're called, the type that the "country set" used to wear in the 80s. Horrible, shapeless things. The "I shoot pheasants, then stamp on their heads" look.

Anyway, he's browsing the aisles, past the shirts, the ties, belts, heading for the shoes, leaving behind a waft of some kind of old-fashioned aftershave. Can't quite place it, but I think my Dad used to splash it round his neck just before he went out to play darts. That's the first giveaway.

"Fabulous shoes. Who makes them?" he says, without looking in my direction.

"They're by Zegna. Z. Zegna. The new sports line."

"Oh, Zegna. Of course. A beautiful brogue."

It's not a brogue, but I don't want to contradict him.

"Quintessentially English," he whispers, as he picks up the shoe and examines it.

Quintessentially English? What does "Quintessentially English" mean exactly? And how can you apply it to a shoe?

"Of course, the Italians have always made the best shoes."

"Actually, Zegna are Swiss," I reply, trying to keep my tone as neutral as possible so as not to alarm him.

He looks round. Noticing me for the first time, it seems—a slightly annoyed look on his face now because I've dared to answer him back.

"I have a house in Switzerland," he says, with just a hint of a sneer in his voice, flaring his nostrils like a panting Grand National winner. "Two, actually."

I want to say, "My mum has a caravan in a field near Newquay," but decide against it.

He looks back at the shoe. "I'll try them on. Fetch me a size eight."

The way he says "Fetch me," it's as if I'm his scullery maid and he's just asked for his bed slippers. I wonder if he talks to his wife like that. "Fetch me a blanket so we can fornicate on the floor by the fireplace." So I fetch the size, offer him a seat and a shoe horn. I contemplate a curtsey.

"How much?" he says, fingering the sole of the shoe.

"Well, they were a hundred twenty-nine pounds, but now they're fifty percent off—so, sixty-four pounds fifty."

"Actually, the price isn't important," he says, quickly backtracking. "Money's not an issue for me."

Ah-ha! But money is an issue, otherwise you wouldn't have asked. This guy is either one of those super-duper-rich guys, the ones who'll spend millions on a yacht but won't buy a round of drinks, or he's not rich at all—just trying to impress. I'm thinking the latter. Which, if you think about it, is even worse.

"All my shoes are handmade. I buy them from the same place as Prince Charles."

"What a coincidence," I reply, not believing a word he's saying.

"Oh, yes. All my clothes are custom-made, too. All my shirts. All my suits. Okay. I'll take them. I'll wear them for driving the Bentley."

Of course! The Bentley. How stupid of me. Well, it was hardly likely to be a Morris Minor, now was it? I wrap the shoes up, place them carefully in a bag, take his credit card, and swipe it through the machine.

"I'm afraid it says 'Not Authorised.' "

"Not Authorised? Preposterous. I've been using it all day." He looks really annoyed now. His nostrils are flaring again, flapping almost.

"Maybe you entered the wrong PIN number. Could you enter your PIN number again?"

He presses the keypad firmly, agitated.

"Oh... It says 'Not Authorised' again."

"That's outrageous! Give me that card. Where's the nearest auto bank? I'll get the cash out and be right back!"

"At the end of Dean Street. On the right-hand side. It's about two minutes' walk," I tell him, pointing outside.

"Right!" he says, his face going redder than an erect penis head. "I'll be two minutes!"

And with that, he marches straight out, strides along Dean Street, and—never comes back.

January 30th, 2007: Chico's Story

"Please don't give up on me," Chico says in my ear. We hug each other in the visitors' room as he is about to be led away by the prison guards. "You're all I have left."

Staring out the grimy window of the First Capital Connect train, I hear Chico's final words in my head. Graffiti-ridden grey factories whiz past as we leave Bedford and hurtle back to Kings Cross.

When we first opened our shop, in February of last year, Chico was one of our first big-spending customers. It's no exaggeration when I say that he probably kept us afloat in the first few months of trading. Then in October, he stopped visiting. No explanation. Just stopped. It went from "Get those size twenty-eights off the racks, girl—Momma's coming shopping!" to nothing. I called his cell phone a few times, but it was dead. It was just so odd—we were just starting to become friends. Then I found out. Chico was in prison. HMP Bedford. Six years for raping three men.

Absurd, of course. Anyone who knew Chico, knows Chico, all seven stone of him, knows that he is completely passive. But unfortunately for Chico, the company he kept turned on him. They demanded more and more money, and when he finally said "no"—they cried "rape." The judge, obviously not well versed in the whole gay client/hooker scene, saw "Black Man Rapes White Man" and put him away.

Never go to Bedford. I repeat, never go to Bedford. It's frightening. But it's the perfect town for a prison. The whole town is a prison. If you were to escape HMP Bedford by lowering yourself over the perimeter wall with your tied bed linen, hit the ground, and look round, you'd think, "Hold on—I'm still inside!" Bedford's that kind of place. It's Alcatraz as far as the eye can see.

Walking through the town, you pass the same shops again and again. Smart Move estate agents. Cash-a-Cheque, Pronuptia Wedding Shop—pawn brokers, estate agents, wedding shops, that's all there is. Row after row of them. It's as if the town is saying, "Sell up! Cash your endowment cheque and leave! Because if you don't you'll end up getting married, and then you'll be trapped here forever."

And the wedding shops. The vile, horrible, wedding shops, with dusty wedding dresses on headless mannequins, ghastly wedding pictures stuck to the shop windows with Blue Tack and yellowing Sellotape. All the brides in the same Pronuptia wedding outfit. All the grooms with their cheap wedding suits, hung-over smiles, and that weary glaze in their eyes, thinking it's something they should do—be one of the lads.

Even the gym. Venice Gym (above a chip shop). How apt—because the whole town feels like it's sinking—sinking in a barrage of overweight mums pushing their overweight kids in their overweight prams to an overweight life to nowhere. And the most depressing part is they seem so "content." Either that or they're Valiumed up to the eyeballs.

The HMP Bedford Prison visitors' waiting area is even worse. It's like their meeting point. A Benefits Office with bars. I'm sure there were more prams in there than inmates, all waiting for their one-hour chat with daddy, their one-hour chat every 28 days.

I hated it. The way they all knew each other. That "I've been coming here for years" look about them, as if it was the local bingo hall. But, at the same time, moved by it—really moved by it. How the wives, the girlfriends, how they loyally stand by their men—carry on with their lives, feeding the kids, living on their handouts, making ends meet.

At 1:45 P.M. we were all called in to be photo'd and finger-printed, told to stand with our arms wide, in single file, while the sniffer dogs circled us for two minutes. Like prisoners.

"If you feel something licking your butt, it's the dog, not me!" said the prison guard cheerfully, a joke he'd probably been using at 1:45 P.M., seven days a week, for 20 years. "Right, in you go! One at a time."

And then I saw Chico. Beautiful Chico. At the back of the room, behind a table, sitting down, near the door. Gone were the designer jeans, the sparkly tops, the Dior sunglasses, the New Bond Street shopping bags; replaced by a pale-blue sweatshirt, stubble, and overgrown hair; his face was frightened, nervous, his bottom lip trembling uncontrollably, his eyes, haunted. Dark, dark, dark.

"Why don't you appeal?"

"Clay, I just can't. I can't go through it all again. It nearly destroyed me. I just want to serve my time and get out."

"But Chico. You're innocent."

"Clay. You don't know what the court's like. They tried to destroy me. The things they said. I wanted to end it all. I just can't go through that again. I just can't do it."

"Here," I said, stretching out my hand. "It says on a sign outside that I can only bring ten pounds in change in here. Can I give this to you?"

"No! No!" said Chico, laughing. "I can't take it. They'll put me in prison."

We cried. We talked. We laughed. The hour came round quickly. By the end Chico's eyes had started to sparkle again. Just the way I remembered.

"I've left you some new clothes with the prison guards. You must write and tell me what you need for my next visit."

"Honey, thank you so much," he purred, showing me his nails. "But all this queen needs right now is a good manicure and pedicure. And in a hundred and thirty-eight weeks' time, I'm going to get it!"

"Are you being treated okay?"

"They've been okay. I wouldn't say I've made friends. Associates, yes. But no friends. But they like me because I can cut hair," he said, trying to hold back the tears again. "This 'Daddy' type keeps bringing me gifts, but I said to him, 'Honey, I ain't doin' no love in here, and no relationships either. The only thing I'm doing here is time.' "

"Be strong, Chico."

"I will. I feel I'll come out of this a better person."

We hugged, pressing into each other as hard as we could.

"I'm fine now," he said, sniffing, pulling back. "It's when you've gone I'll be in pieces."

"I love you, Chico."

"Clay, please don't give up on me," he whispered through the tears. "You're all I have left."

On the train ride back to London, I pick up my little black book and write down everything that happened, feeling slightly guilty, in an *In Cold Blood* kind of way. On the back page I write down Chico's last words. "Clay, please don't give up on me." Immediately after, I write, "I won't, Chico. I promise."

February 2nd, 2007: Fag Lady

There's a small, stocky old woman who frequents these parts.

Very often dishevelled, sporting a number one cut, with round, "barn owl" NHS glasses. She's often wearing a long brown raincoat that glides along the ground behind her, and she always carries a faded Tescos bag. She reminds me of one of those Gateways-era lesbians, butch to the point of being unidentifiable as male or female.

A few weeks will pass by without me catching sight of her. Then, when I least expect, she suddenly pops up everywhere: shuffling past Patisserie Valerie, picking something off the ground in Archer Street, leaning against a porn shop window in Walkers Court. And when she sees me she smiles and talks to me as if we've known each other for years, often starting a sentence mid-sentence.

"...and then she says, 'Well, it's your turn to buy them.' And I say, 'I can't afford them at that price. You must be mad!' Do you think I should have bought them?"

So I'll smile back, or try and respond, and she'll look at me strangely, as if she's just realised that she doesn't really know me at all. Then she scurries off, like an overweight dormouse.

Today, as I tap away at my keyboard in the shop, I catch sight of her outside, crouching down, placing something carefully under the wheel of a car. Then off she goes.

Five minutes later, she's back—same procedure, placing something under the car wheel, rubbing her little hands together with glee, then off again, as if she is about to hibernate and is burying her food for winter.

After her fifth or sixth visit, I sit up in my seat to get a better view. Cigarettes. Half-smoked butts. An ashtray's worth, all gathered in a little mound, and as she arranges them she smiles to herself, looking over her shoulder cautiously, making sure no one has spied her. Our eyes lock for a fraction of a second, but I look quickly away.

Then, once her pile is in place, I watch as she clumsily gets back on her feet, using her hands to push herself up, and proceeds to make her way down Dean Street, stopping passersby.

"Have you got an empty fag packet? 'Scuse me, sir! Got an empty fag box you don't want?"

I sit back down in my chair and start tapping away again, deleting everything I was writing previously, starting afresh with this Fag Lady story.

Moments later, the owner of the car returns, a good-looking businessman. He throws his sports bag into the back seat, jumps inside, and starts to rev the engine.

Oh, no! What's going to happen? Will the car crush the "fag mountain?" Will it just leave a pile of burnt tobacco in its wake? Will Fag Lady return in a flood of tears?

It is a real Hitchcock moment, and I stand up, tempted to rush outside and shout at the driver, "Careful of those cigarette butts, you road hog!" But, miraculously, the driver turns his wheel at such an angle that the whole mound of cigarettes stays perfectly in place.

Then, as so often happens in Hollywood films, just as the coast seems clear and you close your mouth and start munching on your popcorn again, one of those new, motorised road-sweeper vans turns into Dean Street, purring and whirring, sucking everything up in its path. I watch, panic-stricken. The cigarette butts don't stand a chance and they are whisked off, in the blink of an eye, to Cigarette Butt Heaven. Oh, no! This is a disaster. I close my laptop, walk to the shop doorway, and look down Dean Street just as Fag Lady shuffles back into view with a big, beaming smile, holding a cigarette box in the palm of her hand, like one of the Three Kings bearing gifts.

As she gets nearer to her spot she appears puzzled, looking backwards and forwards, up and down the street, as if trying to retrace her steps. Then she walks right up to where her mound should have been, her face forlorn, almost tearful.

I take a step down from the shop doorway toward her, and I'm just about to say "I tried to stop it..." when she spins round on her little blue deck shoes and glares at me.

"You stole my fags! You're always following me and now you've stolen my fags!"

Then she brushes past me, angrily, and, throwing the cigarette box in my direction, shouts, "And stop writing about me! You mental case!"

February 4th, 2007: A Hot Date

A big, butch Texan swaggers into the shop dressed in baggy jeans and a baggy T-shirt. Everything about him says "big"—his voice, his shoulders, his hands, his legs, and, I would imagine, everything else in between.

"How y'all doin'?" he says, in a delicious Southern drawl, the kind of accent that immediately makes me want to dig out my knee pads.

"I need y'all's help. I went an' got me a date tonight with a beautiful woman. She's hot and I just gotta get her in bed."

Oh, God, I love the straight American customers. They know you're the expert and they just want to be styled. No messing. Cash to spend. Zero attitude. Reeking of manhood. So I dress him head to foot in Ermenegildo Zegna—handmade shoes, cargo dress pants, and a button-down shirt with a wool and angora jacket to finish it off.

"If you get lucky tonight, you owe me," I say jokingly as he leaves.

The next morning, Mr. Big Texan comes strutting back in. He walks up to me, slaps a twenty-pound note in the palm of my hand, and, without saying a word, walks straight back out.

February 6th, 2007: A Night to Stay In

I'm sitting in a restaurant on Old Compton Street, Balans. On my own. Back table. Secluded. Just me, my notepad, and a warm double vodka. It's 10 P.M.

The place is a hive of activity. Uptight waiters nursing weekend comedowns mince dangerously past, high on attitude and low on politeness, trying to navigate their feet around the tables and their brain cells around the specials of the day. Young rowdy dyke couples drink beer from the bottle, their mating ritual bordering on violence. A muscle mary loiters at the bar, feigning interest in his friend's conversation while secretly studying his number one cut from all angles in the mirror. Businessmen in limbo, not quite sure what they've stepped into but noticing a lesbian flavour to the evening and deciding to stay. And tables full of East End hen nights, trying to act nonchalant, but itching for attention.

What am I doing here?

My head feels heavy, like a dull ache, from my forehead to my sinuses to my jaw to my teeth. In the midst of a cold. I so don't need to be here.

I try and signal my waiter, but he's engrossed with the hen nights, flattered by their flattery while mentally calculating the tip. They try and tempt him with their drunken pouts and tired lines about "finding the right woman." Their grotesque desperation hovers round their table like a cloud of stale cigarette smoke. I write in my book "I'm so tired of all this." And I don't just mean "this," like this place—I mean the whole Soho life.

When I first came here my writing was warm, naïve, inquisitive. The hookers, the pimps, the rent boys, the dealers—I looked out my window and felt inspired to write. Saw beauty where most see filth. Now I see the filth and it just tires me. I really want that writing back again. I hope it comes.

I think of Ben. Beautiful, sweet Ben. All of 18. I've written about Ben many times. The rent boy outside the shop. There every night. Touting for business. Streetwise, street sharp, Ben.

A social worker came in the shop last week. Poured his story out. And I mean poured. No prompting. It was as if he couldn't bottle it up anymore, the things he'd seen. About the young kids on this street who have maybe six months before they're "taken," appearing in hard-core porn or "snuff." I haven't seen Ben for two months now.

I signal the waiter again. He sees me but pretends not to. Giggling away. Flirting. Thinks he's made it. Serving here. In Balans. The West End. "It's so glamorous, girlfriend. There's always a celebrity here. Someone from *Big Brother*. I may get to work the bar next week!"

My head's pumping now.

I reach into my back pocket and find a plastic wrapper tucked away in the recess. I fish it out, crumpled. Beechams Cold and Flu. I'm tempted to pour it straight into my vodka. Fuck it, I will. Don't care who sees. It doesn't mix well and lies in the bottom of the glass in yellow globules, like infected phlegm. But I knock it back anyway, two gulps.

I think of Chico. God, that trip to Bedford last week. The trips still to come. Locked up in prison for trying to find love in all this squalor. Can't think about this right now.

I feel my head. I've got a slight temperature. Can't seem to shake this cold off. Worries me.

The waiter prances off to clean tables. He's either ignoring me completely or just stupid. Whichever it is, I just want to grab a cocktail from the hen night and pour it over his Superdrug Extra Hold–gelled quiff. But I'm too "heady" to even whimper tonight.

I look round.

There's a couple at the next table. One I recognise from the *QX* hooker section. Mukhtar. "International strip and porn superstar. The biggest cock in porn." He holds it in the photo like a fisherman would a large conger eel. Proud. Moody. Teasing his audience with his "catch." Unintentionally camp with his over-plucked eyebrows and slight "trout pout." He's sitting opposite me, legs slightly spread, and I can't help but look at his package, imaging how he fits all that silicone into a pair of 32-inch briefs. The cock so swollen out of shape it's like an alien cock. ET's. I look at his face, casually, looking past him quickly, so I don't catch his eye. I needn't have worried. His face is expressionless. That porn star "glaze." The only thing that will wake Sleeping Beauty from her spell is the kiss of cash.

I write in my book, "If this motherfucking waiter doesn't get here in two minutes I'm gonna commit a crime." Then, "There'll be no laughs in this blog."

The waiter walks over, smiling, as if he's only just noticed me. It's been 15 minutes.

"Would you like another drink, sir?" he says, his face taking on a slight pinched look as if he's got diarrhoea and he's trying to hold in a fart.

"No, just the bill."

"Dessert menu?"

Just the fucking bill, you stupid prissy queen.

"Just the bill, please."

"Are you sure?"

If you don't get that bill I'm going to throw up all over you, and I've just had your vile Thai soggy noodle dish. You'll look like an oily Medusa and it won't be pretty.

"Yes I'm sure, thank you."

I'm writing SLEEP in big letters in my little black book as he comes back with the bill. He tries to peer over my shoulder at what I'm writing just as I feel the slight tickling sensation of a sneeze in the back of my nose.

I deliberately let it out, full force, without covering my hand. He takes three paces back, not sure whether to hang on for the tip and risk being contaminated.

As I stand, I feel Mukhtar's eyes on me. I look in his direction. He gives me a half smile, half leer. A well-practiced look. I'm almost expecting him to bill me for it.

I'm feeling so grotty and bad-tempered now I'm tempted to sneeze over him too, all over his humongous package. But I settle for a raise of the eyebrows (hey, I may need his client's cash) and walk quickly out, dreaming of my bed, my duvet, sleep, and for this cold to be gone when I awake.

February 7th, 2007: The Rubbishmen
It was late last year when I first saw them.

I was sitting by the window, typing away, babbling on about some local or another, when I saw two strange-looking men walking down Dean Street.

Now it could be said that Soho is full of strange-looking men, but these two were different. Long, flowing hair and beards, dandified dress; it was as if they'd just stepped out of Dr. Who's Tardis, looked around, and said, "You pressed the wrong button, you fool! This isn't 1807, its 2007!" And they had a certain air about them. Like when I first went to Heaven in the 80s and spotted Marilyn. A "nobody" at the time, but you could just tell that a twist of fate could, at any moment, turn him into a "somebody." The same with these two.

So whenever they'd pass the shop I'd press my greasy nose against the window, like the local neighbourhood snoop, and watch, wide-eyed, as they made their way to the French House, wondering who they were, what stories they could tell, or, more importantly, how long it took to grow their beards.

Fast-forward to last month. Whiling away the hours on MySpace, click, click, clicking from one band to another, suddenly, there they were! These strange men had a name. The Rubbishmen.

"We are the arbiters and vanguards of Victorian Punk Revivalism... We currently reside in a Euro wheelie bin in Romilly Street... Please do not use this as a postal address, as it is often emptied," their profile said.

Intrigued, I went to the Colony's monthly cabaret night to see them perform.

The Colony was strange that night. Although I'm not a

regular, the times I've been in it's been empty and I've sat there staring at the artwork on the walls like a spotty Japanese art student in a museum. That Sunday was different. The place was packed. The crowd ranged from students to "literary types," all slightly eccentric; girls, high on God knows what, leaned on their boyfriends or attempted to sway to the rock music, spilling their drinks over unconcerned customers.

When I arrived, the owner, Michael, was already on the small stage, shouting into the microphone. He appeared to have "lost the plot," at one point lying on the floor like an epileptic Johnny Rotten, although, when I looked round, no one seemed too concerned. I assumed he was doing the sound check until he said, "Now, for my second number..."

Between Michael's screeching I caught snatches of conversation. "The Rubbishmen will be back in a minute. They've gone out for a drink." "They're very Dadaesque." "No, I won't be singing. I'll be doing a poetry reading."

Then the Rubbishmen arrived, and a cheer rang around the small room. The atmosphere in the room was not quite electric, more gaslit, but still it felt as if Barbra Streisand was about to take to the stage. Michael screamed, "Ladies and Gentlemen. The Rubbishmen!"

As the little stage was only one step from the doorway, they didn't have far to jump, and, once they'd bashed the drum a few times, they launched straight into their first number, "We are the Rubbishmen." The songs lyrics were quite easy to follow, differing only slightly from the title: "We are the Rubbishmen of Soho, of So...Ho." This made audience participation quite easy.

The second number, which they described as a "mini rock opera," consisted of the words "Gin! Gin! Gin!" repeated over and over again—again, mainly by the audience, who also ad libbed by throwing in lines of their own such as "You are Rubbish, Rubbishmen!" "Rubbage, dear boys! Rubbage!" in between throwing rolled-up newspaper at them.

Ten minutes later, it was all over, greatest hits n' all, and they literally fell off the stage, knocking over the mike stand, the drum kits landing on top of them.

This was followed by Frances, my MySpace friend, the transsexual country singer, dressed in a bridesmaid outfit, belting out a few numbers by Elvis and Cash, ending with "American Pie." By this point the crowd were roaring. I felt like Alice at the Mad Hatter's tea party.

Chaotic, unprepared, surreal, scary, unprofessional... It was fantastic! I loved every minute.

"Close the downstairs door when you leave," said the ticket girl. "We've had a few complaints from the neighbours."

That's style. You know you've made it when even Soho complains about the noise.

February 10th, 2007: Global Warming on Old Compton Street

With all this talk of robins laying eggs in January and polar bears stuck on melting ice floes, you could be forgiven for thinking that global warming doesn't affect the urban environment. Not so. Climate change has hit Old Compton Street.

How do I know this? Well, today we have the first sighting of drag queens on this street. In February! It's unheard of. There hasn't been a drag queen spotted on this street in February since records first began. It's a well-known fact that European drag queens migrate to Tenerife in December and don't return from their sunny climes until at least mid-May.

But there they are; two glorious rare birds. One with long, flowing blonde hair, a wedding dress, and a pink fedora, the other with a floor-length white coat and curly green hair, both being led down the street by a Flyer Boy in tight shorts and a pink shirt, open at the navel, revealing pecs aplenty.

So is global warming really to blame, or have the drag queens simply been blown off course? It's still unclear. However, scientists have today released a statement that says if temperatures continue to rise, Soho may have to prepare itself for not only drag queens in February, but excessive moulting by muscle bears and a swarms of underfed baby dykes as well.

I think Tony Blair needs to know the danger we face.

February 16th, 2007: A "Banging" Brothel

Lying in bed, I am suddenly awakened by what sounds like drunken men running up and down the brothel stairway, just above my head. I look at the alarm clock. 4:30 A.M.

"Bang! Bang! Bang!"

The noise is getting louder, and above the din I can just make out Sue, shouting at the top of her voice, "Get the fuck outta here!"

What's going on? A police raid? I roll over and look at Jorge. Fast asleep. So I reach for my dressing gown, creep upstairs, and peer through the Dean Street window like the local neighbourhood snoop.

As I look to the left, I can just make out a pair of large breasts sticking out of the brothel doorway. In the dim light, bathed in cigarette smoke, they look like mountain peaks surrounded by dense fog. I half expect Julie Andrews to run through them, arms outstretched, singing "The hills are alive"—but instead what comes out is "And don't ever fuckin' come back!" followed by a large smoke ring.

I look across the road, and leaning against the Dean Street wall is a young guy, looking slightly dishevelled, rubbing his crotch and leering.

"You want some of this, don'cha, darlin'?"

"Piss off, you tosser!"

"Come and get it, darlin'. I know what you want!"

By now the guy is rubbing his crotch so furiously it is as if someone has just pressed the Fast-forward button, while to my left, Sue's breasts are thrust out, like armoured chest plates, as if preparing for battle.

"Come on, bitch. Come and get it," yells the young guy, unaware of what fate has in store.

"Right, you fucker, you're gonna get it!"

And with that, Sue runs across the road like a charging rhino and, fists a-flying, catches him smack on the chin. With one punch he crumbles, slipping all the way down the wall. Not content with that, she jumps on top of him, straddles his neck like a sumo wrestler, and slaps him repeatedly around the face.

"Don't ever fuckin' come back!" Sue bawls in his ear.

Brushing her skirt down as she dismounts, she strides back to the doorway, her face set in stone. I quickly duck behind the pillar, breathing a sigh of relief that she hadn't spotted me.

"Clay! You can go back to bed now—problem dealt with!" she bellows as she stomps back up the stairway.

February 24th, 2007: A Celebrity Discount?

A woman's just walked in. She looks familiar. Where've I seen her before? Some show or another? She's famous, I'm sure, although I can't quite place her.

I'm watching her carefully while she browses. Her hair cascades in waves, expensive waves that blend in with the fur on her coat collar. She's talking into her cell phone. One of those loud New York voices. Sassy, ballsy. Very Joan Rivers. A "Don't fuck with me" voice. The kind of American voice you often hear on the tube; oblivious to its surroundings.

I'll give her a minute before I go in for the kill. Not that she'll mind. The Americans are used to it. Unlike the Brits. They run out as soon as you say "Good morning." For some reason they decipher it as "Hand over all your hard-earned money, your pension, your home—now!"

I walk over slowly.

"Just to let you know, everything in shop is fifty percent off the marked price at the moment."

She turns round and looks at me as if I'm a mannequin come to life. "I wanna buy something for a yob!" she barks. I look her in the eye, trying to detect humour. There's none.

"Well, that's nice of you, buying for a yob," I reply cheerfully, trying to mellow the mood.

"Bitch!" she spits back.

Wow! I wasn't expecting that. We stare at each other. Her face is expressionless—either intentionally or cosmetically, I can't quite make out which. And her speech, though direct, is slightly slurred. Prescription drugs? I do know her, though. I'm sure of it. Isn't she one of the judges from *American Idol*? Anyway, whoever the fuck she is, I ain't taking that kind of attitude.

"Well, you said it first," I say.

"Listen, queen, I want some clothes for my son. You gonna help or not?"

Then it hits me. Of course! It's Janice. Janice Dickinson. The so-called world's first supermodel. One of the judges on *America's Next Top Model*. This bitch takes no prisoners. Destroys people with a withering look. She makes Simon Cowell look like a pussyboy. Fuck, Clay, retreat. You're outta your depth here. Dealing with pissy French queens is no preparation for this one.

"Umm. Er. Shall I show you a few T-shirts he may like?"

She doesn't answer, but snatches one off the racks and thrusts it in my direction.

"I'll take this one. Medium."

"Janice, let me get you a new one from the top," says Jorge, appearing from nowhere. He must have clicked straight away. He steps up the ladder. Janice eyes him up as he reaches up.

"Hot ass!" she purrs, and this is a broad who knows an ass or two—Mick Jagger's, Warren Beatty's, Jack Nicholson's...

"Well, most Cubans have hot asses," Jorge replies, looking down. "My name's Jorge."

"J-o-o-o-o-r-r-r-g-g-g-g-g-eh!" she drawls with a Latino twang. "Ha-ba-naaaaaaaaaaa! Get me one of those London track tops too, while you're at it."

I move back. She's scaring me a bit. It's all very Cruella de Vil. Jorge steps back down and hands me the items to wrap.

"What are you working on at the moment, Janice?" he asks.

"Some stupid show about a football player fucking his neighbour," she mutters.

She makes her way to the counter, wobbling slightly, as I start to fold the clothes she's chosen. "Wrap them 'gay'!" she says, watching me intently. "Here, I'll show you." She takes the T-shirt from me and places it inside the tracksuit top. "There. I want gay! gay! gay! It's gotta look gay for the son."

I examine her face carefully while she rearranges the clothes. She's completely unlined. Devoid of makeup. Great surgeon. Still looks fabulous, 37 *Vogue* covers later—and she must be 60 now, her age always something of a mystery. But, there again, she could easily pass for 40; she's got that "negotiable" age about her.

"I love my son. He's not gay, though. Oh, well. You can't have it all. He was deflowered by a midget hooker."

I try and suppress a smile. Where's my little black book when I need it?

"Okay. How much?" she says, throwing notes over the counter as if she's at a poker table.

"Well, these are all half price. So twenty-three pounds for the T-shirt and thirty for the track top."

"Thirty pounds? Are you crazy? What about a celebrity discount?"

"Sorry, there's no celebrity discount here," says Jorge firmly, somewhere behind me, using his years of experience dealing with these pushy celebrity types.

"Hmmm. You bitches are tough," she fires back, attempting to raise a delicately plucked eyebrow. "Okay, throw in a free postcard." She reaches toward the postcard rack.

"They're one pound each."

She stops. Looks across. Smiling fixedly, she reaches for one anyway. Turns back round. Uh-oh. She's about to eat me alive.

"What's your name, kid?"

"Clayton."

"You're tough, mister." She stretches out her hand to shake. "I like that. I like ya."

And as she leaves, promising to come back, I think, with a grin on my face, that, actually, despite the façade, I like her too.

February 28th, 2007: She's Back!

It's a miserable, dreary day outside the shop, hardly any customers; we're both twiddling our thumbs, staring blankly ahead. I catch Jorge's eye. He shrugs. I shrug back. What will break the spell?

I look outside, and my eyes are drawn to two people about to walk in. So I quickly sit up and prepare my Stepford wife "Can I help you?" face.

The first one through the door is a tall, well-built, black man in a tailored khaki outfit. He's sipping coffee. I can't quite see the second person but I hear her talking on her mobile. I recognise the voice instantly. Oh God. It's Janice Dickinson. She's back!

I watch nervously as she walks sedately through the doorway, staring straight ahead, her face, set, like a guest in a Liza Minnelli wedding pic. Then, as if she can't contain herself anymore, she rushes up to the counter, slams her hands on the glass, and shrieks at Jorge, "Was I fucking wasted the last time I was in here?"

"If you were, Janice, we didn't notice," Jorge replies, perfectly composed, without batting an eyelid.

We didn't notice? I look at him with my mouth open. Her eyes were rolling as fast as the balls in the National Lottery!

"That's why I fuckin' love you guys!" she shouts back, and proceeds to run around the shop, frantically pulling clothes off the hangers as if it's the Harrods winter sale. "Dick! Dick!" she shouts at her friend lingering by the doorway. "Dick! Look at this shirt—do you think it suits me?" And she waves him over as she holds up a sky-blue Versace short-sleeve knit.

"It looks like a tennis outfit."

"Good! I love grabbing balls."

What a contrast with Saturday. She's like another person. The last Janice was shaking slightly, rude, obnoxious. Today's Janice is telling us how nice everything is, how she only wants to shop at Dirty White Boy from now on, how she's going to wear our T-shirt on TV tomorrow night.

I decide to take the plunge and give her a compliment. I take a slight step toward her, ready to run at any minute. I'm sweating. The hairs on my balls are standing on end. Like I've got two puffer fish in my pants.

"Janice, you, er... You look better in real life than on TV."

"Fuckin' liar!" she barks back.

"I...I...mean it."

Her face changes, slightly. I think she's smiling—although she could be about to spit.

"I've told you that before, Janice," says Dick.

"Shut the fuck up! He's hitting on me. Let him talk."

Oh, dear. That wasn't quite the intention. Now what to do. Oh, well. I've got this far. So I take another couple of steps forward, grab her by her size zero shoulders, and kiss her on each cheek.

"You know what?" she says, pulling back, all wide-eyed. "I fucking love you!"

And with that, she flies out of the shop, like something from *Bewitched*, shouting so loud the whole street can hear, "Get ready, motherfuckers! I'll be back soon with credit cards!"

March 1st, 2007: Up and Down the Stairway

There are nights when I'm lying in bed, Jorge snoring softly beside me, that I listen to the punters as they stomp up and down the brothel stairway just above my head.

Most of the time they're quiet, just background noise, a noise that slowly works its way into my dreams—a bit like counting sheep, three punters and I'm out. But now and again the stomping can get quite loud and I'm wide awake for hours, wondering whether the brothel's being raided or whether someone's tried to get away without paying again, Sue slowly throttling them between her meaty thighs.

Over the months I've become something of an expert on these nocturnal movements, accumulating enough knowledge to submit a university thesis on the subject. *Prostitution: Seasonal Variations of the Night-time Client.*

What I've noticed, for example, is that whereas the noise before 2 A.M. is low, between 2 A.M. and 3 A.M. it reaches a crescendo, the punters literally running up the stairway. It's as if they can't get their willy out fast enough. In fact, there are times when their running becomes so noisy that I half expect a punter to come crashing through the ceiling, landing on my face—not quite the position he was expecting to fork good money out for, I'm sure.

This 2 A.M. to 3 A.M. crescendo is perhaps to be expected. The clubs empty out and half-drunk horny men are cruising round Soho looking for sex. But what is surprising is that punters run down the stairs just as fast as they run up.

This had me stumped for a while. Why the need to run down the stairs at such speed? Surely, once the deed is done (or the seed is flung), a quiet amble down, cigarette in hand, is called for. Then it came to me. Shame. It's all about running up to get your end away and then running down again to escape, embarrassed, into the night.

One night, settling back down in bed, pondering my "running down with shame" theory, a shameful memory of my own suddenly pops in my head and I'm transported back to the 70s, to an afternoon when I was lying in bed, naked, playing "tents."

Unfortunately, on this particular afternoon, while in full tent-making motion, in walked my Dad. Quick as a flash, ad libbing like a *Give Us a Clue* contestant, my jerky genital hand movement immediately turned into a huge coughing fit. My Dad took one look, his mouth dropped open, and he walked straight out.

To add to my embarrassment, moments later my mum, who would normally just burst into my room, knocked, unheard of in our communal household. The word had obviously gotten out. Clay was an Olympic wankathlete. I stayed in my bedroom all weekend, shamefaced, with my head under the duvet.

In all, my dad caught me in the act three times: the bedroom incident, one I'd prefer to forget about, and once when he walked into his bedroom to find me lying on his bed flicking through a porn magazine (that I'd found hidden under his mattress). The porn mag contained pictures of half-dressed nuns, of all things.

Thinking about this as I lie in bed, the stomping above

my head getting louder and louder, I am very tempted to get dressed, wait outside, and stop the punters as they run out, offering them a piece of schoolboy advice.

"Don't worry, guys, there's nothing to be ashamed of. It could've been worse, she could've been a nun!"

March 3rd, 2007: The Metamorphosis

It was in February of last year that I first saw him.

Something made him stand out—the slight mince as he walked by, the way he ran his fingers through his hair, the fey voice as he chatted on his mobile.

The months trickled by, and my eyes were drawn elsewhere, to the more eccentric, so when I did see him it was just a brief glimpse, just another camp boy finding his way.

Summer came. All the Prides. Euro, Gay, Soho. The sun beat down, our summer stock slowly sold. We weathered the doldrums and hung on in, determined to make a go of the shop, determined to stay.

And then a strange thing happened. When I did catch sight of him, something had changed. I couldn't quite put my finger on it, but somehow he was different. Nothing major, but still, it was enough for me to do a double take. It was as if he was walking more upright, more confident, kind of aware of himself. Like he was starting to shine. And it seemed, as the seasons gradually changed, so, gradually, did he.

Gone were the ripped jeans, the little diamanté-studded jackets, the short, slightly curly hair. Now the face was carefully made up; there was a hint of rouge and eye shadow, shoulder-length hair, lightly tinted, less "boyish" clothing. And as the summer turned to autumn, as the street went from bright to muted, he began to radiate as if in compensation. It was as if he was going through a metamorphosis.

By December I was no longer a stranger in Soho. I'd become a "Sohoite"—getting to know all the locals, the pimps, the prostitutes, the shop owners, people stopping by to pass the time of day; Fall/Winter clothing was gift-wrapped, the winter chill set in, and, as I served what now had become regular customers, I'd glance outside and occasionally catch sight of him. The change was almost complete.

This afternoon, I see him again, and such is the transformation that I have to stop what I am doing and walk over to the window to watch.

I smile to myself. Now it is complete. The butterfly has finally hatched. And, as he flutters past, it looks like he is spreading his new wings. He is smiling. He turns heads. He looks fabulous. Now it is no longer he who walks by, it is no longer he wearing the little jackets, it is no longer "he" I notice—he has finally become "she."

March 14th, 2007: A Collaboration

Late afternoon. A really tall man marches into the shop.

"I'm Paul."

"Hi, I'm Clay," I reply, reaching out my hand to shake.

He looks at me carefully, his expression almost defiant, his hands clasped firmly in his pockets, while my hand hangs patiently in the air like a camp ballerina.

"I know," he barks.

"Um… Take a seat," I say, directing him toward my little red chair by the window.

"No!"

"Please! Sit down!" I insist, thinking he'd not really understood what I'd said.

"No."

Wow! This guy is…different.

Paul's a photographer, the brother of my MySpace friend the glamorous and talented singer Mighty Maggie K. Maggie has put us in touch thinking that maybe my Soho stories and Paul's photos could lead to "something."

Her intervention has come at the right time. I've been

thinking for a while about what to do with all this writing. Was it a diary? Tales of the City? I was open to suggestions. But was I the collaborating type? For it to work I would need to link up with someone unusual, preferably someone slightly unbalanced.

Fortunately, Paul fit the bill perfectly. Fresh from a Spanish prison after being caught smuggling in something a bit naughty, where he made full use of his time by falling in love with a Latino transsexual, Paul has recently had a book published, page after page of breathtaking backstage photos of Duran Duran, capturing the essence of a band as it took its first tentative steps into the 80s limelight.

"So, um, Paul. Would you like to collaborate on a book? Umm...what I mean is—what do you think of my writing?"

"You're the Roald Dahl of the sleaze world."

Well, I didn't think I was ever going to be the new Emily Brontë, but Roald Dahl seems closer to the mark—so the collaboration begins.

On Friday we spend our first day together taking pictures around Soho—Paul with his big "American tourist" camera around his neck, and me, following closely behind, like Lois Lane in a pencil skirt, my little black notebook in hand, ready to blog anything that breathed.

First stop is Great Windmill Street and a notorious brothel situated right next door to Soho Primary School, presumably located there as a warning to the kids of what would happen if you failed your 11+. We venture past the doorway slowly, like giggling schoolboys on their first trip to Amsterdam, the prostitute in the doorway eyeing us up suspiciously.

"Go and ask her, Clay. Go on! This is your area, not mine."

"Oh, God! Do I have to? Okay...hold on."

So I tiptoe over, the prostitute dropping her guard as

I approach, possibly sensing that I'm not exactly "cash material."

"Hi. My name's Clayton. Umm… My friend and I are taking some photos of Soho and we wondered if you'd mind if we took a few shots of you standing in the doorway."

She takes a drag of her cigarette before answering. "What are they for?" she says, flicking back her head, causing the spiralling cigarette smoke to disperse. "You're not from the 'News of the Screws,' are you?"

As she adjusts her yellow tight-fitting top, her breasts spill over, like beer barrels over Niagara Falls.

"Oh no—we're nothing like that. We want to publish a book on Soho, the real Soho, and you're part of the real Soho. I'm from Dirty White Boy on Old Compton Street."

"Oh, I know you. You're that guy who writes in the *London Paper*, aren't you?"

"Yes. That's me."

"I read that story you did about the two old men walking down the street. I like what you write. You see the things I see. It's like you're one of us."

It's like you're one of us. As she talks about her life, the 15 years she's spent working this street, it crosses my mind that I'll probably never get a better compliment than that.

At length, she says, "Okay. What do you want me to do? My name's Regan, by the way."

I beckon Paul over. "Paul, this is Regan. What do you want her to do?"

"Look at me like a punter," he says. "Invite me in. Lift your skirt up a bit. Yeah. Like that." As Paul snaps away, Regan slowly pulls up her miniskirt, giving me my first real glimpse of pussy hair since the school playing fields.

With sex now firmly on our brains, Paul having let out orgasmic cries after every shot, we set off in the direction of Walkers Court.

Walkers Court is, possibly, the sleaziest little alleyway in

Soho, if not the UK. Dangerous, edgy, full of sex shops, strip clubs, and dodgy characters, it makes the corner outside my shop feel like Disneyland. So we snap away merrily for 15 minutes, not realizing that a pack of criminals were circulating menacingly nearby, eyeing up Paul's camera, like sharks circling a swimmer.

From there we run to Brewer Street and the fruit and veg market, which starts on the corner of Peter Street, another one littered with brothels. Here we discover a stall holder who's taken the word *multi-tasking* to a new level by shouting, "Bananas! A pound a pound. Ladies upstairs. It's free to look!"

By now we're almost sleazed out, so after calling the MD of Clonezone, asking him if he'd mind if we took some shots of a few dildoes (the wide-angle lens being put to good use), we make our way through Meard Street.

This picturesque street lined with beautiful Victorian houses, which links Wardour and Dean Streets, is perhaps the prettiest of all Soho's streets. In one of these houses lives the "crucified" artist and frequent brothel visitor Sebastian Horsley, whom I occasionally see striding along past our shop late at night. With his dyed black hair, his deathly pallor, dressed in a black mourning suit and a white shirt with huge collars, he looks like Keith Richards in Nosferatu drag. (As I lie in bed at night, I imagine him on the street behind, luring unsuspecting hookers up to his lair so that he can drain them of their crack-laced blood.)

Paul, meanwhile, is in full paparazzo mode by now, racing on ahead of me, upping the tempo somewhat by running alongside a businesswoman who is desperately trying to get away by shooing him away with her Chanel handbag. He takes shots of her red dominatrix-style stilettos as she runs, while I trail behind, handing out apologies to anyone we pass.

Just before we reach Dean Street, for some reason, I

happen to look up. There, halfway up the wall, about 30 feet up, is a big white carved nose sticking out of the brick-work, and just to the right, the Meard Street sign.

"Paul! Quick, over here! Take a picture of this." I shout, pointing upwards.

"The nose?"

"No, to the right. Look at the Meard Street sign."

"What about it?"

"Well, look just above it."

"Oh, yes."

There, in what looks like sandstone, is the previous Meard Street sign; the words are hardly legible now, faded over the centuries. But if you look carefully you can just make out the inscription: "Meard Street 1732."

By now it is almost six, and as the bells of Saint Anne's church chime away in the distance, we make our way to Frith Street and the Italian district for a large cappuccino, stopping off at the shop en route to say hello to Jorge. I stayed at a friend's house last night, and he called me this morning, acting strangely, overly friendly. As we talk, a sixth sense kicks in, and as I put down the receiver I'm hit by a wave of sadness.

Bar Italia on Frith Street, just opposite Ronnie Scott's, is always busy; guys chatting boisterously beside their motor-bikes, couples draped over each other, gay men pretending to be reading while cruising. This spot is a real culture clash. A melting pot of all nationalities, sexualities, all the "alities" lumped together in a few yards of coffee shops. The perfect spot to take a few photos and capture the vibe of Soho. So we sit down and peruse the street, like cheetahs on a rock ledge.

To our right sits Suggs from the 80s pop group Madness, and, as Paul once took photos of him many years ago, he asks if he'd mind having one taken again. As luck would have it, at this exact moment, the Fag Lady comes stomping down the street. After giving her £2 for her trouble, we're able to get a few nice shots of Suggs with his arms wrapped tightly around her.

"Paul, it's getting kind of late now," I venture. How about we take a few in Soho Square before we pack up? It's quite pretty in there at this time."

So we walked down Frith Street, picking up a newspaper from the *London Paper* man as he passes by with his trolley. I always pick one up just to see if they've published one of my columns. So I flick excitedly to the columnist section, and there is one of mine—nestled, quite conveniently, between a picture of a Victorian toilet and someone ranting on in the letters section about the rise in STDs.

As the sun slowly sets, we sit in Soho Square and Paul snaps away at a pair of beautiful boys sitting on a park bench just opposite, gazing into each other's eyes. It is the perfect way to end the day. It started with sleaze and it ended with love.

March 19th, 2007: "She Doesn't Know I'm Here"

I've got two envelopes in my hand. Neither of them is for me.

The first is handwritten; large, spidery writing spills over the envelope and threatens to travel beyond. It's as if the writer was being hideously tortured, his persecutor holding his testicles in a viselike grip. It's addressed to the brothel upstairs, "Flat 1, 50 Old Compton Street," so that's entirely possible.

The other one's typed, with a plain brown envelope made from coarse recycled paper. It reminds me of the hard, splintery paper we used to have to wipe our bums with at school, the rough treatment we received there even extending as far as the bog roll. The envelope's from the Inland Revenue, another persecutor, and it's addressed to "The Algerian Coffee Shop," the shop next door.

How they both ended up here I can't imagine. So—which to deliver first? The brothel or the coffee shop?

I'm sitting in my little red chair by the window, umming and aahing, when suddenly there's a tap on the window. It jolts me out of my dream state. I look round. Then jump again when I see a squashed-up gargoyle face pressed against the glass, inches from my face, the big oval glasses magnifying the eyes.

It's Pam, the Fag Lady. She's blinking rapidly, which, with her specs, makes her look like a lesbian Benny Hill; although it's quite hot outside, she's wearing her cream mac and holding, strangely, what looks like a Marc Jacobs handbag.

I smile back and, as if that is her cue, she stops blinking, pulls back, and holds up one finger, mouthing the word "money." As we've only just opened, I give her a shrug and her face drops, briefly—then lights up again as she stretches out her arms and mouths the word "cuddles." So I get up from the chair and walk toward the doorway.

"I love you," she whispers, wrapping her arms around me tightly. "Have you got any money?" she says, looking up, her glasses starting to mist up. She has a bit of a dank smell about her but I wrap my arms round her anyway.

"I'm sorry. I haven't. The till's empty at the moment."

She buries her face back into my chest and sighs. "Just cuddles, then." We stay like this for what feels like a minute. Then she slowly unpeels herself and plods off back down Dean Street, stopping after three plods to turn back round and say "What book will I be in?"

"I don't know yet, Pam. I've no idea."

"Okay," she replies, and off she goes.

By now Jorge's back, so I pick the testicle-crushing envelope up from the counter and walk back to the doorway.

"Just popping upstairs to drop this off. Back in a minute."

I look at my watch as I walk round the shop. 1 P.M. The brothel door's open already. I hesitate. The dirty passageway and faded paintwork are not exactly inviting. But, there again, maybe the squalid appearance is all part of the appeal.

I step inside. Read the "Model" sign (which is actually just a piece of paper Sellotaped to the wall). "Gorgeous Ladies. It's Free to Look!" Each letter written in a different coloured pen.

As I reach the first floor I can hear a radio playing—some diva singing about not wanting to go into rehab—and two voices, a male and a female. The female sounds like Sue.

I'm about to shove the envelope under the door, but reconsider. The voices are too close. If I push it under now, there's a chance Sue will see it. If it was Maggie, that'd be okay—but not Sue. Maggie I like. She smiles or waves when she sees me. Sue I'm slightly wary of. She eyes me up suspiciously whenever we pass each other on the street—her huge breasts pointing at me, as if she's got baby machine guns attached to each nipple and they're about to blow me away.

I tiptoe toward the flat door, listening carefully, trying to distinguish the voices from the radio.

"…thought you only wanted half an hour."

"…stay longer…don't worry, I'll pay… I can stay longer…"

" You were the one who says to tell you after your half an hour was up."

"It's okay. She doesn't know I'm here."

She doesn't know I'm here. For some reason I pull back from the doorway, thinking. That phrase, *She doesn't know I'm here.* It resonates.

I take two steps down the stairway. Sit down, slowly. I can still hear the voices but I'm not listening now. I'm in my own world. Looking down at the envelope. Thinking about that phrase.

She doesn't know I'm here.

Oh, yes, she does. She always knows. You think you cover your tracks so well. When she's away for the night. You plan. You scheme.

She doesn't know I'm here.

Oh, really. When you call her at work. When your voice is strangely, unusually happy.

She doesn't know I'm here.

I wouldn't count on it. She knows you inside out. That new position in bed. That meal you took her out for, out of the blue; the plans you make about your futures together, to reassure her. You think she doesn't know that?

She doesn't know I'm here.

She knows everything about you. You're a terrible liar. You cover your tracks so badly. She wants to tell you how badly you lie but she can't bring herself to.

She doesn't know I'm here.

She knows it all. She can read you like a book. She's been trying to ignore it. Hope it'll go away; trying to accept the fact nothing lasts forever and that you must allow for the odd indiscretion.

She doesn't know I'm here.

Yes, she does. She's always known. From day one. It's just that…she's not quite sure what to do next.

I stand up, carefully, holding on to the banisters, leaving the envelope just outside the flat door, and make my way slowly back to the shop.

March 20th, 2007: Mommie Dearest
"Soho became a Royal Park in the Middle Ages and the name actually originated from a hunting cry at the time, 'So-Ho.' "

There's a crowd of people outside the shop at the moment—all ages, nationalities, sizes, wrapped up in scarves, long coats, and woollen hats, listening to a middle-aged tourist guide as she relays the history of Soho. With her angular face, pinched expression, and thinning hair, she bears an unfortunate similarity to a well-plucked battery hen. Even her voice is clipped—short and sharp, as if pecking for seed as she speaks.

"...celebrities lived here. Karl Marx on Dean Street. Canaletto and Casanova also reputedly lived..."

Although I'm hidden, sitting on my little red chair behind the pillar, for some reason I feel as if I'm intruding on her conversation; so I sit quietly and listen.

"By the nineteen-sixties Soho was known mainly for its sex industry..."

Oh, goody. My eyes light up like a naughty schoolboy and I stick my nose around the pillar to watch the crowd's reaction. Two men are smirking and the women all seem to be tut-tutting.

"...number of licensed sex shops, and prostitution is still very much part of Soho."

Suddenly, as if she's been waiting in the wings for her cue, Sue barges out of the brothel doorway like a fearsome Viking warrior, bleached hair trailing behind in her wake. The crowd, mouths open, step aside as she storms through, followed by one of her Eastern European "girls." This is too good to be true. Where's my little black book when I need it? I peer around the other side of the pillar to look at Bird Face's reaction. She squints disapprovingly at Sue from the top of her 1950s pointed glasses.

"Ummm, yes, as I was saying, it's still very much part of Soho life."

Sue, oblivious to Bird Face and the gawping crowd, stands in front of her girl, hands on meaty hips, tapping her Nike-clad foot aggressively. Damn! I'm slightly out of earshot and Bird Face's squawky voice is almost drowning Sue's out, so I'm getting snippets of two conversations at once:

"In the seventies Westminster cut down on the number

of sex establishments..." "I've fuckin' told you about this God knows how many times!"

Told you what? I've gotta hear more, Sue! But what can I do without revealing myself? I know. When in doubt, think Mommie Dearest...

So I reach into the cupboard, fumble around for the Pledge and the grubby yellow duster, step from behind the pillar, and start cleaning the clean window.

"In the eighties the gay community moved here..." chirps Bird Face, trying not to look at Sue, who appears to be getting really angry.

"If I ever catch you doing that again..." Sue growls, pointing her finger at the tearful girl.

Doing what again? What did she do? Keep the tips? Use a bit too much tongue in the fake lesbo scene?

As I've now nearly worn a hole in the glass, I decide to throw all caution to the wind and clean the outside window ledge. But just as I'm positioning myself, duster on ledge, ear in air, Bird Face clucks a "Follow me!" to the crowd and they make their way down Dean Street while Sue, breasts erect and defiant, storms back upstairs, followed closely by her girl. Oh no! I've missed it all!

Disappointed, I turn back round just as Craig, the mad *Big Issue* seller, skips merrily past with a big grin on his face.

"Go and put that one in your little black book!"

March 22nd, 2007: Re-branding

In the past week we have noticed groups of black guys hanging around the shop, discussing the Iceberg window display.

Iceberg is one of the top European designers and is particularly popular with the black community. As every attack we have suffered has been at the hands of young black males, the window display is perhaps giving out a message that says, "Rob us!" Nevertheless, we refuse to be swayed or dictated to; and this week we found that by a subtle re-branding exercise the gangs can be deterred.

Here's what happened...

Jorge's sitting behind the counter. Enter three black youths. They start stalking the shop, acting suspiciously, looking over at Jorge every few seconds, watching him watching them. Their manner becoming slightly threatening and aggressive.

"Where's your Iceberg clothes!" one of the group shouts.

"Yeah! Show us the Iceberg!" says another, sneering.

Jorge looks at them and walks calmly from behind the counter.

"They're over here," he replies, pointing to a row of T-shirts, shirts, and a selection of low-rise jeans. "It's Iceberg's new range. Gay Iceberg. They call it their 'Battyboy' range."

Exit three black youths.

April 1st, 2007: Raqib Shaw

A rainy, gloomy, Sunday afternoon.

It's all quiet in the shop. I'm sitting by the shop window, like a Dutch prostitute, watching the crowds go by. Jorge's flicking through QX magazine, playing "count the Brazilian" in the hooker section. Not a sound between us. Suddenly a strange-looking person flies into the shop.

"Jorge! Jorge! I'm back! HA! HA! HA! HA! HA!"

Imagine, if you will, a 32-year-old, Anglo-Indian Quentin Crisp, dressed in a mélange of stripes, paisleys, prints, with a little psychedelic hat perched on the side of his head— a combination of clothes and colours that only a trained artist's eye could make sense of. Then imagine his laugh, loud and infectious, like a macaw, the most unusual laugh you've ever heard. This is Raqib Shaw.

Raqib is one of our regular customers. I've wanted to write about him for a while, but, to be honest, I've been overawed. He's just so out there, I haven't really known where to start. Give me someone down and out, a hooker, the homeless—and I'm your man! But Raqib? How could I possibly do him justice?

Because, in addition to being the most eccentric person I've ever met, Raqib's also one of the most talented. His own exhibition at the Tate Britain, his work displayed in the Museum of Modern Art in New York—this is an artist who could very well go down in history as one of the greats.

One of his paintings, for instance, *Garden of Earthly Delights,* covers an entire museum wall and depicts an underwater world populated by mythical creatures—part aquatic/part animal/part human. On closer inspection you see that the work is littered with cocks, orifices, ejaculations, animals fucking, all decorated with glitter and semi-precious stones. Another piece, this one a "life size" sculpture, is of a lobster fucking a man with a chicken's head. So you could say that his work is a touch unusual.

Talent on this scale makes me go weak. Although, in Raqib's case, I go one step further. I retreat. So whenever he flies in I immediately start busying myself with the dusting, file an already perfect nail, or pretend to be talking to my mum on the phone about her organic runner beans, anything but face him. Consequently, he and Jorge have become friends while I've become the dumb shop assistant.

But, although I play dumb well, I've had an agenda. I've been secretly recording Raqib's every move in my little black book, which is hidden behind a Takeaway Pizza Express flyer that I pretend to study with a hungry look on my face whenever he looks in my direction.

After six months of this I've managed to rack up a copious amount of notes on this wonderful creature (while also appearing to have a thin crust fetish), and no two visits are ever quite the same...

"Oh, Jorge! Jorge!" shouts Raqib as he runs up to the

counter, throwing his Hermés bag on the floor. "I need to buy some of your beautiful garments!" And he proceeds to pull off his black leather gloves and unravel his pink silk cravat, draping them over the counter.

Jorge smiles back and steps from behind the counter. "Lovely to see you again, Raqib."

"Oh, you too, Jorge dear! Now what've you got for me today?" says Raqib, walking toward the aisles, running a delicate finger along the clothes, inspecting each item with a quizzical eye. As he walks he reveals a small, female Japanese body builder standing quietly behind him. His friend Yoko.

"Jorge! What about these? Do you have these in my size? And these? Oh, I love them all! They're all gorgeous!" Raqib gushes. "I've been running up and down Bond Street and couldn't find a thing. Isn't that right, Yoko dear?"

I peep up from behind my pizza flyer, my nose perched just above the tomato and mozzarella salad, and watch as Yoko nods politely back. She smiles at me, and I lower the salad to chin level and smile back. Seconds later, Raqib's taken about six of our most expensive items to the changing room.

"Yoko dear! I need artistic assistance! HA! HA! HA! HA! HA! Come, Yoko dear! Come, Yoko!"

Yoko follows meekly behind.

"But no picking clothes for yourself, Yoko darling! This is a man's shop and you don't want to look like a butch lesbian, do you, Yoko darling? HA! HA! HA! HA! HA!"

"No, Raqib," replies Yoko, shaking her head.

As Yoko, Raqib, and Jorge head to the back of the shop with a handful of clothes, Raqib's laughter fills the shop. "Oh, Jorge! You must come to my studio again. You can watch Yokie and me as we create beauty! HA! HA! HA! HA! HA! He should come again, shouldn't he, Yoko?"

Deciding to give them some space, I step outside for a moment and lean against the shop wall. A homeless man I recognise walks up to me and leans beside me. I've seen him a few times on this street, and each time we say hello I have this vague feeling that we've met before. He has the type of face you recognise but can't quite place—Spanish, dark-skinned, handsome, but with a couple of teeth missing that I try hard not to focus on.

"I feel really ill," he says, staring across at the bookshop opposite.

"You do? What's wrong?"

"I'm withdrawing."

"From what?"

"Smack. I haven't had a fix since last night. It's awful, man. I feel terrible. Really bad."

"Have you tried methadone?"

"That stuff's nasty. Just as addictive as smack. I just need ten quid to get a fix for tonight. Then I'll feel better."

"I'm sorry. I don't have any cash on me."

"I know, man. Don't worry. I've seen your face. You're okay. You don't need to worry. I'll get the money somehow."

"But is taking more the answer?" I reply, immediately realising that it is a really stupid thing to say.

"It's all I can do to take away the pain, man," he whispers back, before he turns down Dean Street.

As I watch him walk slowly away, in the background I hear Raqib's laugh, and it crosses my mind that I could never be a great artist like Raqib, because the longer I'm here, the more difficult it is to find beauty on this street.

April 5th, 2007: The Groucho Club

It's Thursday night. Almost midnight. We're in the Groucho Club, the celeb hangout across the road from the shop. Waiting list high. Atmosphere low. I'm with my MySpace friend the actor David Benson, his brother, and two of his friends, one the drummer from Duran Duran, Roger Taylor.

David's sitting next to me. We're on a low-level leather settee, sunk into the cushions. There's a glass coffee table in front of us with the remainders of a round of drinks.

We talk easily, excitedly, about film, David's upcoming show, camp icons from our youth, East End straight lads. We've many shared interests; only known each other a few weeks but relaxed as if it's been years.

Every now and again we look across at David's friends, on the settee opposite. They seem almost comatose, through tiredness or drink, not sure which. I watch Roger, closely. He rests his head on the back of the settee, drifting off, and I think back to when I first saw him in concert back in the 80s. Withdrawn, shy, good-looking, the outcast of the group; always the most attractive. But that was many years ago.

He struggles to stay awake. His legs are tucked up on the settee. His hair, dishevelled. His face, tired. His clothes, grungy. The waitress walks over and prods him. Tells him that he can't sleep in here. He wakes up momentarily. Looks round as if unsure of his surroundings. Was he the Duran Duran star who left the band because of exhaustion? It kinda figures. Even when he talks it's with a faraway kind of voice. Anyway, it seems there's no exceptions here, even for stars. The waitress walks off with a stern look, checking on him from over her shoulder. So much for platinum discs.

Then a tall blonde woman breezes in. Dressed in a grey striped dress, with a black handbag that she swings like a deadly weapon. I watch her watching Roger. She focuses. Trying to place him. Knows she's seen him before but just can't quite... There! She's got it. Her face creeps into a smile. A scary smile. She turns around. Heads to the bar. Orders a drink. Then looks over her shoulder. Eyeing up the prize. Thinking.

Now she's walking toward us. This time slowly, in a predatory, cat-like way. I'm talking to David but at the same time watching her every move. Roger must be the most unavailable man in the room, half asleep, but, nonetheless, she sits down on the edge of the settee and pretends to engage his friend in conversation. You can feel the calculated desire from feet away. It's etched over her face. The friend's just bait. I wonder if he realises.

She runs her long fingers through her highlighted hair, laughs—a laugh that if you hadn't been watching her throughout would appear genuine. Then she throws back her head and shakes her shoulder-length hair. It's like a mating ritual. Doesn't notice me watching.

Now I'm asking David about his upcoming Bloomsbury show, how it feels having people he knows in the audience, taking it all in, marvelling at his talent—but all the time I'm watching, watching, as she edges nearer, her hands so close to Roger she can touch him. She can smell the power, the money, the fame, the houses; all within her grasp. She's played this bar for so long for a chance like this. Won't blow it now. Can't. These chances don't come round that often. I read her every move. At least at the brothel across the road it's up front. Here the intent seems so devious.

She turns round. Her face is hard, square almost. Not attractive in the classic sense but with something. Perseverance?

Then she taps Roger on the shoulder. Wakes him. Offers to buy him a drink. Something strong to wake him up.

"Wake up, sleepyhead! I'll get you a martini expresso. Waitress!"

Roger nods. Looks almost cute again. Like he did all those years ago. But helpless. So not aware of what's happening; the web he's caught in. She calls the waitress again. All the time her face set in a grotesque smile. Laughing at anything Roger says, which appears, from here, to be very little.

The drink arrives. She takes it from the waitress with barely a glance, practically forces it down his throat. It's like a horror film. *Fatal Attraction*. He takes a few sips, then rests his head back on the settee and he's out again. Fast asleep. Oh, dear. The plan's failed.

Her mood changes.

David's goes to the bathroom and I pretend to pick at a beer mat. She surveys the room, the people around her, checking to see if anyone's noticed. Then she stands up, tall again, powerful. That steely determination in her eye. For a split second she catches my eye. Her stare, intense. Reading me. *What does he know? What did he see?* I smile back. Sympathetically.

She looks away.

Now she's brushing past the few remaining customers. Leaves. Quickly. It's all very high drama. I want to clap—chase after her and tell her that I haven't seen a performance like that since *All About Eve*. Decide against it. Prostitution comes in many forms.

We finish our drinks. We wake Roger up. We say our goodbyes. We leave.

April 9th, 2007: The Addict

The smack addict started saying "hello" a few weeks ago. Nothing out of the ordinary—just a simple "hello." Just passing the time of day. No different from any of the other street people around here, really. Then one day he stopped to talk. Told me about his addiction.

I remember thinking at the time what a handsome face he must once have had; those deep blue eyes and dark Mediterranean skin. The remnants of beauty. Everything but the teeth. They hang precariously and unpleasantly in his mouth, broken, smashed, and yellow.

Now whenever he sees me he calls my name as he approaches. My eyesight isn't that good so I don't respond until he's close. Until it's too late.

Now, don't get me wrong—he's always pleasant, very friendly; talks to me very calmly. But I'm wary. He's after something. I can sense it. It's hidden behind the smile. The addiction driving him forward. Like he's trying to play me. But he doesn't know that I know. It's like an elaborate game, an intricate but deadly dance of love. He takes a step forward. I respond. He takes another step. I respond. Think *Dangerous Liaisons*. My life under his spell. Victory for him and death for me, if he can just play his cards right.

It started when he asked me for a sip of my coffee. Then it was a bit of loose change for food. Then money for another fix.

This morning he asks me if I need anything. I say, "No, thanks." I don't ask what "anything" is. But I can tell he is confused. Angry, almost. The mask slipping for a split second—like it was all going so well up to that point.

I'm not sure why I'm even writing about him. I suppose because he's been on my mind recently. The feeling that there's someone out there, trying to worm his way into my life, planning and scheming.

It isn't quite over yet, though. He knows it. I know it. There'll be one last try, one last attempt, before we both drift back to our very different lives.

April 9th, 2007: A Coincidence

I'm sitting by the window, laptop open, fingers poised, ready to blog anything that breathes.

Suddenly two tall, well-dressed, Afro-Caribbean men waltz in, smiling and laughing. They light up the shop in an instant and I immediately start typing away furiously, like Barbara Cartland on crack.

"Hi, guys!" says Jorge, cheerfully. "Can I help you?"

"You sure can! This is Richard and I'm Chris, and our motto is 'Thou must shop!'"

"At wholesale prices!" shouts Richard.

"You guys on holiday?"

"I'm from Frankfurt. She lives here," teases Chris as he

makes his way toward the clothes. In seconds he's trying on a green Costume National summer jacket, spinning round in it, opening and closing the lapels. "Momma's taking this!"

He removes the jacket, places it on the counter, and looks over in my direction. "Say, what're you doin' there, bitch? You're always writin' when Momma walks past."

"I'm writing a book about Soho."

"Put me in it!"

I laugh. "I am," I say.

Chris looks across at his friend, who's browsing through the Cavalli section, raising an eyebrow that is so well plucked it makes Bette Davis look like Frida Kahlo. "Honey! Not that! It's too expensive. Shop like a Jew. Here, let me give you tips on Passover shoppin'," says Chris, sashaying over toward his friend while Jorge carefully wraps the jacket.

"Would you like a hanger?" Jorge enquires. "Although I'm afraid we only have wide ones."

"Honey, I've already got a wide one!" Chris calls back. "Hey—I love this hat! Do you like it?"

"It looks great on you," Jorge says, tactfully. "But isn't it a bit hot for hats?"

"Girl, I'm losin' pigment all over my face. I need to keep it in the shade. You know what I'm sayin'? I had chemotherapy for prostate cancer last year. I'm over it now—they saved one ball but it was a difficult process."

"You're awfully young for that to happen," Jorge replies.

"Looks can be deceiving," Richard chips in.

"Do you have a whip handy?" Chris hisses, raising the other eyebrow. "I've been through a lot last year, bitch. I deserve a bit of retail therapy. Okay, I like this shirt," he says, holding up an Iceberg cowboy shirt. "It's very Bareback Mountain."

"The cowboy look is great, isn't it?" Jorge pipes in.

"Honey, it's got me written all over it. Just get me a six-pack, a pickup, and your brother! Now I've gotta get outta here. Momma's broke!"

As they pay for their goods, Chris catches me watching them. In a loud Mexican accent he screams, "You wan' to fock my seester?"

Then they're off, screeching off down the street, reminding me of our first-ever customer, Chico. Beautiful, bubbly Chico.

At that exact moment the phone rings, jolting me back to reality.

"Hello, Dirty White Boy. Can I help you?"

"Clay! It's Chico. Happy Easter!"

April 13th, 2007: Relax. Take it Easy.

I'm sitting in my little red chair by the window, head in hands, looking out. Old Compton Street's packed, but why is no one coming in? The window displays look great—Cavalli in one window and Ferre in the other; the shop's overflowing with gorgeous Spring/Summer collections, Lacroix, Mugler, Basi, Zegna. But all the queens want to do is spend their money on drugs and clubs and swan round in cheap Abercrombie.

I look over at Jorge sitting behind the counter. He's staring straight ahead. Four bad days at the shop and we struggle to speak. He wants to talk bills. I don't want to listen. So we sit here in silence. When takings rise so does the sex, but when they drop…well. It's these moments that you have to try and get through.

I stand up and change CDs. Mika. Freddie's torch handed down. Switch to the slowest track.

"Relax, take it easy…"

I sit back down. Let the music wash over me. Watch the crowds outside. A few minutes pass. There's Pam, the Fag Lady, picking something up off the ground. She looks at it with a childlike wonder. Looks round to see if anyone's watching. Then cups it in her hand and puts it in her pocket, smiling. She'll be in in a minute, wanting money or a cuddle. Quite happy with either. I turn my head. Over there, on Dean Street. There go the Rubbishmen. The longest beards on the street. Out-"bearing" the bears.

"For there is nothing we can do... Relax"

A woman, blonde, straightened hair, walks past the doorway, three paparazzi trailing behind. Like hyenas, they snap at her heels. She's oblivious, in her own world, a Vicodin haze. Dior glasses, Marc Jacobs handbag swaying in time with her StairMastered hips. As she passes, our eyes lock, momentarily. It's as if she's waiting. Some kind of acknowledgment required. Like she's saying, *You should know me.* I arch an eyebrow. I'm sorry, darling. I don't.

"It's as if I'm scared... Relax"

I glance at Jorge. He's scratching his head. Stress. A noise from the doorway. "Hey, guys!" It's the *Big Issue* seller. He holds up a small twig. "I'm from the special branch." Then he's gone. Back on the corner, selling free copies of *QX* to unsuspecting old ladies. Wait til' they're on the tube, flicking through. Especially Mukhtar and his silicone number. Reminds me of a guy in the gym, injects his balls. I try not to look, but the eyes are drawn and the mind is torn.

"It's as if I'm terrified... Relax"

The street's overflowing now. It's 7 P.M. We should be packed. Pulling T-shirts from the shelves, taking up hems, putting darts in First Collection shirts. But the shop's deserted.

"Are we playing with fire..."

Maggie walks across Dean Street, talking on her mobile. Arranging a deal. She's laughing. It must be a regular. She waves. I wave back. We're all hookers on this street. Two middle-aged businessmen follow her up the stairway. "I'll be working late, darling! Don't wait up."

"Relax, take it easy…"

Then, in the distance, as I squint into the sunlight, I see a tall black guy heading toward the door. It's Chris. I stop typing. Look over at Jorge. He looks back. We sit up straight. Please buy something. Anything. We'll be on the street at this rate. Then his fake Mexican accent screams through the doorway.

"Hey, guys! I need a presen' for my beeg seester!"

We relax. Take it easy. Because there's nothing that we can do.

April 13th, 2007: Thank you, Mika!

I stand up and quickly switch the CD back to an earlier track. "Grace Kelly." There. That'll put the shop back in the right mood…

"I try to be like Grace Kelly. But all her looks were too sad…"

"So, guys! You gonna help Momma find a pressie for my seester, or what?" Chris says, hands on hips. "Momma may even spend a little on herself today, 'cos she needs a bit of cheerin' up."

"Why, what's wrong?" I ask.

"The motherfuckin' boyfriend. Or should I say ex-boyfriend. Now, get this. So I have the chemo, lose a ball, and while I'm in hospital, recoverin' from the fuckin' chemo—the motherfucker met someone else!"

"That's terrible!" I reply, ushering him over to the Cavalli section. Oh my—am I about to profit from his misery?

"Too right, bitch! Plus I was his first boyfriend, and you know what he always says?"

"No?" I reply, holding up a £250 purple silk number, my smiling face peering over the top.

"He says he'd never be the one to leave! Then the first chance he gets he's off with a stripper! A Chinese one, too! I mean he could have at least gone Latino."

"I don't know what to say," I say, helping him on with the shirt with one hand, reaching for a pair of couture Ferre jeans with the other, wondering how I can get the Zegna belt round him without him noticing.

"Well, I told the motherfucker. I said, 'You know what, fucker? We ain't never gonna be friends again.' "

"Good for you!" I reply, pushing him quickly past the "50 percent off" sale rack.

"So the fucker goes and writes me out a cheque."

"What for?"

"To leave the apartment. Fuckin' guilt money, that's what it was."

"That's awful. What did you do?" I say, a bit too eagerly, praying he banked it and it cleared.

"Well, of course I took it. And his Rolex. Now Momma's got one for each arm."

"Oh, good for you!" I say, squeezing his foot into an Iceberg sandal.

"He was always jealous of me anyways."

"He was?"

"Oh, yeah. I'm nearly 51. Yes, I know, it's hard to believe. But people always thought I was the younger one. I used to say to him, 'Bitch! You's white and you lie in the sun and don't cream. Whadda you expect?' "

"Well, you certainly look good for your age. And this summer jacket is very age appropriate."

"Plus my life's better 'cos I've moved on. I don't believe in hangin' on to hate...the motherfucker!"

I practically carry him back to the counter.

"Anyways, how much have I spent here? Momma's done a lot of retail therapy, hasn't she?"

"Umm...well." God, please don't freak out if I tell you. "It comes to—"

"Oh, what the fuck! Momma's spent five thousand pounds this month already."

Please spend a bit more!

"And you know what?"

"No, what?" I reply, trying to prise his credit card from his hand.

"It feels fuckin' great! And I'll tell you why. 'Cos it's his credit card! Ha! Ha! Ha! I always say, 'Keep your fist closed and you never get anything in it.' Now I'm the most generous person on earth—'cos I got his cards!"

And as Chris swishes out of the shop, laden down with Dirty White Boy bags, I turn round, wipe my brow, and give the till a big kiss.

Thank you, Mika!

April 17th, 2007: Angela Pasquale

No! It can't be! Not again!

I've got my nose stuck to the window. I'm staring outside. There, across the street, sashaying toward me, skyscraper stilettos click-clacking away, long, luscious brown hair cascading around her shoulders, with a "Don't fuck with me, bitch!" look on her face, is Janice. Janice Dickinson. I immediately dig my hand into my pocket and pinch my right testicle.

Wait a minute. Hold on... Janice doesn't wield a walking stick. And she's not that tall. This woman's at least six foot three. Oh no! She's coming in. Quick, Clay. Act calm. This bitch looks fierce.

The Janice clone swishes up to the counter. But all I see is a beautiful face and a big pair of creamy white breasts that look like they're about to wrap themselves around my neck.

"Girl, where can I get a good butt plug round here?" she shouts in a campy, androgynous voice.

"Ummm, er..."

"It's for my fanny, luv!" she shrieks, seemingly unaware that the other customers are gawping at her in amazement. "I had the cock chopped off last year, dear, but I'm still dilating."

151

"Well, you could try Clonezone, a few doors down," I reply, letting go of my testicle and trying to suppress a giggle.

"You got a tape measure, honey?"

"Sure," I say, reaching inside the desk drawer and handing her the one we use for hemming.

"Mmmm, now what's thirty-five millimetres?" she murmurs as she stretches out the tape.

"Okay, got it. I'll be back in a minute." And she sashays back out.

"Who was that?" I say to no one in particular.

"That was Angela Pasquale," says one of the customers, smiling at me as he leaves. "She's something else, isn't she?"

Two minutes later.

"They are so unhelpful in there. I'd be better off buying a piece of hose."

By now the last of the customers have run out, so I'm able to give her my full attention.

"And you wanna see the size of those butt plugs! How do those boys do it? Asses like Wellington boots, dear! Oh, no—it's not for me. You know what?" she says, reaching over the counter and tapping my arm for effect. "I'll give you a million pounds if you can find anyone in London who's ever fucked Angie's ass. You won't. And you know why? 'Cos no one ever has!"

She reaches behind her head, grabs her hair, and rolls it round her fingers, staring at me defiantly. "It's true! I hate it! Never had a haemorrhoid in my life! And what's with all that smacking business? What's that all about? I used to say to the punters, 'I ain't having none of that!' and they'd say, 'Lady, you got a problem!' I'd say, 'No, honey! You've got the problem—you're the one with the hard-on! Anyway. I don't do punters anymore."

"Why's that?"

"Girl—they all wanna be fucked! Even the straight ones.

And when you're post-op they don't wanna know. Anyway, who cares? Look here," she purrs, pulling down her black leggings, beckoning me down to her nether regions. "They did a good job, didn't they?"

I suppose when you've spent the majority of your life in a cocoon it's quite natural that you'd want to flaunt your butterfly wings—but as I peer down, I can't help but think that what she's been left with is less "fanny" and more "mohair mitten."

"I love my new fanny," Angie coos, as if it's a newborn baby, which I suppose in a way it is.

"What was the operation like?"

She starts to reel off the procedure, from the shaving to splitting the ball bag. Although I'm listening, as I peer into her panties my mind's going back in time, back to my childhood, Angie's voice drifting in and out.

"Five days I had to lie there…"

I'm 12 years old. It's the summer holidays. I'm in the little village of Cheddar. My mum and dad are working in the hotel. I'm on my own, wandering round the hotel, exploring the village.

"You just have to lie there. For five fuckin' days! You can't shit, fart or anything—just lie there…"

The village stretches for a few miles, a long, thin village, nestled between a cleft of rocks known as the Cheddar Cliffs or Cheddar Gorge, surrounded by woods. Like a mini Grand Canyon.

"But it wasn't painful. No, girl! I was morphined up to the eyeballs…"

I'm walking through this narrow pass, staring upwards at these high limestone cliffs, at all this wild, wiry undergrowth on either side of the gorge, when it suddenly hits me. That's it! That's what I'm looking at.

"It looks like Cheddar Gorge," I suddenly blurt out. Accidentally. Oh, fuck!

"I'm sorry?" Angie replies, not really catching on, both of us still peering down.

"Umm. I mean it looks 'gorge'—by the way, I'm Clay!" I say quickly, looking away from her panties and back up to her face, squinting as my eyes readjust to the light.

She pulls her leggings back up and leans on her stick, as if nothing happened. "I know who you are—I work out at the same gym as your boyfriend. I was there at 7 A.M. this morning trying to lose weight."

"You don't need to lose weight. You're perfect as you are."

"Girl! Look at this!" she says, pinching the skin under her arm. "I'd rather die than be a fat bitch. I'd do crystal, but I like my sleep."

"Well, I think you look great. You look like a young Janice Dickinson."

"No, honey, she looks like me!" she spits back.

And she's right. Though Angie is fifty, even without makeup she's still one of the most beautiful women I have ever laid eyes on—sparkling emerald eyes and legs like a gazelle. I watch her closely as she talks, pouring out her life story, telling me about her boyfriend who died last year. "He was 'trisexual.' Try anything. I loved him so much. I'm still a mess. But you know what? A week after he died I'd paid for my sex change and I had the 'op.' I thought, life's too short, and I don't want to lie in my coffin with a cock."

She leans on her stick as she talks (is she still in pain from the 'op'?) and it crosses my mind that I'm in the presence of one of Old Compton Street's real "ladies," a survivor in every sense.

"...and then I was raped by seven men, they punctured one of my tits, and you know what the police said? 'People like you don't matter.' Hey, what's that you're writing? You're always writing."

"Sorry, I'm writing about you. You don't mind, do you?"

"Oh, go ahead, dear! You can write my biography if you want. Say, you ever go to that bear club XXL?" she says, tossing back her hair.

"Umm. Once or twice."

"They hate me there. I can see the venom in their eyes, darlin'. I'm what they tried to stamp out twenty years ago. I remind them of when they used to play with their sisters' dollies—that's why. What star sign are you?"

"Gemini."

"Oh, you'll do well in this town. It's a Gemini town. Two sides. Jorge's a Leo, isn't he?"

"Yes," I answer, not quite sure if I've just been praised or insulted. "How'd you know?"

"I just knew. Lord of the jungle. He'd do well in Rome. My family live there."

"Do they accept you?"

"Kind of. My dad loves me. Although he hated me when I was homosexual. Now I'm a lady, he loves me. But that's Italian fathers for you. You've either gotta be a butch man or a lady. Now he says, 'There goes my Angie. All tits and legs. Watch the men's cocks rise when Angie walks in the room!' I love my dad."

"What about your mum?"

"She doesn't like me 'cos my tits are nicer than hers. I say, 'Mum, you've had your time in the sun—now it's my turn!' So what about you and Jorge? How long have you been together?"

"Oh, about three years. It was a long-distance relationship for the first two. He lived in Provincetown in the US. Actually, we got married there, at the top of the monument. Then he moved over under last year's Civil Partnership Act, so it was perfect timing. We were one of the first cases the US government dealt with under the Act. I'm quite proud of that."

"Well, girl. I really hope it works out. You guys sure put the hours in."

"Tell me about it. We don't have much time to do anything else."

"Anyways, Angie's gotta get going. Which way shall I go?" she says, pointing her stick in the direction of Dean Street. "Hmmm. Not Fashion Street. Central Strada. Not tonight, dear. Had my fill of queens for one day. Present company excepted, of course. Anyway, Angie'll see you soon. I'm off to New York in a week—they love me there. But I'll see you before I go. Ta ra!"

I wave her off from the doorway and watch the crowd part as she sails regally through. The Queen of Old Compton Street.

April 25th, 2007: Angela Flies Away

I'm sitting on my chair, inside the shop, staring out the window.

Across the street I spot Angela. Tall, dark, beautiful Angela. Only it's a slightly different Angela who makes her way toward the shop today. More elegant. More "Hollywood"—the makeup, the hair, the big, dark "Jackie O" sunglasses. She's walks through the doorway, gold-rimmed handbag over her shoulder, talking into her mobile, using her walking stick for support.

"Honey—meet me here. Yes. Okay. I'm in Wide Boy."

"Dirty White Boy," I mouth back.

"Oh, whatever! Yes. On the corner of Dean Street. Okay. Ciao."

She puts her phone in her handbag and sashays toward me, swinging her bag with one hand and wielding her stick with the other. "Girl! I am now a bona fide woman!"

"Why's that?"

"Because today I woke up with my first dose of thrush!" she says, quite matter-of-factly, in her campy, androgynous voice.

"Well, ummm…that's great," I reply, tentatively, not

really sure quite what to say next. "Say, umm. I thought you were going to New York."

"Give me a chance! You trying to push me out the country, or what? I don't leave until Thursday."

"Oh. Okay. Ummm…what will you be doing there?"

"Filming," she purrs, suspiciously, digging a lipstick out of her handbag, which she unscrews, then applies to her lips in a quick, well-practiced movement.

"Really? How glamorous. What kind of film?"

"I can't tell you," she answers, putting the lipstick back in her bag. "It's bad karma until it comes off. Hey, are you writing again?" she fires back, moistening her lips.

"I sure am."

"You're not stealing my lines again, are you?"

"Well, actually…I am. But only because you're part of Soho," I explain, putting down my pen.

"Girl—I AM SOHO!" she retorts, removing her glasses and shaking out her hair, up and down, backwards and forwards, letting her luscious locks drape over the glass counter.

I laugh. "Say, do you know any agents? I think I need an agent," I ask her as she scrunches her hair up behind her head.

"Honey, I've got five agents."

"Five? Do you have a literary one?"

"Yesssssss," she says, in a breathy Marilyn-like voice, narrowing her eyes.

"Can you give me a name?" I ask, hesitantly.

"Mmmm. Why should I? Why should I cross your palm with silver?" and she raises an eyebrow that threatens to slice me in two. "Maybe when I'm back…"

"Angie!" shouts someone from behind. "Darling!"

Angela swivels round, turning to face two guys who've just walked in. The first looks my way. He gives me a look that says, *And you are?* I give him one back that says,

Ask and I'll tell. He looks back at Angela.

"Angie, let's go for coffee."

"Steve, honey, I'm not walking far. I only came out—"

"We can go wherever you want. How about Costa, across the road? By the way," he says, clearing his throat. "I want you to meet my friend Peter. Peter, Angela."

Steve ushers forward Peter, who holds out his hand to shake. Angela looks him in the eye and then looks down disdainfully at his hand, as if she was expecting hers to be kissed.

"Sorry...and your name is, again?" Peter says, smiling, committing his second faux pas in as many seconds.

"Royalty, darling!" Angela replies, breezing past him. "Right, let's go! I need a frappuccino. Pronto! It's too hot to be inside, and my fanny's about to pass out! Ciao, Clay!"

I watch as she sashays back across the street, waving her hand over her shoulder. A Sally Bowles for the 21st century.

As she blows kisses to passersby, I imagine the film that Angela will star in when she gets to the US. Will it be something raunchy? Two hot bisexual Latino studs ploughing her from every position, Angela pouting, always gorgeous, always in control.

Or maybe a comedy—her face hidden by a wide-brimmed hat, the camera starting off at her legs, slowly working its way up as she tilts her head toward the lens. Her opening line: "Unusual places, unusual love affairs. I am a most strange and extraordinary person."

Or perhaps a *Mildred Pierce* type of role. Rags to riches. Angela clawing her way to the top, despite the scheming boyfriend, the devious daughter. The film receiving award after award—BAFTA, Golden Globe, and then the big one. Angela looking fabulous in a simple black Chanel backless number, fighting back well-rehearsed tears as her name is read out, as she rises from her seat, the gasp from the crowd as she makes her way up the stairway, as she finally wraps her manicured fingers around the Oscar, kissing it, holding it above her head, the huge applause, echoing around the world.

"Goodbye, Angela," I whisper as she disappears from view. "If anyone's going to make it around here, it really should be someone like you…"

April 27th, 2007: A Letter

Dear Chico,

Chico, I am SO sorry we haven't been to visit you at your new prison yet. We've been working like dogs in the shop, seven days a week, and just haven't got round to organising it. Actually, I've just got off the phone to the Prisoner Helpline, and it turns out that the Visiting Order you sent me has now expired. Can you send me another one?

So how are things there? Have you settled in? Made friends? I remember you saying on the phone that this prison was bigger than Bedford. Are you able to carry on with your studies? Use the gym? I'm sure you're HUGELY popular, with your hairdressing skills.

Hey, you've been there eight months already! I know time must go very slowly—what was it you said? That you count the time by weeks because it sounds less? But hang in there, Chico. What happened to you was terrible. You were set up. We all know that. But be brave. We'll be here when you come out. Hey, the shop may not be—but we certainly will be!

Hold on, got to stop for a second. Someone's tapping on the window…

I'm back! Sorry about that. Do you remember the Fag Lady? That little shaved-haired woman—the homeless one who's always hanging around Soho? Pam, her name is. She's just told me she won't be in Soho for a while. She's having a toe amputated. I asked her why—but she said she didn't want to tell me. "It's a long story," she said, nearly crying. "I'm going to miss Soho. A lot." Poor Pam.

So, what's my news? Well, not much really. We've been here a year now. The takings are still up and down. Jorge and I are okay, though. We sometimes sit in shop for hours not speaking, worrying about the bills, but we're still a good partnership. He's a dominant Leo and I'm a "get bored easily" Gemini—but luckily we have the same work ethic.

What else? Oh, we've had a few celebs in. Janice Dickinson. You know her? From *America's Next Top Model*? Wow—she was a piece of work. Graham Norton's shopped a few times. Carlos Acosta. He's a principal dancer with the Royal Ballet, and he and Jorge have become friends. Oh, and next week we've got Kathy Griffin coming in to film. I'd never heard of her but Jorge says she's HUGE in the US. Do you know her?

Hey, and I've started writing. On MySpace. "Intellectual Gaydar," Jorge calls it. But it's not really like that. I've met some really nice people from it. I write about Soho and the people who come into the shop, sitting on my little red chair (remember the small one by the window that Jorge's always paranoid about getting chipped?), and I'm there every evening, tapping away, while the hookers lean against the shop window outside. It's a great release—although, to be honest, I'm not really sure what I'm writing half the time. A diary? A novel? It feels a bit weird, too, like posting your thoughts up for the world to see. But I enjoy it—and the people who read it seem to like it.

I've just had a thought, Chico—maybe you should start writing! When things have been tough in my life it's always helped me make sense of things. And with everything you've experienced over the past year—maybe it'd be good for you too. Just a thought…

Okay, I'm going to sign off now 'cos we've got people coming in the shop (at last!). Hopefully they'll be straight. The queens are the WORST buyers. "Does this T-shirt go with my eyes? Jeans? Bedside cabinets?" Give me the straight ones any day. Now there's a phrase we've both used before!

See you soon, be strong, thinking about you.

Clay x

May 1st, 2007: A Bit of Finger

I'm inside the shop, sitting on the glass counter, keeping myself busy by staring aimlessly out the window. Suddenly there's an almighty "CRASH!" as the glass shatters and my ass goes through the counter. I'm trapped inside, sitting on a nest of Thierry Mugler ties like an overweight cuckoo.

"JORGE, HELP!"

"What's wrong?" he shouts, running up the stairway. "Are you okay?"

"Um, I think so," I say, trying to extract myself, checking my ass for cuts. "Hold on... Oh no! I'm bleeding!"

"Where? Your ass?"

"No! Look—my finger! Oh my God! My finger's hanging off!"

"Clay, it's not hanging off."

"It is! Look, there's a chunk missing!" I shriek, pointing to a gash running down my little finger. "Oh my God! I'm losing blood!"

"Clay, calm down. Go and get a bandage from downstairs while I tidy up here. Quickly, it'll stop the blood."

"I want my chunk back first!" I wail, rummaging through the ties while holding my damaged hand up in the air. "It's stuck on a tie somewhere and if we don't find it someone's gonna end up wearing it to work!"

"Clay, go downstairs and wrap the cut."

"I can't. I'm about to faint!"

"GO AND WRAP YOUR FINGER UP!"

"Okay."

Five minutes later I hobble back upstairs, holding my damaged hand in front of me. "Did you find my chunk?" I whimper.

"There is no chunk. It's just a cut. Here, let me dress it properly," says Jorge, taking my hand. "Hmmm. Perhaps more cardio is in order."

"What?" I reply, flabbergasted, snatching my hand away (forgetting I'm meant to be in severe pain). "How can you say that? I'm practically limbless and that's all you can think of to say?"

"Don't you think you're being a bit—"

"Hey! We're back!" shouts someone from the doorway. "And I brought my seester!"

We both look round as Chris and Richard burst into the shop again.

Chris's dressed head to foot in sky-blue Versace with a Louis Vuitton manbag slung over his shoulder. He sidles up to me. "Say, girl! Why aren't you writing?"

"I'll never write again. My finger's hanging off," I reply, waving my bandaged finger at him.

"Oh, poor you," he says, sympathetically, pulling a sad face. "Anyway, I need some new clothes!" He's immediately happy again. "Jorge, that's a mean shirt you're wearing. You got any pretty shirts like that for Momma?"

"Girl! You can't wear that! It's too loud for you," laughs Richard.

"Listen, seester!" Chris purrs back, removing his Gucci sunglasses, turning to face him. "I's black! We wear loud. You can't wear loud 'cos you's half white. So you's half boring!"

Jorge steps from behind the counter and walks over to the Cavalli section, while I, realizing no one's really interested in my finger, sit down dejectedly by the window.

"This is a nice shirt. We have it in black too," says Jorge, showing Chris a fitted dress shirt.

"Momma don't do no black. Especially after the last boyfriend. Motherfucker! Leaving me with one ball!"

"And two Rolexes!" pipes up Richard.

"Does anyone care about my finger?" I murmur from my seat. Richard looks across, gives me a quick smile, then reaches for a pair of Gianfranco Ferre straight-leg jeans from the display rack, while Chris browses the aisles, running his fingers along the shirts until he pulls out a dark purple silk shirt by Lacroix.

"Well, he owed me! Anyways, I'm going to Madrid tomorrow and I'm gonna get me a new man. What do you think?" Chris asks, turning to face Jorge, holding the shirt against his body.

"The colour definitely suits you."

He puts it to one side and carries on looking through the clothes. "The only problem with Madrid is Momma don't like the men."

"What's wrong with Spanish men?" Jorge asks.

"Ewww. Small, with back hair."

"Do these jeans suit me?" asks Richard, draping them against his legs.

"Maybe not," Jorge steps in tactfully. "These ones are more age appropriate," he says, handing him a more conservative pair by Zegna.

"Has anyone noticed I'm close to death here?" I say again, a bit louder.

"Age appropriate? For my seester?" shouts Chris, from the back of the shop. "What did you do—put Pampers in the lining?"

He walks over to Richard and taps him on the shoulder. "Seester, I can't shop no more. Not until I got three cocktails inside me."

"You wanna go drinkies, then?"

"Do bears shit in the woods? Bye, boys! Momma'll be back after three martinis!"

And with that, they leave, blowing kisses in our direction.

"I'm gonna see if I can still type," I moan, reaching for my laptop.

"Are you going to write a blog about your finger?" Jorge says, cheerfully.

"No. I'm going to type out my will in case my finger turns hideously septic."

"You'll feel better if you just write a blog."

"Okay," I sigh. "I'll try." Here goes...

May 6th, 2007: Kathy Griffin

I'm standing by the doorway, watching the crowds, waiting.

I look at my watch. 8:30 P.M. Where are they? They were meant to be here hours ago! The American comedian Kathy Griffin and chat show host Graham Norton are to film in the shop tonight as part of Kathy's new TV series *My Life on the D-List,* and if she doesn't turn up soon Jorge's going to be really upset—he's her biggest fan. 8:45 P.M. Hurry, Kathy!

Suddenly I see a huge crowd of people—camera crews and photographers—making their way down Old Compton Street.

"Jorge, quick! They're here!"

Jorge comes running over to the doorway, jumps up and down, and shrieks, "Oh my God! It's her! It's Kathy!"

Just last week I was a "Kathy Griffin virgin," but after being force-fed 38 YouTube clips, I'm now an official "Kathy whore." In one clip Kathy describes the "gay inhale," her way of recognising her gay fans. Apparently, on a visit to the troops in Afghanistan, while she was searching for a "Don't Ask, Don't Tell" gay man, a guy walked into the canteen with his food tray and saw her. He stopped dead in his tracks with his eyes popping out of his head, and took a quick intake of breath: the gay inhale.

"Now, remember what I taught you, Clay!" says Jorge, excitedly. "As she gets close, after three, we do the gay inhale."

Although the photographers are snapping away furiously now, their flashes lighting up the street, through the crowd we can just make out Kathy being edged toward the shop by Graham.

"Kathy. This way. You'll love this shop," Graham says, as they make their way to the door. "And these guys are big fans of yours."

Within seconds the crowd are surrounding the shop, greasy noses pressed against the windows, people clambering to get inside. Jorge nudges me. "Okay, Clay. Ready? One! Two! Three!"

"HUUUUUUHHHHHHHH!"

"Oh, thank God! I've found my peeps!" shouts Kathy, pushing her way through the crowd toward us. "Get me into that shop!"

Now there're cameramen all over the place, assistants running round with clipboards, makeup artists, photographers, lenses shoved in our faces.

While I flap about preparing for my Gloria Swanson close-up, Jorge reaches for Kathy's hand and within seconds they're chatting away like old friends, while the normally hyperactive Graham Norton looks on bemused, realizing he's met his match, for the next few minutes at least, in Jorge.

"Kathy I'm your biggest fan in Old Compton Street and possibly the only one in the whole of London," Jorge gushes, as the camera crews battle for the prime spot. "Are you here to do another lesbian porn movie with Dame Judi Dench?"

"Oh, no! She's way too cold and frigid. I'm here to do one with the Queen!" replies Kathy with a giggle.

"I didn't know you did a porn movie with Dame Judi Dench!" Graham pipes in, incredulously, turning to face Kathy.

"Go watch it on YouTube, Graham. She's very hairy."

"Don't tell me you're having lunch with your best friend

Gwyneth Paltrow, that anorexic coke-snorting slut," Jorge remarks with a smile.

"No, Jorge! That was Renee Zellweger. Gwyneth's the stick figure with a big head," Kathy says, laughing. "Oh my God—you know all my lines!"

"I've seen everything you've ever been in—as far back as Jerry Seinfeld!"

By now the shop's so busy I have to close the doors, and as Kathy, Jorge, and Graham are the stars of the show, the cameramen start to push me out of the way and I'm relegated to snapping away with my little camera, while Kathy browses the aisles.

"I love your store," she says to Jorge. "How long have you been here?"

"Just over a year. I love London. Although the two things I miss most about the US are you and Martha Stewart."

"Oh yeah—'cause we're so much alike!" Kathy laughs.

"Oh, but you are! Martha slags her guests off just as much as you—but they don't realize she's doing it. You do it behind their backs, 'cos you were raised correctly."

"Yes! It's called manners!" Kathy answers back. "Okay, NOW STOP DOING MY ACT!" They both fall about laughing.

While Kathy and Jorge chat away, Graham starts to look around the shop for clothes. Hmmm. This is being filmed—should we charge him? He reaches toward the Christian Lacroix section. Oh, please, not the Lacroix! He moves toward the "50 percent off" section and reaches for a track top. Phew! Meanwhile, Jorge and Kathy are engaged in a conversation about her act, Jorge transformed into her agent and giving her some comedy tips.

"Whatever you do, Kathy—don't slag off Kate Moss. They worship her here. You'll get a lot of shit."

"Are you kidding me? That's a half hour of my act. Kate's going down tomorrow."

"You'll be sorry!"

"Well, you just know that that Pete Doherty must stink like hell. Ewww! I see him in the newspapers and can smell him on the page!"

As she chats she feels Jorge's biceps. "Jorge, honey—what about these gays on Old Compton Street?"

"What about them?"

"In LA all the gays have six-packs, tits, bodies, and drink wheatgrass. Here they stand with their flabby asses outside Comptons holding a beer the size of a garbage can when they should be saving their tuppences, shillings, or whatever the fuck the money is, to buy new teeth!"

Suddenly a guy pushes his way into the shop and starts reaching for the jeans.

"Is that a real shopper?" Graham asks, smiling. "Or have you set him up for the cameras?"

"Graham! We do have customers, you know!" I fire back, clicking away with my little camera, while my photographer friend Paul zooms in with his paparazzo-style lens.

"Clay! Where's Kathy's gift bag?" shouts Jorge, above the noise. "Kathy, I know the only reason you go to the award shows is to get those gift bags."

"Honey! You know that's right!"

I quickly reach for a Dirty White Boy bag and stuff it with our branded T-shirts. Well, if celebs want freebies then they can do a bit of advertising for us, I figure. I hand Kathy the gift bag just as she's about to reach for a pair of pink Sonia Rykiel low-rise trousers.

"Now, come on, Jorge who is going to wear these?"

"Donald Trump in Palm Beach?"

"Good answer! Someone give Jorge a ticket for my show tomorrow," she tells her crew. "Are you going to come along, Graham?"

"I can't. I've got a date," he replies, pulling a face. "How long are you on for?"

"If no one laughs—ten minutes and my ass is outta there!"

Then with kisses all round, Kathy and Graham turn to leave, while the camera crew follow eagerly behind.

That night, lying in bed, I say to Jorge, "Do you think that bit of publicity will help sales?"

"Who knows..." he sighs. "But hey! At least you've learnt how to do the gay inhale!"

May 13th, 2007: The Stockpot

It's 9 P.M. I've just walked into the Stockpot, the little café at the end of Old Compton Street. It's raining outside and my clothes are covered in a fine mist.

It's practically empty; the few customers are huddled up in the little booths. There's the young black kid with Tourette's, the one who walks up and down the street shouting, "You're a bastard!" He's tapping his foot aggressively as he eats, trying to contain his anger. In the booth behind there's an old man. His fingers move up and down in front of his lips, like he's playing an imaginary flute. Neither of them looks my way; they're trapped inside their worlds.

Deborah, the Spanish waitress, walks past holding a cappuccino and a glass of water. She blows me a kiss. "Cómo estás?" she says. I turn round, spot an empty table to my left, by the window. I take my jacket off, hang it over the back of the chair, and sit down with my back to the wall. There're two guys at the table next to me, deep in conversation—so deep they're not even aware of my presence.

"I'm not upset!" argues the youngest.

I scan the menu. Everything tastes the same, so it shouldn't be a big decision, but because it's been a bad week at the shop, my mind's elsewhere. The great expectations from the previous week came to nothing. Sales plummeted. And all week I sat on my little red chair by the window, like a jilted Miss Haversham, staring at the blank screen of my laptop.

"You are. You've hardly spoken to me all day," says the older guy, perplexed, scratching his beard and leaning back in his chair.

The guy's voice drags me back to the present. Clay—concentrate. I shake my head slightly, trying to focus.

"Okay. I am upset. I'm upset 'cos you won't admit it!" the younger guy pleads. "Look, I can cope with the odd indiscretion—but it seems like as soon as my back's turned you're off!"

I try again to block them out and stare intently at the menu, the prices, the specials, trying to decipher the hand-writing as Deborah walks over. We chat for a few minutes. It's a continuing story. She moans about her job. I moan about the shop. A bonding ritual that unites us. Then her boss, sitting behind the till, calls her name. She rolls her eyes, swears under her breath, takes my order, and carries on clearing tables.

"Baby. I love you. You know that. We've talked about this," the older guy replies tenderly, leaning forward now and reaching for his boyfriend's hand. "If I have sex with someone else, that's all it is. Just sex. It doesn't change what we have."

I glance momentarily in their direction, but tilt my head as if I'm looking out the window at the Hare Krishnas dancing along the street, banging their triangles and tambourines. The younger guy pulls his hand away, not quickly, but quick enough so that it looks like a recoil. Now there's tension. It goes quiet for a few seconds. I look down at my hands, pretend to pick at a cuticle.

"Michael, I'm different from you. I'm built differently. I don't need anyone else. So it's always going to be harder for me."

Michael doesn't reply. He runs his fingers through his hair, down through his beard again. Their body language speaks. On one side it states, *Love me as I am*. On the other it whispers, *I'm trying, but I'm hurting*. I feel for the "I'm hurting." One's been here before. Will never change. Can't. For the other, it's new. It's rejection. Brings back memories.

Michael turns his head toward the door. Sighs. Looks back at his partner.

"Well, what are you saying, Lee? You want us to be monogamous?"

"No, that's not what I'm saying."

"Well, what then?"

"I don't know, Michael. I don't know."

Deborah brings my soup over. Smiles. Leek and potato soup. It's like dishwater with green phlegm. Like drinking from a lava lamp. What tasteless space food must taste like— or not taste like. But it's cheap, and strangely comforting. Reminding me of home. My mother. Growing up. I reach for the pepper so at least it'll taste of something, but it's also a ploy—so I can look across the table and watch Lee.

Above the table he's relatively calm, but below it he's stressed, digging a fingernail into his wrist, oblivious to the pain, to the symbolism. I watch as he brushes a loose strand of hair from his eyes, notice his hand trembling, slightly. Michael doesn't.

I stir my soup, gulp as I swallow, trying to make my presence known, break the spell—but, at the same time, I'm spellbound, drawn in. It's like watching an old Bette Davis film on a Sunday afternoon.

"I remember you once said—once we were married you wouldn't need to do this," Lee says, quietly, but accusingly, his eyes welling up. "And now I feel you're trying to push me to do the same thing just so you don't feel guilty." He scratches his wrist again, backward and forward, faster and faster.

Michael reaches inside his pocket and pulls out a battered leather wallet, places it by his coffee cup. "Lee, we've had this conversation before. It just doesn't work for me. It just doesn't." Now his voice is firmer. "I don't know if it's because I'm hitting fifty or 'cos I'm positive. I don't know what it is. I can't explain it. But I just can't promise something that's not me." He takes a £20 note out of his wallet and leaves it by the bill. "All I know is I love you and I want to grow old with you."

The conversation exhausted, they stand up, Michael first. Head for the door, Michael first. But then, just as they're about to leave, Lee turns round, reaches toward the scarf he left on his chair and, as he does, our eyes meet. I want to smile—but in that split second, while I'm thinking, he gives me a smile instead, a tearful half shrug, half smile that seems to say, *I don't know what to do. But I can't let him go. I can't. I'm too much in love.*

May 21st, 2007: 4:30 A.M.

I'm lying in bed. Wide awake. My mind's ticking over. I roll over, straighten my pillow. Jorge's snoring softly beside me. He reaches for my hand. It's as if, even when asleep, he senses that I'm not. His grip is reassuring. I wait 'til he settles. Then, with my left hand, I reach for the alarm clock on the floor. 4:30 A.M. Fuck!

I wait a minute, then slowly pull my hand free. Slip out of the sheets. Tiptoe over to the desk. Open my laptop. Stare at the blank screen, thinking about the day. Chico.

"Clay, it's my birthday tomorrow," he had said, tearfully, holding my hand as I was about to leave after visiting him in prison yesterday. "I'd had so many plans for my fiftieth. I'd always thought I'd be in some glamorous restaurant, my partner by my side, surrounded by all my friends. Then they'd all stand up, one by one, and say crazy things about me. I never thought in a million years I'd be here."

I run my fingers through my hair. Okay, Clay. Try and stay upbeat. I start typing.

Dear Chico,

Happy (belated) Birthday!

It was great to see you again yesterday.

I know it must have been horrible spending your 50th in prison—but hey! At least you got to spend it with someone special. And a boyfriend too! Who'd have thought! It's a small consolation, I know…but Chico, I was so pleased to hear you'd met someone in there. And who'd have thought that the prison officers would allow you to share a cell!

By the way, I didn't mean to speak out of turn when I talked about the guys you used to bring into the shop; the way you used to buy gifts for them, taking them out for expensive meals and everything. What I was trying to say was that now—in a completely fucked-up way, I know—you've finally met someone who doesn't want you for all that material shit, he just wants you for you. And Chico, that's how it should be. I really hope it works out—he sounds like a dream!

Plus, it was good to hear that the prison's pretty liberal (apart from not letting you have access to condoms). I mean, a "cross-dressing" prison officer and a sex-change prisoner—and all those hunky prisoners walking round with their tops off! What did you call it? "Heaven with bars?" "Like Old Compton Street on a Saturday night?"

"Clay?" says Jorge, sleepily, from the other side of the room. "What you doing?"

"Writing," I reply, in a whisper. "I couldn't sleep."

He grunts a kind of "Okay." I wait a few seconds. Carry on. And I do think it's a good idea for you to take over the administration of that prison gay group, Real Voices, when the current guy gets let out. There's gonna be a lot gay guys who are gonna arrive there completely traumatised. They're gonna need someone like you to show them the ropes. If it was me, I couldn't think of a better person to guide me through.

Now, I know you asked me to write about news from

the shop, but there's really not that much. Nothing too positive, anyway. Shop takings have been up and down. And we've had two black gang attacks on the shop in the last week. It took the police ¾ of an hour to arrive! Can you believe that? But you know us! We ain't gonna let anyone intimidate us without a fight. Hey, if you can get through what you've been through... 'Cos you're my inspiration, Chico. And this shop's gotta be here when you get out. So don't go putting on any weight, you hear? We've got a few pairs of Iceberg jeans here in size 28s and they got your name written all over them!

What else? Oh, yes! There was a huge raid on the brothel above the shop last week. Police in riot gear. The street was blocked off. The madam got carted off. I'm gonna write about it in my blog. Oh, and that reminds me! One of my MySpace friends came up with an idea—that I should print off some of my blogs and send them to you, so you get to read about Soho. What do you think? I hope you'll like them.

So, I won't tell you any more about the shop just now—you'll get to read it soon. Plus, there're a couple of stories about you. I know you said you didn't mind. What did you say? "Don't use my name—use my prison number?"

"Clay?" calls Jorge again.

"What?"

"Come to bed, it's late!"

"Okay. I'll be there in a minute. I'm just finishing."

Chico, sorry, I'll have to sign off. Jorge's calling me to come to bed, and its not often I get an offer like that at my age!

Look after yourself. And hey! Give this guy a chance. I know you're reluctant after everything you've been through—but this could just be the silver lining...

I'll see you next month, baby. Keep strong.

Love, as always

Clay xxx

I close the laptop quietly. Tiptoe across the room. Slip inside the sheets. Reach for Jorge's hand. And moments later, I'm fast asleep.

May 22nd, 2007: Back to the Errands!

I'm walking up Dean Street toward Oxford Street, to the tailor, to drop off the daily alterations. I've got my head down, in my own world, thinking.

Okay, first Pino. Then the Post Office on Poland Street. Then Boots, to get some eye drops for Jorge. Okay. I'll do that first. Down Brewer Street. What's the time now? Then I've got to go to the—

"You! I want a word with you!" a voice suddenly bellows in front of me.

I look up. Do a double take. Gasp. Uh-oh. Angela. Now I'm for it. Oh, well, I suppose it was only a matter of time. "Ummm. Hi, Angela!" I squeak, "How... How was New York?"

"Don't give me that, bitch! I know what you've been sayin'," she fires back, waving her walking stick perilously close to my face. "I was sitting in my hairdresser's the other day and the hairdresser said to me, 'Angie, baby, there's stories about you on MySpace.' I said, 'Realllllllyyyyyy!'"

Is she being serious? She moves in closer, inches from my face. "You've been writing about me, haven't you?"

"Well, I kind of... I did say that—"

"Don't try and talk your way out of it!" she spits. "I've read it. All of it!" She sweeps her stick around for effect.

God. What did I write? Nothing bad, I don't think. Oh yes—there was the bit about... "Well, I...I did say that I write about Soho," I reply, defensively. "And you are one of the faces here."

She looks at me suspiciously, raises an eyebrow. I watch it rise, higher and higher, like a guillotine. Then, unexpectedly, she breaks into a mischievous smile.

"Oh, honey—I don't care! Now if the writing was a pile of shit, then I'd care. You quote me, you'd better be able to string a sentence together. That's all I gotta say!"

"Well, that's good. I mean, that you don't mind—because I wanted to ask you something. Would you mind if I wrote about you? I mean, really wrote about you?"

She leans on her stick as I talk.

"You see all this writing I've been doing about Soho. I mean, I like doing it but it feels somehow that I'm only writing snippets. You know, like mini stories. And that's been okay up to now, but I just think that I've got a bigger story to tell."

"And?" she says, smiling, playing with the handle of her stick, her eyebrow threatening to rise again like a Viagra'd penis.

"Well, I kinda think you'd make a good character."

Clay, why are even telling her this? You can write about whoever you want. Just change the names. But, there again, imagine it... Angela, a Holly Golightly, Sally Bowles, all in the one package. What a star in the making that would be. And me, her Sternberg. Our first hit: *Breakfast at Comptons*. Angela on every chat show in town, Ross, Parkinson, *An Audience With*, while I sit quietly at the back, watching, "finger clapping," planning our next move, always one step ahead of the critics.

"Honey, you can write what you want. I don't mind. But listen, I gotta go now. I've got to be up at five A.M. tomorrow. I've got a big audition. And I mean big!"

"An audition?"

"Yes! Audition! It's a pre-op role—but who cares. No one's gonna be looking down my panties!"

And as she describes the role, swearing me to secrecy, Sally Bowles dissolves before my eyes and it's *A Star Is Born*, with me, James Mason, watching, defeated, from the sidelines as Angela climbs to the top, accolade after accolade.

While I'm left pounding out blogs, for years to come, relying on drink and drugs to get me through.

"So, wish me luck darling!"

"Oh, yes. Umm. Good luck. Let me know how it goes so I can write about it."

"Will do."

"Angie, I've got to go. I've got errands to run."

"Okay. I'm just gonna pop in and say 'Hi' to your husband. Bye, honey!"

"Yeah. Bye."

Oh, well. Back to reality, I s'pose. Okay. Where was I? Oh, yeah. Pino, alterations, then Boots for the eye drops...

May 25th, 2007: Soho Square

3:30 P.M. Soho Square. Sitting on Kirsty MacColl's bench.

"An empty bench in Soho Square. If you'd have come you'd have found me there."

It's the perfect place to sit and reflect. Unwind. Be on my own. The sun's beaming down between the branches of the trees. Everyone's in a good mood; gay couples sprawled across the grass, relaxing, gossiping, flirting, caressing. Music in the air. Huge, bearded men; shirtless, tattooed, pierced. Bear Weekend.

On a bench to my left, an old man rocks backwards and forwards, singing softly, a can of lager in his hand, which drips, drips, drips down his leg. On my right, three young guys, huddled together, deep in conversation.

"I'm not sure what to do," says the one in the middle.

I lean back on the bench. Stretch out my legs. Close my eyes. Feel the sun's heat on my face. My notebook's in my pocket. Toy with taking it out. Decide to just enjoy the moment. As a kid I had so much time on my own—locked in my bedroom for hours, reading, listening to music, drawing. Now, it feels like a luxury to have a few moments like this.

"What would you do if you were in my position?"

I open my eyes, squint into the sunlight, turn my head slightly to look in the direction of the three guys. The one in the middle sits on the edge of the bench, nervously, looking from side to side. He runs his fingers through his hair and scrapes the toe of his shoe in a circular motion on the ground, waiting for a response.

"Well, what did the doctor say?" the friend on his left asks.

I look away. Don't think I'm going to want to want to hear this. Catch the eye of a man sitting on the grass in front of me, studying me. Our eyes lock, for a second, a second more than necessary. He quickly puts his arm around his girlfriend, pulls her head toward his, kisses her—more for reassurance than love, it seems. Looks back at me. I close my eyes.

"He says 'cos my T cells are high and my viral load's low—I should think of starting the Interferon soon."

"Well, perhaps you—"

"I can't cope with this!" the young guy suddenly blurts out, sounding close to tears. "First I'm positive, now hepatitis C—and I'm not even thirty! Now I could lose my hair, my weight…"

I can't listen to this anymore. I didn't come here to be reminded of this. Too familiar. I open my eyes. Pretend to study my watch, as if trying to make my imminent departure look legitimate. Make a move to leave. Then stop. His friend's replies catch me, momentarily, off guard.

"You're gonna be okay, Steve. We're gonna be with you. We're family," pleads the friend on the right.

"Yes, Steve," the other confirms eagerly. "You know you can come and live with me if you have to stop working. For as long as you want. Hey, and if you do lose weight—just think! You'll be able to fit into all my clothes!"

I stand up and glance in their direction. I want to see Steve's reaction to his friends' comments. He's laughing, through tears, being comforted, arms around shoulders. Heartbreaking. On a little park bench in the middle of this busy city, I witness a maturity in their friendship that belies their youth. Wasn't expecting that.

I'm walking through the park gates now, down Frith Street, past Café Nero, head down—thinking back, back to a night many years ago when my first boyfriend told me about his status; how I burst into tears and how he, bizarrely, ended up comforting me.

"Come on, Clay. It could be worse," he said, pointing to the TV. "Look at Sonia. She's just lost the Eurovision Song Contest. Imagine how she must feel!"

How we both held each other, laughing. How laughter gets you through. How when you're laughing you're not hurting. Remembering a review of my MySpace friend Arthur Wooten's book *On Picking Fruit*, a review that went something along the lines of, "If gallantry in our day is defined as facing adversity with screams of laughter, then this book is the most gallant book I know of." How you can apply that line to our lives.

As I reach Old Compton Street I suddenly change my mind. I don't want time on my own. I want my friends round me. Those affected. I dig my mobile out of my pocket and start texting. "Let's do something tonight, a meal, drinks. You decide. Clay x."

I reach the shop. Jorge smiles as I walk in.

"I've contacted a few friends. We're all gonna meet up tonight. For a meal or drinks."

"Great. That'll be fun. If that's what you want," he replies enthusiastically.

It is what I want, I think, remembering the guys on the bench. Right now, it really is.

June 2nd, 2007: Saturday Morning
Lying in bed this morning, preparing to fling myself in the

178

bathroom and readjust the face, I am suddenly jolted out of my semi-conscious state by an extremely loud drilling noise inches from my head.

"DDDDDDDRRRRRRRRRRRRRRRR—"

"What's that drilling noise?" I shriek, jumping up, elbowing Jorge in the ribs.

"Drilling," he mumbles, rolling over.

But this is no ordinary drilling. The walls are shaking, pictures are falling off the walls, ornaments are rocking backwards and forwards on the coffee table, Titanic-style. All that's required to complete the destruction is for Celine Dion to burst into the room singing.

"DDDDDDDRRRRRRRRRRRRRRRR—"

"Jorge! If this drilling gets any closer the shop's going to collapse," I bawl, clinging on to the bouncing bedposts like Angela Lansbury in *Bedknobs and Broomsticks*.

"Not to worry…" he says, burrowing his head under the pillow.

So I jump out of bed, reach for my dressing gown, and, candlestick in hand, tiptoe upstairs and peer out the window to find a gaggle of potbellied workmen digging up the street with drills the size of pogo sticks.

" 'Ere! Sorry, mate!" shouts one of workmen with un-apologetic glee, scratching the plunging cleavage of his well-endowed bottom. "Did we wake you?"

Satisfied that we aren't under attack by a race of under-ground mutants, I am just about to go back downstairs when I spot Angela sashaying across the street, heading for the shop. I reach for my little black book and rush to let her in.

"Angie! How are you?" I gush, gazing up at her like a starstruck fan.

"Fine," she replies, smiling, sitting down on the little red chair by the window. "I've been at home all morning, dilating!"

"Dilating?" I ask, jotting away frantically in my little notebook.

"Yes, darlin'! I may have had the chop but I still have to dilate," she reminds me, seemingly oblivious to my frenzied scribble. "I shove 'Big D' up there, set the timer, lie back, and relax. It's like cooking a hard-boiled egg! Say, where's Jorge?"

"Downstairs, sleeping."

"Oh, why can't I be married?" she suddenly blurts out, crossing her long legs and sweeping her hair to one side. "All they want to do with me is pull it out and wipe it!"

"Er..."

"Do you think it's these tits?" she says, holding them in the air like two plates of quivering milky-white jellies. "My agent told me I should get them reduced. I'm getting too old for tits this big. I'm starting to look like a porn star gone wrong. What do you think?"

"Yes, ummm, yes," I stutter, trying to avert my eyes as her breasts threaten to quiver out of her hands and plonk themselves on my lap. "Say, that's a lovely watch. It's Cartier, isn't it? Is it real?"

"Of course it's bloody real!" she fires back. "Everything else about me is fake, but allow me the jewels, darlin'! By the way, how's the writing going?"

"Oh. So-so," I say, shrugging. "I don't know whether to carry on with what I'm doing or just start a piece of fiction. I'm a bit confused. And the more I think about it the more I can't write."

"Let your Angie give you a bit of advice," she says, blowing me a kiss as she leaves. "Stick to real life, darling. Nothing beats it. Bye, honey."

As she leaves I glance down at my watch. 10 A.M.! Time to open up. What a morning. Celine Dion and a dilating Angie, and the day's only just begun!

June 5th, 2007: "A Floating Queen"

The Queen is currently floating at a dock in Southampton.

Queen Mary, the ship, that is. Not the one with the handbag. And now Old Compton Street is awash with big, loud Americans, cruising up and down, before they set sail again on Thursday.

I love it when the Americans arrive. They barge into the shop, taking over, shouting, jeering, flirting, laughing—deep gruff voices, bodies the size of armoured tanks, and arms like a post-spinached Popeye. There's none of this pinched, tight-arsed attitude of the repressed Brits. They call a spade a spade. If they want you—they tell you. And if you don't want them—hey, it's no big deal; we can still have fun.

I should have moved to New York years ago. Whenever I visit I feel like royalty. Whenever I open my mouth the natives hang on to my every word as if I'm some kind of missionary. Whenever I go out I'm accosted by big brutal men whisking me off to the outer reaches of Hell's Kitchen. Who could ask for more?

I could have found myself a little one-room hovel in the Lower East Side, just like Quentin Crisp, waiting for the opportunity to rule the world, should anyone have thought to ask.

Oh, well. Maybe one day...

June 7th, 2007: The Kiss

I'm standing on the doorstep watching two young guys across the street.

The smaller of the two leans against a lamppost, knee cocked up as a support, while the taller guy presses into him, pinning him to the post.

They're staring into each other's eyes, chatting, smiling, laughing. One's hand strokes the other's arm. One whispers into the other's ear. One body melts into the other. Talking so closely, so intimately, that a kiss appears to be only seconds away. Here it comes...

At first it's gentle. Sensuous. Then, gradually, more passionate, intense. Arms wrapped around each other. Fingers running through hair.

The street's busy, crowds jostling past—families, couples, groups of girls. But as I watch the guys kiss, the crowds become a blur, almost as if they're in fast motion, while the guys kiss in slow.

I'm spellbound.

This is one of the most beautiful scenes I've ever witnessed on this street. Beautiful because it's so natural. Beautiful because it just develops. Beautiful because it's oblivious to its surroundings.

And as they pull back, carry on talking, I look at the crowds to judge their reaction. Interestingly, no one is offended. No one is shocked. And no one bats an eyelid. Which, to me, makes the scene even more beautiful.

I wonder if I'll live long enough to see this scene repeated the world over?

June 11th, 2007: Monday Night

10 P.M. Monday night. Dean Street. Signor Zilli's. Next door to the Colony. Opposite the shop.

It's a humid, sticky night. We're sitting outside. Seven of us. Around a table. Everyone's in a good mood, drinking, laughing, eating. I reach for my kir, watching Raqib, who's sitting opposite me. He catches my eye, cocks his head to one side in a comical way, smiles back.

I've never met an artist on Raqib's level before, so I'm always slightly intimidated in his presence. Stumbling over my words. Unsure of what to say. Raqib's from another age. Out of sync with this one. The Indian Quentin Crisp comparison doesn't do him justice. His laugh is so infectious—it comes in machine-gun rapidity. His dress, so out there—colour combinations, scarves, hats, brooches, huge rings, all jumbled together in a fashion I've never seen before. His mind, working on a slightly different level to those sitting around him. A bundle of eccentric energy that threatens to bubble over into chaos at any second.

His smile drops. He studies me for a second. Leans forward. "Clayton, my dear," he says, batting his eyelashes. "How, if one may ask, is the writing going?"

I'm hesitant. Feeling slightly awkward, that someone of his ilk would be interested. "Oh, okay," I mumble back.

"Those pieces I read," he whispers. "You paint, too..."

He leans back in his chair, raises an eyebrow, stares at me as he rolls a cigarette, licking the Rizla. Nodding. Then he breaks the spell, suddenly blurts out, "You must come to my studio next week! I'm picking up Colombian peonies at Heathrow at the weekend. By next week they'll be in full bloom and I want you to be there to enjoy the subtlety of the colours."

I watch him closely to see if this is a joke. It's not.

Then, suddenly, out of nowhere, a gang of men rush up to the little doorway right next to our table. We all look round. Startled. Flashes, in rapid succession. Waiters make their way outside. Customers stand up.

"Kate! Kate!" shouts the tall photographer, blocking the doorway with his huge lens. "Look this way!" And he click, click, clicks his huge camera at a slightly dishevelled Kate Moss and Pete Doherty, who run out of the Colony, heads bowed, jumping into a silver car that's appeared out of nowhere, that speeds away, leaving a pack of rabid photographers in its wake.

I look around the table. Everyone's on their feet, watching, laughing, pointing. Everyone, that is, except Raqib. He's still seated. Composed. His face not showing any emotion. I look around the table again, everyone's happy to have seen a couple of celebrities. Cracking jokes. Boisterous. Talking loudly. I look back at Raqib. He's in his own world.

What is he thinking? Then I see it—as he gazes up at his friends. It's nothing he would verbalise, of course. He's far too polite for that. But, it's in his eyes. Embarrassment. At their crass reaction.

Wait... There's something else flickering over his face as he looks back down at his plate. Sadness? What for, I wonder. Himself? What may lay in store? The fickleness of celebrity? How it can overshadow art?

Whatever it is, he doesn't say. He sits quietly, patiently, waiting for everyone to be seated, then carries on talking again, about life, art, culture, as if nothing untoward had just taken place.

June 13th, 2007: Angela's Basic Instinct

"I didn't get it!"

I look up from my magazine as Angela swishes into the shop, all Hollywood starlet—tits, curves, and long, long legs.

"Get what?" I ask.

"You know—the role. The audition."

I pull a face, close my magazine. "Oh, no. Angie. I'm sorry."

She steps in front of the fan, her mahogany locks flying behind, like a windswept Kate Winslet on the Titanic. "I'm not that bothered," she says with a shrug, shaking her head from side to side. "Could you really see me on Coronation Street, uprooting to Manchester? I don't think so."

"I know, but—"

"Oh, honey! What will be, will be. It's all one big game anyway. I learnt that after the last role."

"What last role?"

"*Basic Instinct 2*," she replies nonchalantly, as she holds her hair up behind her head, striking various model poses.

"Wow! You were in *Basic Instinct 2*? I never knew!"

She stops. Arches an eyebrow that brushes the ceiling. Looks at me suspiciously. "Honey—there's a lot about me you don't know."

"Yeah, but *Basic Instinct*! That's big!"

"Not for me!" she says. "All my scenes were cut."

"They cut you out?"

"Everything but the trailers. Mind you, do you think the powers that be were gonna show Sharon Stone blowing a trannie? I don't think so."

"But, still, what an experience…"

"We were at the premiere and she says, 'Angie,' she says. 'Angie, this was meant to be my comeback role and look what the bastards did to it! But we'll bounce back. Don't worry. We're old pros, you and me.'"

I like Angela.

I'd noticed her over the years, of course—on the street, looking fierce, brandishing her walking stick, holding court. But when she first came into the shop she intimidated me. And, rather than talk to her, I retreated. Blended in. Observed from a distance. Until gradually, week by week, I stepped into her line of vision.

"Are you upset?"

"About what?"

"Not getting the part?"

"Oh, God. Not at all. There're far more important things in life. That's miniscule in the grander scheme of things. I've been through a lot worse that that…" Her voice trails off, but hints at more.

She takes a seat. Crosses her legs. Smiles. Looks up at me. Radiating the kind of beauty some women spend thousands trying to achieve. Then, slowly, she starts to open up. The loud, protective persona is put to one side.

"You see, Clay, I don't play victim. I know who I am. I'm not a woman. And I'll never know what it's like to be a woman. How could I? I'm a transsexual."

"You've had quite a difficult time, haven't you?" I say, choosing my words carefully.

"The past year and a half has been the worst. Since I had the chop. I lost a boyfriend. Friends…" Again her voice, her eyes, drift away.

"I remember once a group of guys were chasing me and one shouted, 'Not bad for a geezer!' So I stopped, turned round, and said, 'Well, at least I've changed my looks. You'll always be an ugly fat cunt!' Then he threatened me with a knife and I just stood there and said, 'Go on, then. Kill me. Go on, do it!' Honey, it's just intimidation and I don't run from that anymore. It's important to stand up. You know what I mean, Clay?" She looks back at me, locking eyes. "Then there's the hormones. I'll be on them for the rest of my life. Do you know what that does to your moods? Do you know how many post-op transsexuals end up committing suicide?"

"I don't…" I mumble.

"That's not me. I've got a path to follow. And like I said, I don't play victim." She stands up to leave. "Clay, I'm fifty. There's really only one thing left for me to do with my life right now."

"And what's that?" I question, in a hushed voice, hanging on to her words, wondering what else could possibly be left.

She takes a step toward the counter, leans over, places her mouth next to my ear.

"Get these tits reduced!"

Then she shakes them in my direction, blows me a kiss, and sashays back out of the shop.

June 17th, 2007: HRH Sue

Sue's outside the shop.

Sue's rarely on the street, managing the brothel upstairs taking up much of her time, so when she does venture out it's an event. I sidle up to the window and, notebook in hand, peep from behind the window frame, watching with bated breath.

What I'm watching her for—it's hard to explain. You have to live here to understand the reverence held for Sue in these parts. For the crowds rushing past, singing, drinking, laughing, arguing, the sight of an overweight brunette (the bleached mane being strictly a winter look) dressed in a mustard-coloured, tight-fitting tracksuit, is no reason to stop and stare. But for me, and the rest of the Soho milieu, it's different. We understand the hierarchy. Who kowtows to whom. Who's who in the pecking order. And Sue is royalty on this street. Top of the food chain.

Seeing her now, it's like sitting in your local launderette and you suddenly spot the Queen rinsing out her smalls. Sue has that kind of local power. In fact, I've often sat here late at night watching the pimps, the hookers, the dealers stand aside like courtiers, as Sue waddles by with her late-night shopping. Respectful. Reverential. Soho's own Trooping the Colour.

When we first moved into the shop, not yet accustomed to Soho etiquette, I committed a cardinal sin. After a huge leak, I went storming upstairs to complain, and Sue calmly turned off the offending tap and then politely offered me, by way of recompense, a free blow job, just as a neighbour would a bag of organic carrots from his allotment. But, and here's where I made my big mistake, I never took Sue up on the offer, and for months after she eyed me up with suspicion. It was as if I'd refused a knighthood. I was "Sohostracized."

Thankfully, after a year, Sue and I have now reached a mutual understanding. I don't step on her turf, nor does she mine. If we catch each other's eye, I'll smile, contemplate a curtsey, and bow my head in respect—never speaking unless she speaks to me first, never attempting to touch the royal person. When she last caught my eye, she actually smiled back and it was then that I knew I'd finally been forgiven and would be allowed back to court.

I'm thinking about this now as I study her—on, coincidentally, the other Queen's birthday. The window's steaming up slightly from my breath, so I wipe it with my sleeve, as Sue chats away on her mobile unaware that there's a tall Rastafarian eyeing her up from behind, starting to circle.

Un-oh! Royal protocol is about to be breached. Where's Sue's bodyguards? Ladies in waiting?

I rush to the doorway.

"What you lookin' for, darlin'?" the Rastafarian grunts aggressively, with a drunken leer.

Sue, accustomed to such intrusions, having had to deal with commoners in the royal bedroom many times before, calmly finishes her call, puts her mobile back into her Tescos bag, and gives her attacker a steely glare that makes him take two wobbly steps back.

"SEX!" she barks back. "NOW PISS OFF!"

The Rastafarian, caught unawares, unsure of how to react, grumbles an apology and slinks away.

I look at Sue, gazing at her in awe.

O Sue. Long may you reign in these parts. Long may you govern your people. Long may you watch over us. HRH Sue. I salute you.

June 19th, 2007: A Scary Start to the Day

The sun is streaming through the shop windows. Summer's hit Old Compton Street.

I look out the window. It's only midday and already the street's busy. Hare Krishnas singing away, drag queens mincing away, gay men cruising the day away. Costa coffee shop is packed, every chair outside taken. Couples, gay, straight, all nationalities. A Soho melting pot. I unbolt the door, pull up the grates, smiling. Hey, this could be a good day. Then, suddenly, I stop. Catch my breath. Take two steps back...

Oh, God! It can't be! The face that launched a thousand nightmares. It's Ann "Doris Karloff" Widdecombe!

Ms. Widdecombe, former Shadow Home Secretary and Conservative MP for Maidstone and the Weald, known for her ardent opposition to gay rights, is staring right at me. I immediately slam the door shut. Duck down. Cross myself and reach for the *Yellow Pages*. E... E... Ex... Here we go. Exorcisms.

What's she doing here? Has the name "Dirty White Boy" made her hackles rise? Come to close us down for being too gay?

I peep up above the window ledge and watch as she walks slowly past the shop, down Dean Street, the sound track to *Jaws* going round my head. Duh-duh. Duh-duh. Duh-duh-duh-duh.

Then she stops. Just outside the brothel. Oh, no, Ann, please! I know times are hard for the Tories, but still... Although, hold on. Wait a minute. Isn't Ann famous for still being a virgin at 59? So what's she doing outside the brothel? Looking to get broken in? Heard that Sue's a swinger? Her tongue action second to none? Surely not.

Intrigued, I crawl on all fours to the door, open it carefully, and, crucifix in hand, peep round the corner. Oh. Okay. Now it makes sense. Hovering outside the brothel doorway there's a film crew, cameras, lights, and makeup artists. Ann's being interviewed. As I watch, an assistant walks past with a clipboard under his arm.

"Hi, what's the programme?" I ask him cheerfully.

"Oh, Ann's doing a show."

"What about?"

"Prostitution."

"I see... Sympathetic, I hope."

"Well..." he replies, tentatively. "The one after's about benefit fraud, so..."

Oh, no! Sue! Quick—run for your life! The Wicked Witch of Westminster is coming to get you!

June 24th, 2007: Overheard

7 P.M. Overheard—coming from the brothel next door: a man shouting up the stairway as he runs out, "I ain't paying shit! No one told me she had a cock!"

June 25th, 2007: Customer of the Day

A rather large black guy with small Benny Hill glasses comes into the shop this afternoon. He walks round slowly, looking at me cautiously.

"Our Spring/Summer sale has just started, so everything's now fifty percent off the marked price!" I say, cheerfully.

"I know a lot about selling clothes," he grunts back. "I used to work in a filofax factory and it was my job to punch the holes in the paper so you could get the binder through."

June 28th, 2007: Pride London

Standing by the shop doorway, watching the crowds drift by.

The street's getting busier. Pride is just a couple of days away. Soho's melting pot is starting to bubble over. Loitering outside Costa, a gang of big, buff, "chemically enhanced" Texan bears; canoodling against Soho Books, Wimbledon "rain delayed" dykes; and dodging club kids, drag royalty, and a scattering of excitable Flyer Boys, euro-laden Mediterranean queens.

Across the street, nervous straight tourists struggle with maps and over-sized coffee cups; the growing realisation that a quick detour has taken them straight inside the loins of So(ho)dom, a picture worth taking.

And just by the shop doorway, the *Big Issue* seller seizes the moment, flogging *QX* and *Boyz* magazines to unsuspecting old ladies who will no doubt be in for a nasty shock when they flick to the hooker section on the train home to Worthing.

Inside the shop, its all Go! Go! Go! The Spring/Summer

50 percent sale has begun; selling First Collection Iceberg couture with one hand, placing sandbags by the doorway in preparation for the gay onslaught with the other.

By tomorrow night Soho will be completely cordoned off. A Women's Stage erected in Romilly Street, with DJ and festival stands positioned in Soho Square.

Thus Old Compton Street braces itself for yet another day of madness, mayhem, and men, men, (wo)men.

Happy Pride, everyone!

June 29th, 2007: "They're Getting Rid of the Fags!"

2 P.M. I'm sitting behind the counter, looking out the doorway, waiting for the day to begin.

An old man totters past. He stops. Looks inside. Smiles. Then, holding onto the doorframe, takes a step up, gradually making his way slowly toward me, adjusting his tie and patting down his wispy grey locks as he gets closer.

"They're getting rid of the fags!" he suddenly announces in a clipped, disapproving voice, as he rests one slightly trembling pale hand on the counter, taking a yellow silk hanky from his top pocket with the other.

"I'm sorry?"

"I don't mean us, dear!" he says, lightly dabbing his forehead. "They're not getting rid of us! I mean the smokes. You know—no smoking in public. Starts next week. Can you believe it?"

"Oh yes, of course. I'd almost—"

"I never thought I'd see the day, ducky, I can tell you," he says. I watch as he licks his forefinger, running it up and down an eyebrow that is as clipped as his voice. "Where're we gonna smoke now? In the loos?"

"I'm not sure—"

"You can't smoke in there, dear. Not round here, you can't. Oh, no! Too many men in there doing 'the business.'"

"You're probably right," I reply, trying not to laugh.

"The air'd be thick with smoke. Thick with it! We'd have to feel our way round the bog. The queens would love it, of course. But what about those of us who just want the urination—what would we do? Oh no—not in the loos. We can't have smoking in the loos."

"Plus it'd leave a bit of a smell," I remind him.

"Well, there's gonna be a bit of a smell in there anyway, dear. It's a bog! What'd you expect?" he fires back, throwing back his head and holding on to his tie for mock effect.

"Ummm..."

"Oh I couldn't *bear* it in mine," he says, pulling a face. "My loo's sparkling. Always has been. Well, you never know when you'll have the visitors, do you? Imagine them leaving and saying, 'Did you see the brown?' Oh I couldn't bear that. Couldn't think of anything worse!"

"Er..."

"I use the bleach. You know the spray one? Oh, yes. Every night. Leave it to settle. By the morning it's all gone. Gets rid of it all. You could eat off it come the morning."

"That's, er, nice."

"Talking of which, it's time for my smoke. Not for much longer though, hey? I never thought I'd live to see the day. Oh, well. Bye for now, ducky. Bye."

And with that, he totters right back out again.

June 30th, 2007: Pride London
5:00 P.M. The phone rings.

"Hello, Dirty White Boy. Can I help you?"

"Clay!"

"Chico?"

"Hey, honey!"

"Chico! How are you?"

"I'm good. What about you? I heard about the bombings. Is everything okay there?"

"You heard about it?"

"Yeah. We have a TV in the cell. It was all over the news."

"It was scary. The whole of Piccadilly was cordoned off. They found a Mercedes loaded with gasoline, gas canisters, nails..."

"Isn't that near you?"

"Just round the corner. And you know it's Pride today, don't you?"

"Of course. You must be mobbed."

"Oh, it's heaving! The street's absolutely packed. Police everywhere. 'Cos you know everyone descends on Old Compton Street once the march's finished."

"I remember. You making loads of money?"

"Not really. Just keeping our head above water."

"Really?"

"Yep. I'm never really sure how long we'll be able to stick it out. Plus no one really shops on days like this. They're too busy getting drunk. The only customers are the ones who've had a drink spilled over them."

"Honey, if I was there I'd be throwing red wine over everyone!"

"Ha-ha! Say, Chico, how's it going with the boyfriend?"

"Okay."

"You don't sound so sure..."

"Well, he's a bit demanding. But thing's are fine."

"You still in love?"

"Yes... Anyway, I don't want talk about that, I wanna hear about Pride. Tell me all about it. What's going on outside? What's happening?"

"Well, first thing this morning, do you remember the cute Hungarian boys from the Algerian Coffee Shop next door?"

"Honey, how could I forget?"

"Well, they came in this morning with a big tray of home-made cocks made out of clay. Cock pipes, cock ornaments, cock badges—they gave us one each with our name on."

"How cute!"

"Mine's got a big red bell-end."

"I've heard!"

"Ha-ha! Then, about midday, the lesbian drummers started bashing away outside the shop for about an hour!"

"Oh, God! Bet you loved that! What else?"

"It rained all morning so it was a bit slow to start, but now—well, can you hear it?"

"It sounds like a riot going on! Come on! Tell me everything! They only let you speak for ten minutes here."

"Okay. Well, it's the usual. You know…"

"Clay, speak up. I can hardly hear you."

"Sorry. Can you hear me now?"

"Yes. That's better."

"Well, I'm standing on the doorstep, and everywhere you look there're muscle guys, bears, drag queens, every nationality. Chinese girls kissing Muslim girls, young guys with old guys, suburban dykes, Brazilians, guys with their tops off, dancing, leathermen being led down the street on chains, guys in kilts, straight girls, families, kids, men dressed as fifties flight attendants, everyone drinking…"

"God, Clay I really wish I was there…"

"Ahhh… You will be, Chico… You will be… Before you know it. You'll be out soon."

A young guy dressed in army fatigues and a football shirt approaches.

"Hold on a sec, Chico. There's someone here. Yes. Can I help you?"

"Do you know where I can get a whore around here?"

"A whore?"

"Yeah…"

"Look around you. The street's full of 'em!"

"No, I mean a woman."

"Oh. Okay. Umm… Have you tried the brothel upstairs?"

"Yeah."

"Well?"

"They want forty pounds. Where can I get one for twenty-five?"

"Well, there're a few more brothels down Peter Street. You could try there."

"Are the girls pretty?"

"Sorry, I've never done a survey. It's not really my specialist subject."

"Uhhhh. Okay, mate."

"Bye."

"Clay, who was that?" Chico pipes in.

"Some cute young guy looking for sex."

"And you couldn't help?"

"He only wanted to pay twenty-five pounds. I'd want diamonds!"

"So, come on, what else? What's going on now?"

"Oh, okay. There's an ambulance across the road for the 'G' queens."

"Anyone pass out yet?"

"Not yet… Then, this is weird—there's been two guys come in so far, both from the States, who've been reading my stuff on MySpace. First thing they wanna see is the little red chair where I write!"

"Honey! You should sell it on eBay!"

"You could be right." I say. "What else. Oh yes. We've had a few drag queens come in, customers of ours. But you know what it's like when guys do drag—you can't work out who's under there. Jorge knew, of course. He can tell your waist size and leg length at twenty paces. So this drag queen comes in and Jorge says, 'Hi, Peter!' and I say, 'How'd you know it was Peter?' And he says, 'Thirty-six-inch legs, twenty-eight-inch waist!' "

"Did he guess your size the night you met?"

"Oh, yeah. He's always been able to sniff out a large!"

"Clay, you're too much! Hold on. Oh, okay. Clay, they're saying I've gotta get off the phone now. Oh, honey, I miss you guys."

"Chico. Send me another visitation form. I'll come and see you next week."

"Okay, honey. Bye. I love you."

"Bye, Chico. I love you too."

"Happy Pride!"

July 12th, 2007: Trying to Write

1 P.M. Staring at my laptop. My fingers lightly fingering the keys. Thinking.

"Hey, man! I was hopin' you'd be here!"

I look up. It's Tariq, the crack addict. He shuffles into the shop, holding a faded Safeways carrier bag, which he plonks down on the floor next to my chair.

"Look what I got!" he rasps, with a Fagin-like leer, opening the bag, revealing a mound of plastic air fresheners. "You got a cat?"

"Umm, no," I reply, carefully, trying to tear my eyes away from the one black tooth left in his mouth, which rests precariously on his gum like an ancient shipwreck. "And I don't really need any air fresheners at the moment. But thank you anyway."

His face turns, frighteningly, from *I really like you* to *I really hate you*, in the blink of an eye.

"I gotta have the cash, man," he pleads, aggressively. "I just gotta!" The last "gotta" is almost spat in my face.

I shake my head, shrug my shoulders, and watch as his eyes, which moments ago had a spaced-out, faraway kind of look, narrow, turning venomous. Oh, dear. I get the feeling we won't be exchanging Christmas cards. Then he snatches his bag off the floor and stomps back out of the shop, barely able to contain his anger.

I take a deep breath. Hover my fingers over the keyboard

again, waiting for a thought to—

"Clay!" shrieks an androgynous voice from the doorway. I stop. Look up again. Angela.

"I'm not stopping. I've just come to say goodbye."

"Goodbye?"

"You know!" she says, pulling a face, sweeping her gorgeous locks to one side. "My breast reduction! Duh! It's tomorrow. At four P.M."

"Oh yes! Of course," I say, apologetically. "I almost forgot."

Then she cups them, one in each hand, as if about to start juggling. "Say goodbye to the girls!" she says, bouncing them up and down. "Hopefully they'll be adopted and find a good home."

"Bye," I laugh, waving as she leaves. "Good luck, and call me when you're up for visitors!"

I look at my watch. God, I've hardly written a thing. Close my eyes. Okay. Why not just write about who's been in the shop this morning? Of course! So I'm just about to start when in bursts—

"Hey, Clay! It's your seester!"

"Chris!" I reply, looking at him, at my laptop, and back to him again, trying to keep my train of thought. "Where've you been?"

"Frankfurt. But I'm back. And look!" he says, stepping to one side, revealing his friend Richard. "I've brought you a little something. Well," he whispers behind a cupped hand. "Maybe not *that* little."

"Hey, Clay!" Richard pipes up from behind Chris's back.

Seconds later they're both picking up jeans, shirts, T-shirts, vests, holding them up for size, comparing fabrics, colours.

"Chris, did you go out on Pride night?" I ask as he tries on an Iceberg sandal, admiring it from each angle.

"No, honey. I had to go to Morton. Whiteville. Girl,

you'd think they'd never *seen* a black woman before! I felt *so* at home," he sighs sarcastically, pointing his toes and looking at them with admiration. "All night it was 'Can you fetch me a drink?' 'Here's my coat!' "

"What do you think I could get away with wearing?" Richard queries, as he rifles through the Lacroix shirts.

"A mask!" Chris replies, reaching for a pair of Thierry Mugler dress trousers, which he holds against his legs.

I nod approvingly. "You should try those on."

So he skips off to the dressing room. Two minutes later he's back, twirling round.

"They're low-rise," I remind him, raising an eyebrow. "You should be wearing them on your hips. You're wearing them far too high."

"That's my tight ass," he purrs back. "It makes everything go high."

"There's some real bargains here!" says Richard excitedly, heading off toward the dressing room with a handful of jeans over his arm. "When's the next sale?"

"January!" I shout back.

Chris reaches for a snakeskin belt and wraps it round his waist. "She'll be dead by then!"

"With that belt, just so you know, the guard needs to land in the centre of the hole."

"Oh, she likes a guard in the centre of her hole!" Richard shouts from the other end of the shop.

"How long've you two known each other?" I ask Chris with a grin on my face.

"Twenty years. I was sixteen. Waiting at a bus stop and this dirty old man pulls up and says, 'Get in!' "

"That's a lie!" Richard fires back as he models a pair of conservative Rykiel jeans that appear to be a touch too tight.

Chris looks at him, hand on hip, shaking his head. "Honey! You can not wear them! Not with your fat ass! Remember! We black. We hung. And we got the big ass!

Plus we got no money!" He turns round to face me, whispers behind a cupped hand again. "Well—I have. But she hasn't. She mixed race."

Ten minutes later, laden down with bags, they're off, waving goodbyes, blowing kisses.

So I sit back down. Okay, where was I? Oh, yes. Here we go. Then, just as I'm halfway through the first line about Tariq, in walks the Fag Lady—

"Can I have a cuddle?"

July 20th, 2007: Angie's Girls!

"I'm back!"

I look up. Standing in the doorway, Angela!

"Well. What do ya think?" she says, the sun streaming through the copper highlights of her shoulder-length hair.

I gaze at her, transfixed. "You look absolutely…amazing!"

And she does. More "Janice Dickinson" than Janice— the legs, the hair, the lightly made-up skin, and cheekbones cut so deep you could do yourself damage caressing them. She walks toward me, gracefully, all 6'3" of her, using her silver-headed walking stick for support: Dirty White Boy transformed into a catwalk.

"Well, go on, then!" she insists, as she nears the counter. "Say hello to the 'girls.'"

I stare at them, up at her face, at her breasts again as she gives them a quick shimmy, thrusting them toward my face.

"Umm…er…hello, girls!" I mumble, fighting for air.

"Come 'ere!" she says, pulling me out of my seat, leading me to the dressing room like a schoolboy about to be deflowered. "Follow Angie!"

"Where…where are we going?"

"The unveiling, of course. After all, you are their godfather!"

Then she whips back the curtain, pushes me inside, pulls back the curtain again and turns round to face me with a glint in her eye. Oh, dear. What's she going to do? I giggle nervously as, in one quick, well-rehearsed movement, she whips off her top and black bra, letting her breasts spill out, like barrels over a waterfall.

"Oh, thank God for that!" she sighs with relief. "I have to wear this support bra for six weeks. I feel like a bandaged mummy! Anyway—how do they look?" she asks, looking at me, hands on hips, raising a quizzical eyebrow.

I stare at them, not knowing whether to tweak them or bury my face in them. "They look...well, I haven't seen a pair up this close since er...the school playing field. But they look really... Can I touch them?" I ask eagerly.

"Of course. Go ahead!"

I reach forward, fingers twitching like a rampant Benny Hill.

"Come on! They won't bite!" Angela urges, stepping forward, as I lean back to focus.

"Wow!" I murmur, cupping one in each hand, tempted to juggle. "Angie! They feel just like real boobs!"

"Well, thank God for that!" she replies, looking down at them like a proud parent. "Mmmmm. Now we're lesbians."

"I... I...suppose I'd better get back," I say nervously, laughing, not really sure how to hand them back.

"But you like them, though?"

"Oh, they're gorgeous. The perfect size!" I reply, admiring them as you would puppies in a pen. "So in proportion. And they don't look too 'Posh' either."

"Oh, God! I hope not," she says, horrified.

"No, yours are really natural," I say reassuringly as she reaches for her bra while I continue to hold them.

"Hey. By the way, where's Jorge?"

"Downstairs," I answer, getting hand cramp. "On the loo. He's had the runs all week."

"The runs?"

"Yeah, we ate at Zilli's. You know the Italian place across

the street? He had the lobster and he's been on the loo ever since."

"Well, let's get him upstairs. Pronto! Angie'll cure that."

"You can cure his diarrhoea?" I ask, incredulously, handing back her tits, one by one, watching her push them back in her bra, my fingers still twitching like crab claws.

"Honey!" she jokes as she adjusts her bra clasp behind her back. "You may be writing about me on MySpace but there's a lot about me you don't know."

"Really? Like what?"

She grins. "You'll see."

We step out of the dressing room and make our way to the counter, Angela shouting down the stairway. "Jorge! Jorge! Get that pink ass of yours up here!"

"What are you going to do?"

"I'm a healer," she says, turning round.

"A healer?"

"Yes, a healer. I'm ruled by the moon. Men are ruled by the sun. But Angie's ruled by the moon. That's why I'm a bit down at the moment. For two days after a full moon Angie's not herself. But!" she fires back, with a grin on her face, waving her walking stick perilously close to my face. "She can still heal!"

"Sorry. I don't get it. You're gonna heal Jorge's bum?"

"Yesssssss," she drawls.

"What is it?" Jorge pants, running up the stairway.

"Hey, darlin'!" Angie says with a big smile.

"Hey, Angie! What's goin' on?"

"Come here!" she orders, reaching her stick toward the stairway, placing the crook of the handle round Jorge's neck, dragging him up the last few steps. "Come to Momma!"

"What…"

Seconds later, Angela's wrapping her arms round him, Jorge resting his head on her new breasts.

"What's all this about?" he asks, through a mouthful of silicone.

"SSSSShhhhhh," says Angela. "Angie's healing you. Don't speak!"

We stand there for about 30 seconds—Jorge's face buried; Angela, at least a foot taller than Jorge, resting her head on top of his, focusing; me watching Jorge's bottom for, well, I'm not sure what. Then she takes Jorge's face in her hands. "There."

"Oh, no!" Jorge winces, pulling a face. "I gotta go again." And off he runs back down the stairway to the toilet.

"Angie, do you—"

"Shhhhhh."

I watch as she meditates, eyes closed, momentarily. "Okay. We're done. Job done. Or 'jobs,' in Jorge's case."

"You mean he's cured?"

"Should be!"

"Jorge!" I shout down the stairway. "Jorge! Are you, er, solid again?"

"I think so," a voice cries faintly from somewhere far below.

"Angie! It worked! Yippee! No more chicken soup and loo roll!"

"I'll see you soon, Clay." She laughs.

And I watch as she swishes gracefully back out of the shop, giving me a Liza-style wave over her shoulder as she hits the street.

July 25th, 2007: Leslie

"A single macchiato to take away, please?"

"Okay," grunts the bored Spanish waiter, digging his finger inside his ear.

I hand over a few coins, wait for the change.

"Anything to eat?" he mumbles, as he pulls his finger out, examining a small yellow lump stuck to the dirty nail.

"Er…perhaps not today."

"Oh, do hurry, ducky!" a clipped voice suddenly pipes up from behind. "Let's not take forever, shall we?"

Where do I know that voice from? I turn round and face a small, old gentleman dressed in a beige three-piece suit with a white handkerchief flowing extravagantly from the top pocket.

"Hi! I know you. You came into my shop a couple of weeks ago. You're…"

"Leslie. Les-Lie!" he enunciates, delivering the words as a schoolteacher would to a room full of unruly boys. "And I don't want any of this 'Les' business. Can't abide all that name shortening."

"Nice to, er, meet you, Leslie," I reply cautiously, reaching over to shake hands. "I'm Clay…Clayton, from Dirty White Boy, across the road."

He looks down at my hand disdainfully, not offering his, and continues talking. "Is that coffee?" he asks suspiciously, nodding at my cup.

"Yes, I—"

"Bona! I'll join you," he says, with the hint of a smile. "A coffee and a fag, outside. We'll rest the lallies and watch the rent go by."

"Rent?"

"Oh, don't play the innocent with me, dear. You've been round the block almost as long as I have," he says mockingly, flicking back the fringe of his Brylcreemed grey coiffure with a well-manicured forefinger. "Don't tell me you haven't seen 'em?" He motions toward the window.

"You mean the—"

"The Third Worldies, dear. The hookers. Straight off the boat and straight on the game! It's shocking, it is. The glossies are full of 'em. Showing their cocks and bumholes to the world. Thank God I left all that buggery business behind. That's what caused the piles, you know!" He turns to face the now clean-fingered, and wide-eyed, waiter. "A black coffee."

"Anything to eat?"

"No. Just the coffee. And don't be over-generous with the granules. I want a 'pick-me-up' not a 'keep-me-up!'" He turns round again. "Get some chairs, would you, ducky?"

I take a seat outside. Moments later, Leslie walks toward me, like a haughty old Dame, carrying his cup in front of him with two hands, blowing on the coffee as he approaches.

"Ahhh. That's better," he sighs, settling gingerly into the seat next to mine. "Oh look, there's one now!"

"What?"

"Rent!"

"How do you know he's—?"

"Vada the eek, dear! Don't tell me you've never seen 'er. She's been trolling round here for years, fiddlin' with the basket."

"I don't think I've noticed—"

"Well, you wanna pay a bit more attention, then, don't you? Wandering through life with blinkers on."

I suppress a giggle, trying to stay composed. A few seconds tick by. We reach for our coffees, take sips, and place them back down in unison. I wait a moment, wanting to delve deeper. Then decide to just go for it, asking as politely as I can. "So, umm, where do you live?"

"And what's that got to do with the price of eggs?" he shrieks, fluttering his eyelashes.

"Nothing, I just…"

"Bloomsbury, if you must know," he answers calmly, reaching for his coffee again. "Got me own flat. All paid for. And no, I'm not on the national handbag. I live off me own pension, dear. Oh yes. I've always been very self-sufficient in that department."

Then I have an idea. "Leslie, I write about Soho. Would

you mind if I went across the road and got my notebook so I could take a few notes?"

He arches a very fine, almost invisible eyebrow. "What for?"

"Well, I could write a blog about you—"

"A blog? You want to interrogate me and then put me in a *blog*?" he sneers, throwing back his head, his eyes hovering just above his flared nostrils.

"Yes, I was thinking—"

"Well, think again! I ain't divulging nothing!" he snaps back.

"Sorry, I didn't mean to offend you," I say apologetically.

"Well, you just did!"

He licks a finger, running it up and down his eyebrow, a habit he seems to perform when thinking, and I watch as his eyes narrow, examining mine just as studiously. "And will my name be in this *blog*?" he asks sarcastically.

"Yes. Unless of course—"

"What is it you write about, exactly? 'Cos if it's all about bumming I'm not interested!"

I bite my lip, trying to stop myself from laughing again.

"No it won't be—"

"I do have a reputation to keep up, you know. I'm a member of the Bloomsbury Association."

"I promise, it's nothing rude."

"And I make donations to the Royal Opera House—so I don't want anything soiling the name, dear. You 'ear me?"

I lean across the table, smiling, trying to reassure him. "Honestly, Leslie, it's nothing that would compromise your reputation."

"Hmmmmm. What is this *blog*, anyway? One of these sex sites, is it?"

"No. It's nothing like that. It's more like a diary."

"A diary! Oh, she wants me in her diary now, does she? And who's going to be reading this *diary*?"

"Well…anyone who wants to."

"Anyone! You write a diary for the whole world to see? Who do you think you are? Anne bleedin' Frank? I've never heard anything so stupid in all my life. You should be locked up. In my day we kept our business to ourselves."

"Leslie," I say, laughing, "I just want to ask you a few questions about Soho, you know, the history. I'm sure there'll be people who'd be quite interested in reading about it."

"Oh, you do, do you? And who might they be?"

"Well, my MySpace friends, for a start."

"Ducky, I haven't got a clue what you're talking about. My. Space. Friends. If I were you I'd give them space, space from that bleedin' diary of yours." He runs his fingers through his hair, pauses. Looks at me. "Oh, go on, then, get your notebook if you must. But I'm warning you—nothing on—"

"—the bum thing. Of course not."

So I jump out of my seat, rush across the road into the shop, grab my little black notebook out of the desk drawer, and run back to the coffee shop, just as Leslie's getting up to leave.

"Sorry, dear," he says mischievously, mopping his brow with his hanky. "Another day, perhaps. I do have stories to tell, but it's time for my lie-down. Bye, ducky!"

I sit back down, watch him totter off toward Wardour Street, open my little notebook, and try and remember everything he's just said…

August 2nd, 2007: Leslie Returns

12:47 P.M. Jorge's outside cleaning the windows. I'm sitting behind the counter, looking out.

I watch the *Big Issue* seller cross Dean Street. He stops. Leans over the drain. Vomits. Projectile. A hosepipe full of food shooting from his mouth. He wipes his mouth on his sleeve, then waves to Jorge, who, with a look of horror on his face, takes two steps back. Looks like it could be an eventful day.

"Well, if it isn't Anne Frank!"

I look over toward the doorway. "Leslie! I didn't expect—"

"Never expect, ducky, and then you won't be disappointed. Now go and fetch your notebook. But I'm warnin' you!" he says, wagging his finger at me like a past-her-prime Miss Jean Brodie.

"Don't worry," I laugh, reaching into the top drawer of the desk. "I know. Your reputation!"

I open my book, flick to a clean page, pen at the ready, and watch as he removes his blazer, placing it on the floor beside his battered leather shoulder bag. Then he eyes up my little red chair suspiciously, brushes it with his hand, and sits down, gently.

"Well, thank heavens the sun's out," he says, smoothing out the creases on his trousers while peering out the window at the blue sky. "All that rain was getting right on my tits!" He turns back to face me. "Now dear, what is it you want to know, exactly?"

Hmmm. Now he puts it like that, I'm not really sure. "Well, nothing specifically," I reply cagily, more interested in the flow of the conversation than any need to direct it. "I just wanted to—"

"You said you had some questions. Don't tell me I've minced all the way over here for nothing," he sighs, his pinched expression now more reminiscent of a *Gosford Park* Dame Maggie.

"No, I'm just, er…"

He rolls his eyes. "Gawd help us! You should have your own chat show. Okay, let me do the askin', then. Why are you writing this diary?"

I don't answer for a second. Start doodling in my notebook, not used to this kind of question. "Well…I… For a start, I enjoy it." I pause again. "Then, I suppose, I want to document my time here in case…well, I'm never really sure how long we're going to last."

"Okay. A fairly reasonable explanation," he says, as if it isn't reasonable at all. "And tell me again, who's in this diary?"

"Oh, you know… Soho characters, the people who come into the shop, people on the street."

"And what about your fair self?" he says, tilting back his head, his eyes narrowing as he studies me. "Do you make a guest appearance?"

"Now and again. But it's not really about me, it's more about—"

"But it's a diary, isn't it?" he interrupts, changing positions, resting his elbow on his knee so that his hand cups his chin, a delicate finger stroking his cheek.

"Well, it started off as one but now it's more about other people," I answer, slightly defensively.

He leans forward inquisitively. "And why is that, pray tell?" he coaxes, in a sing-song voice.

"Ummm. They're more… I just feel more comfortable writing about other people."

Silence.

He drums his fingertips on the counter. I chew the end of my pen. Maybe I should elaborate… "It's just that there're more interesting characters here than me. That's all."

There. That'll shut him up.

"So you don't think you're an interesting character, then?"

"Yes, but…"

Where is he going with this?

He reaches forward, taps me on the leg. "It seems to me, dear, if you don't mind me saying, that you'd be quite happy to interrogate me, publicise my dirty laundry for all and sundry, but not the other way round. Am I right?"

Clay—stick up for yourself! "I do write about myself

now and again. I did a piece last week."

"About?"

"Ummmm, when I was a kid."

"The past. What about the present?"

I look at him, dumbfounded. He looks back, one eyebrow arching, like a crossbow about to snap.

"Quid pro quo, ducky."

"Sorry?"

He smirks. Leans further forward. Eyebrow higher still. "Well, here's the deal as I see it. If you tell me about you, then I'll tell you about me. How does that sound?"

I watch him, carefully. This is how Jodie Foster must have felt with Hannibal Lecter. "Okay…" I reply, cautiously. "What do you want to know?"

"The point is, ducky, it's not what I want to know, but what you're prepared to tell."

His eyes widen; he nods, as if to reiterate what he's just said. We stare at each other for a few seconds. Feels longer. A mind game. This isn't what—

"Time up!"

"Sorry?"

"I said, time up." He stands, slowly, using the counter as a support, reaches for his blazer, smiling. "Leslie's going to leave you with that little thought."

"You're leaving? Again?"

He drapes his blazer over one shoulder, his leather bag over the other. "Ducky, we both have personal stories to tell that revolve around this shop. When you're ready to tell me yours, then I'll tell you mine." Then he throws back his head, running his fingers through his perfectly groomed hair, and gives me a camp little wave with his fingers. "Enchanté, my dear!"

And with a sparkle in his eye and a grin on his face, out he goes.

August 3rd, 2007: Customer of the Day

Young guy: "How much is this polo shirt?"

Me: "It was a hundred and thirty pounds but now it's fifty percent off, so—sixty-five."

Young guy: "Okay I'll take it. It's for my boyfriend. It's his birthday."

Me: "Well, I hope he likes it!"

He digs his mobile out of his pocket, calls the boyfriend.

Young guy: "I've just bought a lovely shirt for your birthday, so you'd better get me something nice for mine..." Pause. "How much did I spend?"

He pauses. Looks at me. Turns his back to me and whispers, "Well, let's just say I didn't get change out of a hundred and fifty pounds. I know. I shouldn't have, but you're worth it!"

August 5th, 2007: Employee of the Day

2 P.M. Sunday. I'm sitting behind the counter.

A bearded guy walks in—white T-shirt, camouflage trousers, rucksack on his back. He smiles. I smile back. He browses the racks for a few minutes, pulls out a Dirty White Boy vest, walks over to the counter.

"I'll take this."

"Okay. That's half price. Thirteen pounds fifty," I say cheerfully.

As I wrap the vest he takes off his rucksack, plonks it on the floor, bends down, rummaging inside for his wallet.

"What time do you finish?"

"We're open 'til eight."

"You wanna go out?" he asks, expectantly.

"Ummm. No, thank you. I can't tonight."

"We can go to the cinema, a bite to eat, whatever you want. Just the two of us."

"I can't. Sorry," I reply, a bit firmer. "I've got a partner."

"Okay, I'll see you at nine o'clock outside Compton's!"

"You're persistent, aren't you?" I reply, laughing.

Then he stands up. Looks at me strangely. And carries on talking into his mobile.

August 6th, 2007: Monday Morning

"Clay!"

"What?"

"Clay! Get up here NOW!" Jorge screams.

Fuck! This can only mean one thing...

I'm running up the stairway. Round the corner. Adrenaline. Heart beating. Breathless. Mouth dry. Top step. Scanning the shop. And there it is—10 of them. Jorge trying to push three of them out the door. The others screaming abuse. "Fuckin' batty boy!" Steaming the shop. Grabbing clothes. It's all happening so fast. Like when you press Fast-forward on a DVD. A blur. And I'm frozen, for a split second. Not knowing what to... Clay! React!

I rush to the doorway. Push them out. The others follow behind. Shouting. Swearing. Threatening to come back. Kill us. I shut the right door. They leave. Laughing. Jeering. All except one.

He stands in the doorway, in front of me, staring. Still. Silent. Expressionless. Just me and him. One hand lingering near his right pocket. And everything stops, momentarily. I'm looking at him. He's staring at me. Like he's been here before. Knows what to do next. I can feel it. See it in his eyes. What will the next moment bring? What direction will it take? Whose life will alter as a consequence?

"Try coming back without your gang, you piece of shit!" I shout, unlocking the bolt, breaking the spell, shutting the other door in his face.

I turn round, reach for the phone. Someone kicks the doorframe, hard. "Fuckin' queers!" I dial 999, calmly, strangely. Jorge sits down next to me, his head in his hands.

Monday morning on Old Compton Street.

August 12th, 2007: The Raid

BANG! BANG! BANG!

"Oh my God!"

BANG! BANG! BANG!

"Jorge! Come up here!"

Jorge runs up the stairway. "What? What is it?" he says, out of breath. "Has your ass gone through the glass cabinet again?"

"No! It's the brothel upstairs. There's some kind of banging going on!"

"Well, there would be. It's a brothel!"

"No, not that kind of banging! Listen!"

BANG! BANG! BANG!

"There! I told you!"

We rush to the window just as 10 (hot) policemen in full riot gear, guns in hand, burst open the side door and storm up the brothel stairway, leaving another six (even hotter) policemen posted outside.

"Look!" I say, pointing to the Dean Street crossroad, which is completely blocked by police vans. "What do you think's going on?"

"I'm not sure."

"GET YER BLEEDIN' HANDS OFF ME!" Sue's voice suddenly bellows from above.

Within minutes there's a huge crowd outside, the police holding them back, customers streaming out of the Groucho Club, everyone staring at the commotion. Even the paparazzi, bored with waiting for a grainy pic of some C-list celebrity, swivel their huge telescopic lenses toward the brothel.

"YOU'RE ASKING FOR IT!" yells Sue again, and we both look up to the ceiling thinking she's about to come crashing through, chest first.

Then it all goes quiet. The banging stops. Sue stops. Everyone stares at the first-floor window. What's going on? My mind's racing. Have the policemen got bored and decided to have a bit of fun? A full-blown police orgy taking place just a few feet above our heads?

I'm still fantasizing about what they're doing with the handcuffs when there's an almighty "CRASH!"—the sound of a door being broken in. I rush outside. Peep round the corner, where I'm confronted by a burly policewoman (no makeup) who barks "GET BACK INSIDE!" in an accent that appears to be half Essex, half pit bull.

Suddenly, all hell breaks loose. Shouting, screaming, swearing, and what sounds like a grand piano being pulled down the stairway.

"GET THE FUCK OFF ME!"

"Lady, we're just doing our job!"

I press my nose to the window just as Sue is being pulled out by four policemen. She grips the sides of the doorway, cursing and spitting, her breasts thrust forward like a ship's carved figurine.

PC Pit Bull runs over, prises Sue's hands from the doorway, and three policemen push her from behind, bundling her into the nearby police van. The crowd cheer, while the photographers snap away with delight.

Meanwhile, one by one, the rest of the police stomp back down the stairway, big plastic bags over their shoulders, which they throw into the back of their vans. Then they slam the doors shut, turn on their sirens, and speed off into the night, proud that they'd just saved the world from mortal danger.

Gradually, the crowd disperses; the photographers go back to their hidden spots, their lenses directed back at the Groucho, and Old Compton Street carries on again as if nothing's happened.

The next day, standing on the doorstep, watching the passersby, thinking about the previous night's activities and who our new neighbours would likely be, I catch sight of a big blonde woman stomping toward me, a bottle of

Lucozade under each arm, like mini torpedoes. No! It can't be...

"Hi, Clay!" says Sue, with a big grin on her face as she makes her way back upstairs. "How's business?"

August 12th, 2007: Words of Wisdom?
"You know this shop has a bad vibe, don't you?"

"So many businesses have failed here."

"This shop is in a great location. But every one seems to close after a year."

"Do you know your shop is haunted?"

Hardly a day goes by without someone coming in and imparting comforting words of wisdom. At first we ignored it, thinking hard work, experience, and a good business brain would pull us through. But after 18 months, it seems that there's some truth in all this.

So I sit here, in an empty shop, thrashing out blogs, until my fingers are worn down to stubs and blood drips into the keyboard, focussing on the world outside the window—while Jorge, as if auditioning for Mommie Dearest, throws himself into cleaning the already clean surfaces.

Then, at night, we lie in bed, cuddled up in the damp basement, amongst the rats, drifting off to the romantic sound of someone having their bottom slapped in the brothel above, wondering if we'll last the month, let alone the year.

So, by way of a comparison to the "Isn't life on this street one big, exciting laugh a minute" type blogs which I seem to have, inadvertently, posted, I offer you this one by way of an alternative, so that, should one day these blogs come to an abrupt end, you'll know why.

August 15th, 2007: The Stockpot (in Two Acts)
Jorge and I are outside the Stockpot, the little café at the end of Old Compton Street.

There's a queue to get in—a large group of Americans,

the guy at the front bearing an unfortunate resemblance to Herman Munster. As they appear to be waiting for a large table to match, we push past, taking seats at the back, scanning the menu that I can now recite in my sleep.

Hmmm. Should I go for the spaghetti carbonara or the... I look up. Herman's lurching toward us. Oh, don't sit here! It's cramped enough as it is.

Too late.

He collapses into the next chair, revealing a small, old, mousey-looking man quivering behind him, who takes the seat opposite.

What's interesting about these two is how different they are. Herman's as large as Mouse is small; as loud as he is quiet; as confident as he is nervous. Complete opposites, except for matching thick metal collars soldered around their necks. Lovers? Members of an international slave sect? I nudge Jorge in the ribs, point toward them under the table. He ignores me and stares straight ahead—which I take as *Yes I know. Please don't talk to them.*

The Spanish waiter approaches.

"The roast beef," barks Herman, as if chairing a Parliamentary debate. "Is it rare?" (Bear in mind this is the Stockpot, where all main courses are under £3.)

The waiter scratches his head with his pen, looks puzzled, more used to being asked whether it comes with cabbage. Herman frowns, drums his fingers on the table impatiently. Mouse examines the pepper pot, Jorge's still staring ahead, and I start picking my nails with a fork.

"What I want to know is, is the beef pink or grey?" Herman growls, his drumming fingers getting noticeably louder.

The waiter looks nervous. Herman sweeps a strand of Ozzy Osbourne hair behind his ear and Mouse starts rocking like a mental patient in a straitjacket.

"The beef!" Herman bellows, the drumming fingers

sounding like stampeding horses. "I want to know how it's cooked?"

I clear my throat. Decide to do my bit for the United Nations. "This is the Stockpot," I explain cautiously.

"Meaning?" Herman replies, turning round, flashing me a look that could strip paint.

"That it isn't the Ivy."

He glares at me, stops drumming, jerks his neck strangely, like a "neck orgasm." "Well, I can tell *that* by this awful street!"

"I think you'll find that the Ivy isn't on the best street in town either," I fire back, feeling quite protective about our turf.

Oh, dear. What have I done? Herman's nostrils flare, nose hair wafting like net curtains, and he does the neck thing again. Mouse starts shaking like a virgin about to be deflowered by a humungous penis, and Jorge kicks me under the table. How not to throw a dinner party.

Now, if this was a play (think Beckett), this would be the end of Act One—because nothing really happens again for another 20 minutes. (Did anything happen in the first 20? I hear you say.) So pop to the loo, knock back a G&T, and buy yourself a tub of ice cream.

Ring! Ring! Okay. Time up. Back to your seats. Curtains up. Act Two.

So, we're all eating. Mouse's staring at his food, Jorge's racing through his, and Herman's telling anyone who'll listen what terrible airports we have. Then, just as Herman's draws his first breath in 10 minutes, about to start on our transport system, Mouse pops his head up, takes his big chance, and, looking at Jorge, blurts out, "Are you a body builder?"

It all goes quiet. Mouse squeaks, bobs his head back down, and starts tapping his fork on his plate like a child ODing on additives. Herman does the neck thing. And Jorge, a forkful of food in midair, looks from Mouse to me and back to Mouse again. "Well, I—I was at one time."

Suddenly, it's as if Jorge's answer has opened up the floodgates, both of them suddenly bombarding us with questions.

Herman: "So where do you live?"

Clay: "On this awful street. In a shop basement."

Mouse: "Did you ever compete?"

Jorge: "No, I just did it for a hobby."

Tap. Tap. Tap.

Herman: "I live in Budapest. Have you ever been?"

Clay: "Ummm, no, I haven't."

Nostril flare. Nose hair waft.

Mouse: "Have you heard of the body builder Shaun 'Dino' Davis?"

Jorge: "No, sorry."

Tap. Tap. Tap (faster and more excited).

Herman: "I'm looking to live in a basement in Budapest. Preferably with no windows."

Clay: "That's nice."

Neck thing.

Mouse: "What about Zach 'the Freak' Khan?"

Jorge: "No. Can't say I have."

A crescendo of Tap! Tap! Tap!s.

Then, having run out of questions to answer, we pay our bill, get up to leave, and are just about to walk off when Mouse, with an "it's now or never" look on his face, gazes up at Jorge longingly and shrieks, "I'd love to see you pose! Naked!"

Squeak. Moan. Neck thing.

Applause. Encore. The End.

August 17ᵗʰ, 2007: Having a Three-Way (Conversation)
"Hello, Mum, it's Clay... Yeah, things are okay. Sorry I haven't called you, I've been really busy... Yes, he's fine. How's Dad?... Good. Give him my— Yes, you did tell me...

Mum, you've told me this already... Mum, I've heard this... Can you hold on a second? A customer's just walked in... Hi! Leslie! Nice to see you again!"

"Hello, ducky! What's going on with all this naff weather? Plays havoc with the riah."

"Leslie, could you hold on for a second? I've got my mum on the phone."

"Oh, don't mind me, dear. I'll just sit down here and vada the omis."

"Sorry, Mum... Yes, you've told me that story. Mum, I've really got to— I'm *not* always putting the phone down on you!"

Leslie giggles. "Ohhh! She's having the tiff with the mother!"

"Sorry, Leslie, I'll be with you in a second. I've just got to—"

"Get rid of the mother! 'Ere, what's 'er name?"

"Frances... No, not you, Mum. I'm talking to someone in the shop... Yes, I know you don't like... Okay. Hold on... Leslie, my mum told me to tell you that it's not Frances, it's Frankie."

"Frankie! Oh, I love the name Frankie! Tell your mother, when I was stationed in Africa I shared a bunk bed with a Frankie. Terrible wind! Oh, it were awful. 'Cos he had the top bunk, you see, and it used to waft. I told him, I said, 'Give us a break, ducky, and lay off the Spam!' But he wouldn't have it."

"Mum, the man in the shop... Yes... Leslie... You knew a Leslie? Hold on. Leslie, my mum says she knew a Leslie in the war, stationed just outside Plymouth, and he had terrible wind too!"

"It wasn't me, ducky! Tell your mother it wasn't me. Oh, no! I've never had a problem in that department. I've always been very polite in the bum area. I always leave the room to blow off."

"Mum, it's not the same Leslie. He says he's never had a problem in that... Okay, hold on... Leslie, my mum's saying do you have a sister called Vera?"

"No sisters. But I did know a Vera. Lived at the end of our street. As rough as ninepence. Oh, she was butch, dear. You didn't want to mess with Vera. She'd have your guts for garters!"

"No, Mum, I don't think this one was married. I'm really going to have to go now, Mum... I promise... Bye, Mum..." I put down the receiver. "Phew! Leslie, sorry about that."

Leslie stands up.

"Now where are you going?"

"Well, I can't sit here waitin' round for you all day, ducky! I've got other queens to have the chat with. You've had your ten minutes' worth!"

And out he goes.

August 28th, 2007: Angie Flies Away Again

"I've come to say goodbye!"

"Goodbye?"

"Yes. I have to fly away again," Angie purrs, pouting in front of the fan, her eyes hidden behind a huge pair of black sunglasses. "It's time for my MOT."

"What do you mean?"

"My checkup, honey! It's a year ago today I had the box fitted. So I'm gonna be in hospital for two weeks of tests."

She places her handbag on the floor next to my chair.

"Where do you go for that?" I ask.

"Thailand. They do all the best fannies in Thailand. Here, take a look at this," she says, elbowing me out of my seat and logging on to a sex-change website. "This is the one I had," she says, her finger resting on a long, cavernous example. "Isn't it beautiful?"

I peer over her shoulder. "It looks, er...like a very pretty oven glove."

She ignores me, carries on staring at the screen. "Hmmm. I might ask them to make me a bit less fleshier while I'm there. Maybe a half-inch off either side."

"So you won't be here on the sixth September, then?"

She looks up, removes her sunglasses, fixing them in her hair. "On the sixth September I'll have a surgeon's face between my legs!"

"That's a shame. I thought you might want to come to Sebastian Horsley's book launch with me. Do you know him?"

"Of course I know Sebastian. He's very charming."

"You know Sebastian?" I gasp.

"Yes," she replies, halfheartedly, engrossed in the screen. "Honey, do you think I should have some lipo while I'm at it?" She pulls the skin underneath her toned upper arm.

"Angie, there's nothing there. You look gorgeous the way you are!"

She swivels round, crossing her long legs, like that scene in *Basic Instinct*. "Clay! Look at this!" she says, sweeping her hand from her head to the floor. "The way I am has taken work. A lot of work. You think all this comes easy? No. It's hours and hours on the Stairmaster. Discipline, honey. Discipline." She picks her handbag off the floor, smiles, puts her sunglasses back on. "I know what you're thinking. I may be shallow, but at least I'm beautiful and shallow."

She stands up. "I have to go. I've got a dilating date with Mr. Big."

She walks to the door, then stops. Looks back over her shoulder, lifting her sunglasses again. "I'll be back in two weeks. Get ready for another unveiling!"

She gives me a wink and out she goes—head held high, down Old Compton Street, handbag swishing from side to side.

I stand by the doorway, waving her off. Admiring her for what she's still going through. Then, just as I'm about to go back in, I notice someone walking toward me. I stop. Squint. No! Is that Sue? It is! But it's nothing like the Sue I last saw…

August 29th, 2007: A Happy Ending

It's late.

I'm sitting inside. Usual spot.

A young girl. Could be my sister. Just outside. A small red bag slung over her shoulder, the type they carry at school. Probably from school. She on one corner, pimp on the other. They chat. Laugh. Then he nods and she approaches a man walking past. "Business?" she asks him. He hurries on. Head down. And she blows into her hands to keep warm. Asks if she can go home.

Across the street a little old Chinese woman fishes inside a dustbin with her umbrella, pulls out a brown paper bag, opens it, finds a half-eaten muffin, puts it in her pocket. Smiles. Then reaches in again. Deeper now.

And just behind me, a businessman walks out of the brothel, looks right, left, marches briskly on, phoning home. "Sorry I'm late, luv. Been out with the lads."

A little bit of Heaven. A little bit of Hell.

Then Soho Books closes. The lights dim, the shutters are pulled down.

Now everyone's gone. The street's empty. Just me.

In a second I'll close my laptop. Walk downstairs. Take a tablet. And, in minutes, sleep.

Dreaming, dreaming of a happy ending.

August 29th, 2007: A "New Sue"

So I'm standing in the shop doorway when a vision in white fleece and leggings approaches. Who could it be? She's smiling at me, so she seems to know who I am. Hold on… It's Sue!

Now, when I last saw Sue she looked completely different.

A mass of mammaries, matronly hips, with thighs that could crush a small country and a bum to finish it off. But this Sue...well... She's grinning not growling, walking not waddling, half the woman she once was. Literally.

"Sue! You look...amazing! What happened?"

" 'Ad a bypass, din't I."

"A heart bypass?"

"Stomach."

"You had a stomach bypass?"

"I 'ad to. Doctor made me. I was gettin' really bad back pains."

"Well, you look fantastic!"

And she does. I'd never have guessed it was her; and, dare I say it, nestling in that face, the face that launched a thousand blow jobs, is quite a pretty woman.

"Thanks," she replies, nonchalantly. "I've lost nearly four and a half stone."

"That's incredible!"

"That's what the punters are sayin'. Although some of them are missing the old titties."

I take a quick peep. Oh. I see what she means. They're definitely now more "pancake" than "projectile." Oops! She's spotted me. Back to the face.

"But you must feel a helluva lot better?"

"Well, I'm still gettin' the pains, but I've always been a greedy bitch so I 'ad no choice."

"So you can't eat much now?"

"I keep tryin' to shovel it in but me stomach's shrunk so much I end up pukin' it back up!" she says, smiling.

Sue smiling! Wow! Sue never smiles. Never. The only time I've ever seen Sue smile was when she pushed a drunk out of the brothel, giving him a big right-hander, smack on the face. As she made her way back upstairs she gave me a quick smile, as if to say, *No one fucks with Sue!*

But now look at her! From super size to size zero. Sue's

become a swan. But, with all this weight loss, will she still be a force to be reckoned with? Will she still be able to guard her patch? Or has HRH Sue become just another hand (job) maiden?

As we chat, a dishevelled-looking guy with a can of lager in his hand peers up the brothel doorway. Sue stops talking. Looks over. Her face changes. Eyes narrowing, hands curling. Uh-oh! Wonder Woman in a shell suit about to attack.

"Hey, you!" she yells. "Fuck off outta there! It ain't a halfway house for the friggin' homeless, ya know!"

Hmmmm. I think it's safe to say that Sue's position on this street is still very much in place.

September 2nd, 2007: Soho Square—Leslie's Story

"Well, fancy seeing you here, ducky!"

"I didn't know you came here!"

"Oh, I'm here all the time, dear. It's my favourite spot."

"Yeah, it's peaceful isn't it?"

Leslie takes a seat on the bench next to me, crosses his legs. Then leans back, breathing in deeply, exhaling slowly. We don't speak. For a minute. A comfortable minute, as we take it in.

Another minute passes by, one I'm more conscious of, and I try to think of something, something to start us off.

"We don't have to speak," he says, as if sensing my discomfort. "Although I know you're itching to put something in that diary of yours, aren't you, Anne?"

I laugh. "You know me so well."

"No, not really," he says, raising an eyebrow that seems to frame his face. "But that's okay. I knew someone just like you many years ago."

Leslie's different today. Friendly. A glint in his eye, like he's decided today's the day he's going to tell me something. So I sit quietly as he licks his forefinger, the way he does, running it up and down his eyebrow, the way he does, up and down, up and down. And as I watch, I'm transported back, a kid again, watching my mother sitting in front of her bedside mirror, as she pencils in her eyebrows, up and down, so precise, so steady, wanting desperately to try it for myself, but having a vague feeling, and not really sure why, that it'd be wrong to ask.

I snap back to the moment. "This person... Why was he like me?"

"Because he was guarded," Leslie replies, guardedly. "Because he was a writer."

Then his finger stops still, on his eyebrow, paused and poised, while he too reflects, he too is transported back.

I wait a few seconds, feeling there's more to come, if I just prompt. "Where did you meet?"

"What, dear?" he says, as if coming out of a spell, looking slightly confused.

"The writer. Where did you meet him?"

He hesitates. Smirks. "In your shop," he bats back nonchalantly, looking down at his brogues, which he points like a ballerina.

"In my shop? You met him in my shop? What a coincidence!"

"Not really. Why do you think I've been coming in? It ain't just to vada your eke, ducky! There's memories in that shop of yours."

"What kind of a shop was it?" I ask eagerly, full of questions, ignoring his sharp tongue. "How long ago?"

His face lights up. The first time I've seen him look this happy.

"Oh, it wasn't a shop back then, dear. It was a restaurant. Not a posh restaurant, but still... It was somewhere to be seen. Italian. What was its name?" He licks his finger again, this time using it to pat down his hair. "Torino's? Something like that. Full of gangsters and celebrities and musicians, it was. Full of 'em, dear! I even saw Charlie Chaplin in there once. Oh, and the place was alive. Remember, this was the

60s," he reminds me. "The Beatles were living above the French House. The first rock and roll clubs on the street. It was so exciting back then..." He trails off again, lost in memories.

"And that's where you met?"

"Yes. Yes, that's where we met. Sitting in my usual spot. Your spot!"

"My spot?" I reply, leaning closer, engrossed in the story.

"Where you write that diary of yours, ducky! That was my spot. Just by the window. I'd sit there for hours. Just watching the trade mince by."

"And that's where you met..." I repeat, trying to direct the conversation and get a name.

"Where I met Charlie," he says, looking across the park, deep in thought.

I'm just about to ask him if they were friends or lovers when, again, he seems to read my mind.

"We were lovers," he says, smiling. "And then... And then, one day, he broke my heart." The smile disappears.

Silence.

I reach over to touch his leg. "I'm sorry."

He recovers quickly. Dismisses my words. Recoils. "Oh, don't be sorry for me, dear. What will be, will be. Plenty more where that one came from!"

Although when I look at him, closely, into his eyes, I sense there wasn't, ever again. Now I understand why Leslie is the way he is. It's all fitting into place.

"Did you love him?"

"Of course I loved him!" he fires back, reaching for the white hanky hanging from his breast pocket. As he dabs at his eyes, I look away, feeling awkward, not sure how to react.

"Of course I loved him," he says again, quieter now. "But the bastard was too scared to let it happen!" He sniffs. "Five years, we were together. Five years! Then, one day, out of the blue, I received a letter saying he still loved me but he'd got married. And I never saw him again."

I look toward the park, back at Leslie, back to the park. Then he grips the side of the bench, rises slowly—as I thought he probably would, as if he'd given too much.

"There, that's enough for today. You've had your story," he says, stuffing his hanky back in his pocket and walking slowly, slowly away.

September 4th, 2007: I've Been Rumbled! Again.

Oh, dear. I've been rumbled again. More of my characters have found out I've been writing about them.

I thought MySpace was meant to be this huge entity; you post something up and then it's gone forever, floating around in space, ready to zap itself up ET's bottom, never to be seen again. Apparently not. It's either not as huge as I'd imagined or ET's had colonic irrigation, because my little blogs have just plopped back out and are now splattered all over Soho. And now Sue's found 'em! Yes. I know. My sphincter went tight, too.

So here I am, in my usual spot, staring aimlessly at my fingers, which are taking a well-earned rest on my keyboard, when suddenly there's a Tap! Tap! Tap! on the window. I turn round.

Uh-oh! Right in front of me, faces pressed against the glass, stars of stage and semen, Sue and Maggie!

"Come 'ere!" Sue mouths seductively, with all the allure of Hannibal Lecter on a dinner date. "I wan' a word with you!"

Forgive me, Father, for I have sinned. I slink toward the doorway, hands in pockets, holding on to my testicles for dear life. This can only mean one thing. Someone has "blog blabbed."

"Er... Hi, girls! How, er...how are you both doing?" I squeak, looking to Maggie, normally the "tart with a heart," for support.

She glares back, her breasts already in firing position. "We're okay. *Considering*."

"Yeah," Sue growls, taking a step closer. "*Considering*."

Yikes! By now I'm standing in a huge pool of urine, which gushes out the shop doorway, down the street, into a nearby drain. Sue takes another step closer. "A little bird has told us that you've been writin' stories about us."

"Yeah! On the Internet, innit!" snarls Maggie.

Okay, I give up. It's no use. There's no way out of this. So I take my hands out of pockets, ready to sacrifice my testicles in the name of art. "Yes. Yes. I have," I admit. "Nothing bad. But, yes, I have been writing about you. I'm writing a book about Soho and you two are in it. Do you, er…mind?"

Silence.

I close my eyes. Wondering how I'll break it to Jorge that I'm now a eunuch. But—nothing. I open one eye. They look at me, then at each other, and then back to me again.

"Course we don't mind, darlin'!" Maggie says, laughing.

"Nah, we don't mind!" says Sue good-humoredly. "We're already on there, luv! Log on to punternet.com. They've got some really good reviews on there 'bout us. Apparently we're the best maids in the business!"

"Yeah! We got five stars!"

And with that, they make their way back upstairs, giggling away like two naughty schoolgirls.

September 12th, 2007: June 18th, 1964

Leslie's sitting outside Costa.

A coffee. A cigarette. Elbow on the table. Gold buttons on his blazer. A white hanky in his breast pocket. Stylish, camp, and immaculate. A cross between Dame Maggie and the end-of-the-pier comedians who used to frequent the one gay bar in my home town.

As I watch, a truck drives slowly past, a waitress steps outside to clean the tables, and Pam, the Fag Lady, shuffles by. It's like a film set. All it needs is for a director to say, "Okay. Let's go for another take," and then the story will unfold. Which it does when I step outside…

"Leslie!"

He turns his head, for a second not quite recognising me. Somewhere else.

"Oh, hello, dear. Sorry, I was…"

"Somewhere else?"

"Yes."

"Can I join you?"

"Of course. Pull up a pew. Rest your lallies," he says, moving the table a fraction so that I can squeeze round.

"Maybe I should get a coffee first."

"No, here—have this. I can't drink this foreign muck."

So I sit down. Take a sip. Look back toward the shop.

"Want one?" Leslie says, offering me one of his cigarettes.

"No, thanks. I… I just wanted to say, the last time we met, sorry if—"

"Oh forget it, ducky!" He dismisses my apology with a camp flick of his wrist, as if brushing away an irritating fly. "It was just a silly old queen reminiscing. Let's not talk about that again."

"Why not?"

Uh-oh. Wrong thing to say. He narrows his eyes, arches an eyebrow, like the wicked stepmother from a Disney film.

"Because, ducky, there're some things that are just best left—that's why not! When you get to my age—and you ain't that far away—then you'll know what I'm talking about! So let's just leave it, shall we?" He twists his head sharply to one side as if an odious fart has suddenly wafted under his nose.

I try and suppress a nervous giggle. "Okay."

It goes quiet. Momentarily. Then he starts tapping his nails on the table. "Oh, typical you! If I'm not spilling the beans then we just sit here in silence."

"No it's not that—I was just thinking…"

"And what, pray tell, is ticking away in Anne Frank's brain today?" he asks, cupping his chin in his hand and fluttering his eyelashes like an aging pantomime dame.

"I was just wondering…" I reply, choosing my words with care. "If it's a story that's best left, then why do you keep coming back here?"

He leans back in his chair, clutches his tie as if I'm a mugger about to snatch his pearls, his nostrils flaring open like windsocks. "You, my dear… You wanna try sticking that beak of yours where the sun don't shine!" he admonishes. Then he leans forward again, prodding me with his forefinger. "Although," he adds, mischievously. "I'll admit. You do have a point." He looks at me studiously, clicks his fingers. "Okay! Let me explain. Do you have a favourite film?"

"Yes."

"And how many times have you watched it?"

"I don't know. Ten. Twenty."

"And why do you keep watching it? It's not as if you don't know the ending, is it?"

"No. I suppose it's because the more I watch it, the more details are revealed."

"Exactly! Well, all of this…" he says, sweeping his hand across the street. "This is *my* favourite film. And coming here, all those details, they all come flooding back."

I nod. "Oh, okay. I understand. But, have you really been coming here for forty years?"

"Of course I haven't been coming here for forty years!" he fires back. "What kind of stupid question is that? What do you think I am? A nun on a pilgrimage? No, ducky. I was here when it was glamorous. Not the tatsville it is today."

He reaches for the cigarette pack on the table. Takes one out. Lights it. Takes a short, sharp drag without inhaling, blowing the smoke quickly, upwards. "Actually, I've avoided this street for years. Years I've avoided it for, dear! Then a month or so ago, I was trolling along, and somehow I ended up back here." And for a moment he drifts off, two well-manicured fingers holding the cigarette poised near his lips. "Then I saw you tapping away in that window of yours, writing that damn diary, and it all came back... How we met, where we used to sit. And now I just can't let it go..."

He stares at the shop, alone in his thoughts.

I reach for my coffee, and he snaps back, taking another vicious drag of his cigarette. Like a scene from an old Bette Davis film. Then he looks back at me suspiciously. "Oh, you've done it again, haven't you? Dragging my story out of me. You devious little witch—taking advantage of a kind-hearted old queen like me. You'd have me pension too, given half a chance, wouldn't you?"

I laugh. He stubs his cigarette out. Grins. "Now, I hope you're gonna remember this because I ain't repeating it!"

"I'll try."

"And if this goes in that Space diary of yours..."

"MySpace."

"Whatever! I want me name changed. You 'ear? Something exotic. Nothing common. And don't shorten it, either. You know I can't abide that."

"Ummm...it's a bit late now."

But he's not listening anymore. Just staring at the shop. Doesn't speak for at least a minute. Then he starts. Quietly.

"I was quite the dish back then. Foundation on the visage. All very dolly. Sitting in my usual spot. When in walked Charlie. June, it was. June the eighteenth, nineteen sixty-four," he says slowly, staring intently ahead. "And I looked at him. And he looked at me. And I just knew. Do you know what I mean?"

"Yes. Yes, I think I do."

"He asked if he could share my table, and then he just sat down, and I thought, bloody cheek! And that was it. It was as quick as that. The best five years I've ever had. Sounds naff, doesn't it? But it was. Didn't realise 'til it was over that I'd never have that again. Well, you don't, do you? It didn't cross my mind. We were having so much fun... It just didn't cross my mind."

I'm looking at him as he talks, while he stares at the shop. It's all playing out in my mind.

"Out every weekend, we were. Mambo's on Greek Street—Lord Montagu's hangout. The 2i's, where Tommy Steele sang. And always your shop to eat. It was always your shop. But you know what? I should have known something would go wrong. It was just too good. And that's not real life, is it?"

He looks at me. Runs his fingers through his hair. "I was okay with it. You know? The gay thing. But he wasn't." He pauses. Lets the sentence linger.

"Oh, in Soho we were fine, but once you stepped outside it was a different story. Persecution comes from within, you know. That's what I used to say to him. And you know something else? All the time, he was seeing women. I mean, really seeing them. Sleeping with them. And I just turned a blind eye. Because I knew what we had, I knew he couldn't get it from them. So I just let it go. I suppose I thought, Well, if I make him choose, what if he chooses the easier life? Because it was still illegal back then, you know. So I just put up with it." He sighs. "I suppose that seems weak to you, doesn't it?"

"No. I can relate to that."

"You can?"

I don't answer. Look away. Wait for him to continue.

"So, when I received the letter. Although it was a shock and I was upset n'all, in another way I knew what he was battling with…had been battling with."

"And you never saw him again?"

"Never. He changed jobs. Flat. Everything. I could've tried to track him down but I was just too hurt by then. And I couldn't beg. It would've been the final kick in the teeth. Maybe if I'd have known back then that…"

He reaches for his cigarettes again, about to light one, then decides against it, carries on staring at the shop. "All these years I've tried to blank it out. All these years. But this past month, it's as fresh as…"

There's a vibration in my pocket. My mobile. I pull it out, look at the number. The shop. Jorge's voice. "Clay, can you come back so I can pop out?"

"Coming!"

I put my mobile back in my pocket. "Leslie, I've got to—"

"I know, dear. You've got to go. Don't worry. Get back to your shop."

"Are you—"

"Nothing wrong with me, dear! Nothing another fag and a proper coffee won't fix. Go on—get back to work! Plenty of handbag to be made on a day like this."

"Bye, then."

I stand up, am just about to leave, when he touches my hand. I look from our hands to his face.

"It's good to talk, dear," he says, smiling. "Thank you."

So I walk back to the shop. Sit down. Look across the street and watch as he smokes another cigarette. Then I open my laptop and start typing. Remembering everything he's just said. Letting his story gradually unfold…

September 12th, 2007: An Hour Later
A coffee. A cigarette. An old queen.

Sipping. Smoking. Staring at the shop opposite. Dabbing his eyes with a white hanky. Thinking. Then he rises. Slowly.

Using the table as support. Straightens his tie. Pats down his hair and starts walking.

After a few yards, he stops. Looks back. For a few seconds. He sees someone typing by the shop window. He runs a finger across an eyebrow. Sighs. Then turns round and walks slowly on.

Home.

He hangs his jacket behind the door. Takes a key from his pocket. Stares at it. Silent. Walks toward the little door underneath the stairs. Opens it. Reaches inside. Pulls the light cord. Lowers his head. Steps inside.

He looks round. Treads carefully amongst faded cardboard boxes, looking, looking; moving one box on top of another until he finds the one he wants. Then he stops. Hesitates. Picks it up. Blows dust off the lid and places it on the floor, removing an old brown envelope.

A deep breath.

Trembling, he pulls out a handful of faded black-and-white photos. Two men. Suits, ties, Brylcreemed hair, smiling. Smiling in every photo. Carnaby Street, Wardour Street, and then, last one, sitting inside a restaurant on Old Compton Street. Smiling.

"Charlie," the old queen whispers, his voice as shaky as his hand. "Oh, Charlie…"

I finish typing. Close my laptop. Look out the window, down Old Compton Street. Smile. "See you soon, Leslie."

September 28th, 2007: A Talk on the Wild Side
3 P.M. My mobile rings.

"Clay, where are you?" says Jorge.

"Having a coffee at the gym."

"I wish you'd been here a few minutes ago."

"Why?"

"Guess who just came in?"

"The Queen?"

"Close. Holly Woodlawn."

"Who?"

"Holly Woodlawn. The drag queen legend. Andy Warhol's Factory superstar."

"Oh, no! I missed her! I knew she was in town. I can't believe it! Tell me everything. Hold on, let me get my notebook... Right. Go on. What did she say?"

"Well..."

"I want to hear everything!"

"Clay, I'm thinking! Okay. So I'm sitting behind the desk and I look up and see Rupert in the doorway, and he's supporting this frail Latin man."

"Man? She wasn't in drag, then? What was she wearing? What was her hair like?"

"Let me think..."

"I need all the details for my blog!"

"Okay, Clay. I'll tell you everything. Just give me a minute. Let me just think back to when they first stepped through the door..."

"Hola!" a voice calls from the doorway.

I look up. See two men—Clay's friend Rupert and a frail man who holds on to the doorframe with one hand and beckons me over with the other, his fingernails painted a vivid purple. Who's that? He looks vaguely familiar.

So I stand up. Walk over. And as I get closer I notice a shock of receding red hair, shades of burgundy dress, a man in pain, as if about to fall if Rupert wasn't there to support him. And then I notice his eyebrows. Perfectly plucked. Eyebrows that J-Lo would kill for. Eyebrows that could only belong to—

"I understand you speak Spanish," the frail man says in an American accent.

"I do. I'm Cuban," I reply.

"I'm Puerto Rican. That makes us sisters."

I smile. He smiles back.

"I told you I'd find a Spanish speaker for you," Rupert whispers into the man's ear, before introducing us. "Jorge, this is Holly Woodlawn. Holly, meet Jorge."

"Oh, Holly doesn't need an introduction!" I say, laughing, switching to Spanish.

Holly grins. "I haven't spoken in Spanish for ages."

"But you're from Miami Beach. My home town."

"Oh, my moon was never over Miami, my dear. I left when I was very young."

And leave she did. A journey everyone my age knew by heart.

Holly came from Miami F-L-A,
Hitchhiked her way across the USA,
Plucked her eyebrows on the way,
Shaved her legs and then he was a she...

"Holly, I know. I've read everything about you. I've read every Warhol art book, every biography. I know everything about Edie, Joe Dallesandro. I know all about you crazy guys."

She laughs. "Yes, those were the days."

"When I was growing up in Palm Beach there was a rich socialite there who became one of Warhol's 'girls.' What was her name? I just can't think of it."

"Candy Darling?" Holly asks, raising one of her celebrated eyebrows.

"No, not Candy," I reply, shaking my head. "A socialite..."

"Oh! Oh! Baby Jane Holzer!" Holly says excitedly, almost toppling over.

"That's it! Baby Jane Holzer. Isn't it strange, though, when the Factory finished she went straight back to Palm Beach—back to the 'ladies who lunch.' "

"They all returned, dear. Eventually," Holly reminds me.

"Yes, it was like nothing ever happened."

"Yes—her and Edie. They were Warhol's socialite trophies. The real upper class."

As she talks, I visualize her at the Factory, the place covered in a sea of aluminium foil, no surface left uncovered—Holly talking incessantly in her Nuyorican accent for hours on end, with Andy occasionally adding, "Oh, yeah. That's great."

"What about Robert Morso? What happened to him?" I ask, desperate to hear anything about that period that I don't already know.

"Robert Morso?" Holly replies, looking puzzled, trying to place the name.

"You know. Warhol's head silk screener. He went on to do his own series called Morso Torso, full of beautiful naked men encrusted in wild glittery colours."

"Yes, of course! Robert. But you know there were so many silk screeners back then. Andy never lifted a finger," Holly says, speaking in English again. "I don't know what all the fuss is about with all these fake Warhols."

"The Warhol Foundation has to approve them, I believe," Rupert points out.

"Yes, but he didn't do them, anyway. So what's all the fuss about?"

Then Holly starts to flick through the rack of postcards, taking one out, the one showing the "Model" sign next door.

"That 'Model' sign refers to the brothel just above our shop. Please, it's yours," I offer.

"A brothel postcard? For me? How appropriate."

Rupert smiles. "Holly, Jorge moved here from Provincetown."

"P-town? I performed there once," she says, directing her gaze back at me. "With Jackie Curtis. We were in a play called Women in Revolt. Back in the seventies."

"Really? I was at school in Miami back then."

As she recounts more stories, my mind drifts back to the

days when I was first reading about her, when I was at high school. Cardinal Newman in Palm Beach.

I was the poorest kid there. My 1973 Mustang Fastback laughed at. My only extravagance, my Halston outfit—a black turtleneck and a slick black Italian suit that I'd saved up for teaching tennis to rich little brats. But although they all looked down their noses at me, I knew more about art history and the good life than all of them put together. I'd lived that life in Cuba before we were forced to flee when I was a child. The houses. Drinking out of Baccarat glasses. The fact that I'm drinking out of a Dixie cup now will never change those fantastic memories.

I look back at Holly. It's funny, just as we were fleeing Cuba for Miami, she was fleeing Miami for New York.

"Jorge, we must go," Rupert says with a smile.

I snap back to the present.

"Sorry, I was, er…somewhere else. Thank you for coming in, Holly. You brought back such good memories. And can I just say, you're not like today's drag queens—all dress and little talent—you were always a true star!"

"Thank you, Jorge," she laughs as she turns to leave, grabbing Rupert's arm again for support. "Oh, and darling, by the way, I still am!"

And with that, the most famous drag queen the world has ever seen hobbled slowly out the door and back down Old Compton Street.

October 3rd, 2007: Drama at the Post Office
Poland Street Post Office.

Two Indian women are serving behind the counter, chatting away, seemingly oblivious to not only the queue that stretches all the way out the door, but also the pandemonium in their midst. Kids crying, hoodies arguing, pit bulls barking, women tut-tutting. A full-scale chav riot about to ensue at any moment.

Then, just above the din, a voice cries out, "Oh, do hurry it up, dears! I think you'll find Ramadan finished three weeks ago!"

The women immediately stop talking, look over. Then one walks slowly toward the counter, behind which stands an old man, eyebrow arched, a pinched expression on his face, one hand on hip and the other leaning on a long yellow umbrella.

"I'm sorry to drag you away from such important tittle-tattle," Leslie says sarcastically as the woman approaches. "But I want to die of old age in my bed, not stood 'ere waiting for a stamp!"

Gradually the crowd stop talking. Nudge each other. Grin. Even the pit bulls pull up chairs to watch the spectacle.

"What do you want?" the woman asks disinterestedly as she takes a seat.

"I want to send this package first class to Manchester," Leslie says, pulling a brown padded envelope from his jacket pocket and plonking it on the scales. "Although, judging by your efficiency, I'm sure our definitions on what constitutes first class differ wildly."

The woman narrows her eyes and sighs, then looks at the scale monitor. "Seven pounds fifty."

"Seven pounds fifty?" shrieks Leslie, turning around dramatically to address the queue of people behind him, who by now are giggling away at his performance. "Seven pound bloody fifty? I want it delivered in a van not a bleedin' limousine!"

She stares at him impassively.

"It's daylight robbery! That's what it is!" he screeches, whipping the package back off the scales. "If everyone used second class there'd be no need for first!"

Then he grabs a 10-pound note out of his leather wallet and shoves it quickly under the window as if it's riddled with a deadly disease. "Here! And I want a receipt too, if it's not too much to ask!"

Without flinching, the woman prints one off and pushes the receipt and the stamps back under the window, staring back at him.

"And?" says Leslie expectantly, eyebrow arched as high as a railway tunnel.

"And?" the woman repeats blankly.

"Listen, dear," he says, tapping the dividing window with his umbrella. "I don't know how it works in your culture, but in ours, once you've finished serving a customer, it's customary to say 'Thank you,' or 'Have a good day.' It signifies the end of the transaction. Then both parties can continue on their merry little way."

"Thank you! Have a good day!" the woman fires back aggressively.

Uh-oh. Leslie's eyes widen, his nostrils flare, and everyone in the post office takes a deep breath as he leans toward the window, fire coming out of his ears.

"You wanna learn some good old-fashioned British manners! That's what you wanna do, Miss Gandhi!" he hisses back.

And with a sudden swish, almost a pirouette, he spins around again, brushing past the crowd, unaware that everyone in the post office is looking at him wide-eyed, jaws hitting the floor. Then, just as he's about to swan out the door, he catches my eye.

"Oh, hello, ducky!" he says, smiling, as if nothing untoward had taken place. "Gorgeous day, isn't it?"

October 8th, 2007: An Early Christmas Present

Pam, the Fag Lady, is one of the characters of Old Compton Street. A small, squat woman in her late fifties with closely cropped hair and "barn owl" glasses, Pam usually starts begging at midday and finishes once she's collected enough money for a packet of cigarettes and a bed for the night at the Dean Street hostel. She invariably stops off at the shop.

If we've had a good day I'll give her some change, but if not, when she pops her head around the door, I'll hold up the palms of my hands and shrug. Then she'll smile and say, "Okay, just a cuddle, then." So I'll walk over, put my arms around her, and she'll rest her head on my chest for a few seconds, then off she goes again.

Here she comes now…

"Sorry, Pam. Not today. We haven't sold a thing yet," I tell her as she stands in front of the shop doorway, smiling strangely.

"I don't want money," she replies excitedly, grinning from ear to ear, shuffling from one foot to another as if in dire need of the toilet. "I got a Christmas present for you!"

"But it's only October, Pam."

"I know, but I might not have any money at Christmas," she says, chuckling, shuffling toward me, pulling a black cardboard box from her faded Tescos bag. "Open it!" she squeals, thrusting the box in my direction and staring at it with glee.

"What is it?"

"Something nice—I bin savin' up for it! Open it!"

So I open the box and pull out a wooden doll dressed as a nun. "That's, er…nice, Pam. Thank you. I've, er…always wanted a nun doll."

"You haven't finished! Unscrew her head!" she orders, staring at the nun.

So I unscrew the nun's head and, lo and behold, inside the nun there's another nun, slightly smaller, this time without her habit.

"Now unscrew it again," she cries, practically jumping up and down.

And so it goes on, nun after nun, a nun in a corset, a nun in a bra and panties, until I'm left with just a tiny naked nun in my hand.

"Do you like it? Do you like it?" she cries, like a kid at Christmas. "I saved up for it!"

240

"Pam, that's very sweet of you," I reply, popping the nuns back into each other. "But really, you shouldn't have."

"Well, we gotta look out for each other on this street," she reminds me, wagging her finger. Then she gives me a big, beaming smile. "Now, can I have two pounds, please?"

October 10th, 2007: He's Here!

Wednesday morning.

I'm sitting by the window, buffing my nails, catching up on world politics in *Boyz* magazine, when in walks…

"I had to come in and see you, ducky. Oh, I had to!"

"Hi, Leslie. What's the matter?"

"He's here!"

"Who's here?"

"Charlie!"

"Charlie?"

"Yes, Charlie! Are you deaf?"

"You mean your ex?"

"Yes, Charlie! My ex! Who'd ya think I meant? The Prince of bleedin' Wales?"

"Where is he?"

"In London!"

"I thought—"

"Dolly saw him. Gettin' on a bus in Charing Cross Road, he was. This is your fault!"

"My fault?"

"Oh, don't play the innocent with me, dear. It was you who got me thinking about him again. All those years together. This shop. And now he's back! You've willed this on me, you have!"

"I didn't do a thing!"

"Well, I wouldn't put it past you. Now what am I going to do? Oh, I'm ruined. Ruined, I am!"

"Hold on. Calm down a minute—"

"Calm down? Calm down, she says! How can I calm

down? I was hoping he'd be dead! But he's here! Oh, Gawd 'elp us! Get up, dear. Give a queen a seat."

"Here you go."

"That's better… Ohhh! I just thought! What if he's read that Space diary of yours?"

"MySpace."

"Oh, whatever. What if he's read it? 'Ere, what did you put in there about us?"

"Nothing—"

"You lying little minx!"

"I've just been writing what you've told me."

"Where's me pills? You're driving me to a stroke. That's what you're doin'!"

"Do you want some water?"

"No, I don't! You've done enough damage! Rubbing my name through the dirt. Spreading evil gossip. I told you I've got a reputation to think of."

"I only—"

"I'm a contributor to the Royal Opera House, don't you know!"

"You told me. Listen, Leslie, I—"

"Oh, don't you 'listen, Leslie' me. If you're behind all this I'll 'ave your guts for garters! Don't think I won't!"

"Leslie, if Charlie's in London—how's it my fault?"

"Because I wouldn't be 'ere talking about him now if it wasn't for you! Honestly, every time I turn me back there you are—you're like trapped wind! I'll 'ave that drink now."

I hand him a glass of water. "So what would you do if you bumped into him?"

"Slap him round the face. Tell him how much he'd aged. How married life obviously wasn't all it was cracked up to be."

"You wouldn't!"

"Oh, yes, I would! Then I'd tell him I came into a lot of money when he left but now it's nearly all gone and what's left's going to a cats' home."

"You've rehearsed this, haven't you?"

"Course I've rehearsed this! What do you think I've been doin' the past forty years? Making peace with it? I did think about tellin' him that I'd met a Russian prince, but thought that might be a bit much."

"Possibly."

"Oh but it's been a terrible state of affairs, it has. I haven't slept a wink." He sighs. "Anyway, enough of him. How are you, my dear?"

"Yeah. I'm good."

"What about that writing of yours? Don't think I didn't see you makin' notes just then."

"Well, I'm still doing it. Oh, by the way, I signed a book contract last month with a US publisher—based on my MySpace stuff."

"I told you! I told you all this writing would be worth it one day!"

"You were the one who said—"

"Rubbish. I've encouraged you every step of the way. I was only sayin' to Dolly last week. I said, 'Dolly, he writes this diary and shows it to everyone.' "

"What did she say?"

"She's a 'he,' dear. Dolly's me sister."

"Oh, okay. What did he say?"

"She said, 'What's the world bleedin' coming to!' I told her, I said, 'Dolly, dear, it's all changed since our day. They use computers these days. That's how they find boyfriends.' 'Computers?' she said. 'What happened to good old-fashioned cottaging and a troll up the heath?' She's getting on a bit, is Dolly. Anyway, what were you saying, ducky?"

"I was telling you about my book—"

"Oh, yes. When's it coming out?"

"Next—"

"Now, you just remember what I told you, missy. You put me in it and I want me name changed. Something exotic."

"I'll remember."

"Charlie was a writer. Oh, yes. He'd write for hours, he would. About art, art history. All these 'pop artists.' 'Installation' things. I said to him, 'If you can't hang it on the wall I'm not interested!' But he loved all that. Actually, it was Charlie that got me into opera."

"Really?"

"Of course 'really.' You think I'm making it up?"

"I meant 'really' as in 'how interesting.' "

"Mmmm. But he loved his art, did Charlie. Very creative, he was. Oh yes. Creative in *all* areas, was Charlie."

"What do you mean?"

"In the bedroom department, dear! Do I have to draw you a flow diagram?"

"What did you do?"

"I'm not telling you, you filthy homo! Oh, but he loved all that dressing up stuff. Underwear. Outfits. Anyway, that's enough tittle-tattle for today. Can't be doin' with thinking about all that messy business. Not at my age. That's what did the back in."

He stands up, slowly.

"Are you going now?"

"Of course I'm going now! What do you think I'm doin'? Warming up for a yoga class?"

"Okay, Leslie. I'll see you soon."

"The way you're hauntin' me at the moment, dear, I've no doubt you will. Anyway, lovely seeing you again, dear. TTFN, ducky! TTFN!"

October 16th, 2007: How to Visit a Brothel

I live and work below a brothel, and having spent many a long hour sitting by the window watching guys come and go or chatting with the "girls" who work above, I feel I am in a very good position to write about the etiquette on how to visit one.

This is very important stuff, so pay attention. Here goes...

Rule 1: Dress

Dress for the occasion, or at least wash. I know you're not going on a date with Nicole Kidman, but put yourself in the girls' position. They have to deal with smelly drunks, unshaven drug addicts, and, heaven forbid, men in corduroys. So do them a favour. Shower beforehand. And, as the genital region is likely to feature quite prominently in your love tussle, special attention to this area wouldn't go amiss.

Rule 2: Approaching the brothel

When walking past the Dean Street brothel do not on any account look nervous. Do not stop, retrace your steps, or dither. The fact that you've got this far would indicate that you're "begging for it." Sex is just like breathing and we all have to breathe. So, once you see the neon sign, march confidently up the stairway and don't pay any attention to the nosy old queen gawping at you through the window next door (me).

Rule 3: Brothel rules

All financials arrangements are conducted beforehand, and the price varies according to what you pick from the menu. Don't haggle. This isn't a car boot sale. The price is what the price is. If you can't afford £50 go and see the Italian hooker who haunts Peter Street. "She" will be happy to oblige.

Rule 4: Check for orifices

While we're on the subject, how many times have I heard a man running down the stairway shouting, "No one told me she had a dick!" Oh, at least once. Do not assume that every hole has a silver lining. They don't. Some have stitches. If in doubt, ask to see "the goods." This isn't Benetton. You can't have your money back if it doesn't fit.

Rule 5: Orgasms

"Ohhhh, yeahhhh, baby! You're so big! Give it to me, big boy!"

On hearing this, do not assume that the woman below you wants to be kissed/married/taken on a date. I hear it echoing down the stairway 24 times a day.

Rule 6: Leaving

Don't run out. If you want to run in, okay, fine, but running out equals guilt. Here's what to do... Once you've mopped up, pop your Viagra'd penis back into your greying Y-fronts or oversized boxers (you can tell this isn't a gay brothel, can't you?), pull up your slacks, button up your polyester no-iron shirt, and then, calmly, breathing deeply, make your way slowly back down the stairway.

Once outside, don't be nervous—march briskly on, just as you would if you were leaving your local bank after making a small deposit. (Which, in effect, you just have.)

N.B. Again, pay no attention to the queen with his nose stuck to the glass. He's bored to tears and is just trying to fill in time.

October 20th, 2007: Winter

The tables are empty outside Pulcinella. The owner stands in the doorway, dejected, hands in pockets. At Costa it's the same. Just one person sitting outside, like the Little Match Girl, her hands wrapped round her coffee cup for warmth. Winter hits Old Compton Street.

Pam passes by.

"Sorry, not today, Pam."

She looks at me, waiting for a change of heart; trudges on.

David the dealer shouts through the doorway, "Hi, Boss! Where's your partner?"

"In Miami, visiting his Dad. He's been very ill."

"Oh..." he replies, staring at the floor, probably thinking back to his own mother, who died the month before. "That's too bad, man."

Two drunks fall against the window as I type. Although they're just inches away, in their oblivion, they don't see me.

Then one grabs the other and helps him toward the brothel doorway. They get as far as the first flight of stairs before they're out again; the ferocity of Sue's voice has a strangely sobering effect.

The phone rings.

"Clay?"

"Jorge?"

"You okay?"

"Yeah. You?"

"I'm okay."

"How's your dad?"

"He has good moments." Jorge sighs, his voice trailing off. "Do you want me to pick you anything up?"

"No. I don't think so."

"How's the shop doing?"

"Don't ask."

"That bad?"

"You know, I wouldn't blame you if you decided not to come back..."

"No. I'm ready to come home."

"Okay."

"What're you doing?"

"Writing."

"How's it going?"

"I dunno... Okay, I guess."

"Clay, go to bed. It's getting late."

"I will. I'm just finishing."

"What are you writing?"

"Nothing interesting... Just the view from the window."

"Okay. I'll call you tomorrow before I leave."

"I love you."

"Me too."

"Say it!"

"I can't. Family are here."

"Chicken!"

He laughs. "Bye."

"Bye."

I finish typing, close down my laptop. Take one last look outside, then head downstairs to bed.

October 21st, 2007: An Interview

As I busy myself this morning with the very important task of picking a cuticle, a voice suddenly pipes up, "Hi! I'm Siddharta Lizcano!"

On looking up, expecting to find a tropical disease, I am surprised to find instead a tall, studenty-looking man.

"I'm creating an audio guide for the Internet about Soho," says Sid excitedly. "And I want to interview you." With that, he thrusts his microphone into my mouth as if it were a sexual organ.

"How lovely," I say, gagging, wondering if I should start bobbing my head.

"Now you probably don't know too much about this area—so don't worry, just answer as best you can."

"Okay, I'll try very hard," I promise.

"Now the first question is: Soho is known for its diversity. In your experience do you think this is true?"

Not wanting to waste my moment of fame on a yes/no answer, and anticipating not drawing breath for at least another 20 minutes, I take a deep lungful of air and begin.

"When I think of diversity, I think of the local inhabitants, people like Pam, the Fag Lady, the homeless woman who trawls these streets from morning to night. I think of Angela, the stunningly beautiful post-op transsexual. I think of people like Sue, the madam from the brothel upstairs, who rules this corner with an iron fist."

Sid's mouth drops open.

"Then there's the Rubbishmen, the Victorian Punk revivalists who live in a Euro wheelie bin in Romilly Street. There's

Dr. Vas Deferens, the local sex therapist. Then there's the dandified artist Sebastian Horsley, who is famous for shagging over 1,000 prostitutes and being crucified in the Philippines. Then we have the—"

"Do you know all these people?" Sid gasps, taking a step back.

"Of course. They're my friends."

"Oh, okay. I'm not sure this will be suitable for the website."

And with that, he runs out.

October 22nd, 2007: A Kashmir Brothel

Within the art establishment, Raqib Shaw is now the new British sensation.

Although artists like Tracey Emin and Damian Hirst garner more publicity, the private and publicity-shy Raqib prefers to let his work speak for itself. Which it did last week at the Sotheby's auction. His monumental painting *The Garden of Earthly Delights*, which he originally sold for £12,000, went for £3 million, outshining the works of Bacon, Warhol, and Banksy.

As Raqib rarely leaves his studio, whenever he visits the shop it's an event, and when he steps in I reach for my little notebook, discreetly scribbling under the counter as he tiptoes daintily around the aisles, selecting clothes as if he's a couture *Supermarket Sweep* contestant. In fact he buys so many I invariably have to deliver them to his studio the following day in a taxi.

On the outskirts of Islington, bordering gloomy Old Street, on a fairly nondescript street of ugly warehouses and lonely, graffiti-ridden bus stops, the contrast between what's outside and what's inside Raqib's studio couldn't be greater. Dorothy is about to step inside the Land of Oz...

"Ring! Ring!"

There's a shuffling inside. I sense someone looking at me

through the spy hole. I smile politely. Then the bolts are pulled back—three, four, and the door slowly opens.

"Clayton! Darling!" shrieks Raqib, his head peering round the crack. "Come in! Come in!"

His dress is just as eccentric when he is in work mode as when he steps out. A black silk scarf wrapped round his head like a turban, a multi-coloured negligee (or is it a kimono?), beneath which peep pink ballet pumps.

"I was just finishing my yoga," he giggles, wrapping his arms around me as if I was a long-lost brother.

On entering his studio the first thing you notice is the beautiful Baccarat chandelier. It dominates the space. On closer inspection it's disturbing, wrapped in barbed wire, with barbs piercing little hand-made birds that drip blood down their breasts.

I try and follow Raqib's train of thought as he talks, but at the same time my eyes race around the room: ornate candlesticks, long tables piled high with sketches of skewered babies, Holbein-inspired paintings encrusted with diamonds, emeralds, and sapphires adorning white, white walls.

This is the studio that curators from the Guggenheim in Venice and New York, MoMA, the Tate, and the Royal Academy have been desperate to visit. The art world realizing he's their future cash cow.

"Oh, Clayton, darling. I never take their calls. The art world's a nasty place. It's all Money! Money! Money! Let them wait. No one will have my paintings until I'm ready. I'm Mother Goose sitting on her golden eggs!"

And then he laughs—that strange laugh of his that's half macaw, half hyena.

"Come, let's go down to my boudoir," he sings, skipping down the centrally placed staircase to his basement living quarters.

The basement is hard to describe. It's not just an assault on the senses but rape up the bottom by a very large willy.

In the middle of the room a huge tree sprouts from the cement. In each corner exotic plants stretch out their tendrils, weaving in and out of antique furniture. One wall is covered in china tea sets from long-dead British royalty, all draped in more barbed wire and little dead birds. The lighting is low, from huge church candles hidden behind see-through drapes that partition the huge room—a room decorated with large silk cushions, cavernous sofas, and velvet-draped chaises longues. The smell of incense, intense. Think Kashmir brothel mixed with Victorian opium den.

As we talk, it crosses my mind how grounded and completely unaffected he is, considering what he's achieved at such a young age. He is more interested in talking about my writing than his own work, a conversation I find slightly embarrassing given his stature.

"Raqib, you live here, you work here, don't you ever miss the outside world?"

"Oh, no, my dear! Outside is violent and cruel. I have taken the beauty inside my head and transported it to this room. Why do I need to leave?"

"Company?"

"I have my assistants. Although I forbid them to speak while we work. I pay them well, but forbid them to speak. We need total silence to create."

"What about a partner? A relationship?"

"Clayton, my darling, this is my relationship," he says, laughing, sweeping his hand toward one of his paintings. "Alas, we are forever chained."

As I go to leave, I look around his "Factory," wondering if this studio will be written about in years to come. It's certainly a place I'll never forget. Remember the name Raqib Shaw. His golden eggs are about to turn platinum.

October 24th, 2007: The Top Hat

Somerfields on Berwick Street, "hooker alley." Not the type of place you'd expect to find a vampire.

There I am, browsing the aisles, trying to decide whether to go for the coconut macaroons or the Fondant Fancies, when it suddenly goes cold, as if someone has just dropped an ice cube down my back.

I shiver. Look round. Empty. That's strange.

Then, as I'm about to reach toward the shelves, out of the corner of my eye—a flash of red and black by the doorway. Then it's gone. Just as quick.

I rub my eyes. This is getting weird.

So I reach toward the shelves again, and as I do I see a tall, black top hat glide past the aisles. I watch, fascinated, as it floats past one aisle, then another, then another, getting closer and closer, like a shark fin slicing through water. Then it stops, abruptly, on the aisle in front.

Only one person would wear a hat as tall as this. Sebastian.

Sebastian Horsley, artist, writer, and failed suicide, lives behind the shop. Meard Street. Number 7. The house with a sign on the door that reads: "This is not a brothel. No prostitutes live here." Always in black—the suit, the shirt, the swept-back dyed hair. Tall. Very tall. And pale. A deathly pallor. Like a faded junkie rock star in undertaker drag. Only once have I ever seen him in daylight. I'll never forget…

It was early morning, back in January of last year. I was opening the door to the shop and suddenly I felt a "whoosh"—a "whoosh" and a smell of old mothballs. And as I looked round I caught a glimpse of a black apparition flying past. The feet barely skimming the pavement. The face set, stern. Pushing through the crowds, as if trying to get back to his coffin before daybreak; shielding his face from the sun.

Over the months that followed I heard strange stories

about this tall, dark figure. His name cropped up again and again on the street. A rumour here. A dark secret there. All very *Salem's Lot*. How he'd become infamous after subjecting himself to a crucifixion in the Philippines, refusing pain killers as he was nailed to the cross; painting pictures of what he'd been through. How he'd once owned a brothel and shagged more than 1,000 prostitutes.

So whenever I'd catch sight of Sebastian it was an event. Just like seeing Sue. And I'd rush to the window, pretend to polish the already clean windows, and watch, wide-eyed, as he whisked unsuspecting hookers back to his lair.

And now he's here. I peep round the corner.

Sure enough, there he is, scanning the shelves, muttering to himself. All decked out in a long, black, velvet evening suit, crimson waistcoat, and pointed boots that curl up at the front. The devil doesn't wear Prada. I duck back.

What should I do? Speak to him? He's bound to see me if I stay here. I peer around again. Take a deep breath. Clear my throat. "Sebastian!"

He turns. Slowly. Stares at me. His eyes taking a moment to adjust. Grins.

"Clayton, by the skimmed milk! What a pleasure!"

"How are you, Sebastian? I haven't seen you since your—"

"Book launch. Yes. The book that launched a thousand shits."

"Er… Yes. I really enjoyed it, and the reviews were amazing."

"Not all, my dear. Not quite all," he corrects, shaking his head. "I received a 'pink pounding' from that faggot whore newspaper called *QX*. It's odd, the fags having a pop, isn't it? You would have thought us minorities would've stuck together."

I try to reply, but as I look into his eyes, they widen, and I'm transfixed, hypnotized inside deep, dark pools.

"Actually, my darling, I feel I am doing them a service. Riddled with self-loathing, it must be a happy distraction finding someone they hate more than themselves. I'll be off to a gay sauna later on to extract revenge." He giggles, a little camp giggle behind a cupped, bejewelled hand.

"Oh, by the way," he purrs, stroking a rouged cheek. "I read that brothel piece of yours on MySpace." His eyes narrow as he looks me up and down. "Wise words indeed, Mr. Clayton. I've been to that place hundreds of times. Although I haven't been for a while, as the women were getting rather flat-chested. And, as you know, I hate flat-chested women. I always think it shows such bad judgment."

He reaches forward. Strokes my arm. "I have one further tip to add to your brothel etiquette, although I fear it's unique to me. Would you like to hear what it is?"

"Yes, yes, of course," I stammer.

"When I'm done I always walk down the stairs half undressed. Then I pause in front of the doorway of the Groucho and slowly pull up my flies. I do think that the most important thing is to be whatever we are without shame. Don't you agree?"

"Yes. I—"

"I thought perhaps you would," he says, smiling, taking a step closer. "Clayton, let us go to the Colony, or the Colon, as I call it, when I return from Ireland. I am off to do some promotion. Appropriate, really. Ireland is a country full of genius, but with absolutely no talent."

As he turns to leave, he waves, a fey flutter of his delicate fingers, and blows me a kiss.

"Until then, my dear…"

And then, in the blink of an eye, he's gone.

October 31st, 2007: Thong Man's Secret

Thong Man's been visiting the shop for over a year, and his visits always follow the same pattern. After the usual pleasantries are exchanged—"How's the shop doing?" "Isn't it getting cold?"—he immediately gets down to business, walking slowly past the underwear section, running his hand up and down the row, lightly fingering the garments, both of us acting as if nothing untoward is taking place.

Occasionally, he'll find a piece of underwear to his liking, and when he does he'll take it carefully off the hanger and hold it up to the light, mesmerised, marvelling at the design, the cut, the fabric.

Months will pass by without me seeing him, and then I'll be sitting by the window and there he'll be, peering through, checking to see what new brands we have in stock.

Only, today is slightly different. Not only does Thong Man actually come into the shop again, but he also reveals a secret...

"Hello, Clayton!"

"Oh, hello," I reply cheerfully, looking up at the old man standing in front of me, patting down his wispy grey/black hair. "I haven't seen you for a while."

"It has been a while, hasn't it... How's the shop doing?"

"Not too good. It's been a really difficult couple of months."

"Oh, dear. Well, maybe things will improve with the run-up to Christmas," he says encouragingly, his eyes already drifting toward the underwear rail. "Do you have anything new in?"

"I think you've seen everything we have. Oh... We have ordered a new line, though. Take a look at this," and I hand him a catalogue, full of semi-naked men, which he flicks through excitedly.

"Oh, I love the camouflage jockstrap on this one," he gasps, admiring the model lying provocatively, if slightly unrealistically, across an armoured tank. "The colour combinations are perfect. They've really got their finger on the pulse."

"So has he!" I point out, laughing, looking at the model's hand, which lingers over his pouch.

But Thong Man pays no attention. He's in his own world. "Will you call me when they come in?" he murmurs, turning the pages of the catalogue with a trembling hand.

As I still don't know Thong Man's real name, I hand him my pen and notebook and ask him to write his details down. I watch as his hand shakily spells out the letters.

C-h-a-r-l-e-s

I stare at the name. "Charles?"

"Yes."

I look him in the eye. "Your name's Charles."

"Yes, it is," he says again.

I wonder... "Charles, how long have you been coming to Soho?"

"Oh, a long, long time. I used to do all my socialising here. In fact, I used to come to this shop when..."

And as he speaks, I drift back, back to a conversation...

That was my spot. Just by the window. I'd sit there for hours... It's where I first met Charlie..."

I look back at Charles. "Sorry, umm, what did you say?"

"I said, I used to sit just—"

"By the window?"

Charles looks at me. "How did you know?"

I don't reply for a second; thinking back again...

"Oh, Charlie loved all that dressing up stuff. Underwear. Outfits."

It must be him! I clear my throat. Wondering how I should proceed. "I think... I think I know someone you might know."

He studies me. Turns his head slightly to one side. Runs his fingers through his hair, puzzled. Should I ask him? Okay. Here goes.

"Do you know Leslie?"

His hand stops. Halfway through his hair. For a second

256

no one speaks. Then Charles says, "You know Leslie?" He is shocked.

"Yes."

"You've seen him?"

"Yes."

"He's still alive, then?"

"Yes."

He grips the counter with both hands, his knuckles white, tense against the glass. "Do you have his number?"

"I'm afraid I don't. I bump into him quite a lot, though. He comes into the shop—"

"How often?"

"Every week or so."

He looks down at the floor, deep in thought. I wait for him to speak. "I suppose he told you...that I let him down... badly," he says, his voice barely above a whisper.

"We were lovers... And then... And then one day he broke my heart."

"It was such a long time ago," Charlie says. Then he sighs. Deeply. Looks back up. Alert again. "Would you do me a favour?"

"Of course."

"When you see Leslie again would you give him my number?"

"Yes. Yes, I will."

"Tell him... Would you just tell him to please call me. To please call...Charlie."

I nod.

"Thank you. Thank you. I would be very grateful."

I watch, in silence, as Charlie buttons up his black raincoat, smoothes down his hair, looks back at me, and makes his way out of the shop, walking slowly down the street.

As he passes Costa, he stops. Looks back. As Leslie once did. I wave. Smile.

Then he turns around and he's off again, past Pulcinella, American Retro, until he's finally out of sight.

I sit down. Pick up my notebook. Look down at Charlie's phone number.

Leslie, you're not going to believe this…

November 4th, 2007: Round One

Sunday morning. Two hours ago…

I'm standing by the doorway, people-watching, thinking about the day ahead, when a smartly dressed old man in a cream suit and tan brogues walks slowly out of Costa coffee shop, heading in my direction.

"Hello, ducky! Fancy seeing your visage!"

Oh, no! I wasn't expecting to see him just yet. I shove my hand in my pocket. Fiddle nervously. "Leslie, I've got something important to tell you."

He arches an eyebrow. "You're not pregnant, are you?"

"No, it's—"

"Not a good idea at your age, dear."

"Listen—I really need to tell you something!"

"Well, spit it out then, ducky! I haven't got all day!"

"I'm trying!"

He stares at me. "It's a death, isn't it?" he gasps, clutching his tie.

"No it's not a death, it's—"

"Oh, I haven't been to a good funeral in ages! I was only sayin' to Dolly last week, I said, 'Dolly, dear, will you hurry up and pop your clogs—I've got a lovely herringbone suit that I could—' "

"It's Charlie!" I suddenly blurt out. Leslie looks at me in amazement. "He came into the shop."

Silence.

Uh-oh.

Then his eyes widen, his nostrils flare like cave holes, and he takes a dramatic inhale of breath. "WHAT?" he shrieks, his voice going up three octaves. "What do you mean, Charlie came in the shop?"

I shrug.

"No. No, you're wrong, dear," he says, shaking his head dismissively. "What would Charlie be doing in your shop?"

"He came in to... He came in to look at the thongs."

"Oh, my good God! That's Charlie!" he screams, slapping his hands to his cheeks, his mouth falling open like Munch's *The Scream*. "Get me a seat quickly—I'm fainting!"

So I reach for his arm, grab him around the waist, and lead him carefully inside, directing him toward my little red chair by the window.

"There you go. Do you want some water?" I ask, turning toward the stairway.

"No, I don't!" he snaps back, lowering himself into the seat. "Oh, Gawd 'elp us! Where's me pills?"

He digs into his breast pocket, pulling out a small brown bottle which he taps into the palm of his hand, throwing his head back dramatically as he knocks back a tablet. Then glares at me. "Now you just come here, missy—I want to hear *everything*!"

I step forward, cautiously, expecting to be turned to stone at any second.

"When did you see him?" he demands, his face screwing up like Witchiepoo from *H.R. Pufnstuf*.

"Well, he came in a few days ago and he gave me his phone number..."

He claps his hand to his mouth. Gasps again. "You've got Charlie's phone number? How dare you! You keep your thievin' hands off my Charlie! You hear me?"

"Leslie, he gave me his number to give to you."

"Where is it?" he barks. "Give it to me!"

I reach toward the desk drawer and take out my little black notebook, placing it on the counter, turning to the page with Charlie's phone number.

"There!" I say, pointing at it.

He looks down. Back up at me.

"And how did he know we know each other?" he says, spitting out each word.

"Well, I...ummm, he told me that he used to—"

"I knew it!" he fumes, his eyebrow arching higher by the second. "I knew you were up to something. Right from the first time I ever set eyes on you. Those shifty eyes of yours."

"No you've got the wrong—"

"You drag me in here. Steal my story. A defenceless old queen like me. Then you track down Charlie... There should be laws against people like you. It's harassment, that's what it is! Well, I'll have no part of it. Do you hear me?"

He stands, gripping the counter for support. "You tell him when you see him—*if* you see him! Tell him I'm dead!"

Our eyes fall to the notebook. I have a feeling I know what's coming next, so I quickly reach forward—but too late. Leslie snatches the notebook from the counter, rips out the offending page, and tears it viciously into little pieces, throwing them in the air like a snowstorm.

"Leslie, I think you're overreacting—"

"Overreacting? Overreacting, she says? You shove my life story on cider space!"

"Cyberspace."

"Whatever! Then you drag up all these old memories. Who do you think you are? Eamonn bleedin' Andrews?"

"I think you're being—"

"You can think what you want, dear! As far as I'm concerned there is no Charlie. And if he comes in again, I'm dead! Do I make myself clear?"

"I can't do that. I've already told him—"

"Told him what?"

"That I see you."

"Well, then you can bleedin' well tell him that you *won't* see me, can't you?" he shouts, digging a hand into his jacket pocket, pulling out a yellow silk scarf, which he sweeps around his neck in a gesture that is so Bette Davis I can't help but giggle. Then, in a last show of defiance, he kicks at the paper on the floor and flounces out of the shop.

I look out the window and watch as he sails past Soho Books, pushing past Pam, the Fag Lady, who, picking a bad moment to ask for money, is almost knocked to the ground.

Oh, dear. Well, that could have gone better. Still, at least now he knows.

I bend down, gather up all the pieces of paper, arrange them in order on the counter and reach inside the desk drawer for the Sellotape.

Round One to Leslie!

November 9th, 2007: Charlie Calls

The phone rings.

"Good afternoon, Dirty White Boy!"

"Is that Clayton?"

"Speaking."

"Clayton, it's Charles... Charlie."

"Oh... Hi!"

"I'm not disturbing you, am I?"

"No... Not at all."

"I was just calling to find out if..."

"Leslie had been in?"

"Yes."

"Ummmm..."

"He has, hasn't he?"

"Yes, he has."

There's a pause.

"It didn't go well, I take it."

"It kind of...er, no. Not quite."

"Oh, dear... I thought over time he might..."

"I think he's still...a bit hurt."

Silence.

"Do you know when he'll be back?"

"I'm not sure."

"You gave him my number, though?"

"I tried…"

Silence again.

"It's strange…" he sighs. "The split was so…sudden. I've only got one photo of us together. Standing outside your shop, funny enough."

"When it was a restaurant?"

"Yes. That's the only photo I have. I don't even know what he looks like anymore…"

"Oh, Leslie always looks immaculate. He's dresses really well, very dapper; his hair's always perfectly in place; and his nails are so—"

"Yes! Yes!" he replies, as if remembering. "He had a thing about his nails. Nails and eyebrows."

He pauses. "I'm sure he told you that I got married."

"He did. Yes."

"It's hard to explain, but it just wasn't right back then. Two men. Not for me, anyway. Too many eyes watching. And Leslie… Well, he was just so… I know you think I'm a coward."

"No. No, actually, I don't. Things were very different. It was illegal; there were no role models—"

"Exactly! And I just wasn't the political type. Not like Leslie. Not that he ever attended meetings or anything. Just his stance. You know. His personality. The way he faced the world. I just couldn't be like that."

Another silence.

"I'm so sorry, Clayton. You must have things to be getting on with?"

"Not really. The shop's empty."

"It's just so silly."

"What is?"

"This. At my age," he says, sighing again. "I really don't know what I'm expecting."

"What we all expect, I suppose."

"What's that?"

"To find a companion, a soul mate, to fall in love."

"Yes. That's... Do you have a partner?"

"Yes. My business partner, Jorge."

"The Cuban gentleman?"

"Yes."

"Oh, of course. And... And are *you* happy?"

"For the most part. This shop creates problems, though—stress, that kind of thing. And the sex life goes up and down according to the takings. But...we're supportive of each other."

"Supportive..." he repeats, as if contemplating the meaning. "You must really love each other."

"Yes... We do."

"What would you do if you were in my position?"

"Charlie, that's not for me to—"

"I know. I know. I'm sorry. I shouldn't be asking."

"Well, there's not much you can do. It's really down to—"

"You're right. This is about Leslie, not me."

"I think, given time, he may come back, but—"

"But I may have hurt him too badly. That's what you mean, isn't it?"

"Hmmm. Well, he does have a touch of Miss Haversham about him," I joke.

"Clayton, I'll hang up now. I've taken up enough of your time."

"Charlie, can I just ask... Why didn't you try and track down Leslie before?"

It goes quiet again, momentarily.

"I don't know... Guilt? The fear that he may already be dead? Then I had some personal problems..." He clears his throat. "But maybe that's why I've been coming to your shop the past couple of years. You know, reliving old memories."

"So it's not just the thongs, then?"

He laughs.

"Oh, by the way, we've got that new range in."

"What?"

"The camouflage thongs!"

"Oh, I can't think about thongs at a time like this!" He laughs again.

I laugh too.

"Clayton, would you do me another favour? If he comes in again would you…"

"Yes. I'll give him your number again."

"You still have it?"

"Er, yes. Yes, I do."

"Thank you. And maybe I should… No, no it doesn't matter. Goodbye, Clayton. Thank you so much."

"Goodbye, Charlie."

I put the phone down and look out the window, wondering. Wondering what Leslie's thinking, wondering if he'll ever come back…

November 13th, 2007: Tuesday Morning—a Postcard Arrives

Dirty White Boy

50 Old Compton Street

London. W1D 4UB

10th Nov

Hello, Dear,

I'm staying at Dolly's cottage by the sea to recuperate.

Trolling down the prom vardering the omis, I'll be.

I'll come and see you the night I'm back. Wed 21st.

Keep it free, ducky… Meal on moi!

P.S. Oh, and if you're reading this thinking this is just Leslie's way of apologising, you'd be absolutely right—

it is!
Leslie

November 13th, 2007: Imagining

An old man walks along a seaside promenade, ignoring passersby, head down, thinking—thinking about someone he once knew.

As he walks, his hands dug deep inside his well-cut coat, a sheet of newspaper blows toward him and wraps itself around his leg, fluttering in the wind.

He stops. Tuts. Reaches down, glimpses the headline, "A Storm is Coming Soon."

Suddenly, as if pulled by invisible hands, the paper breaks loose and flies away, up into the air, over the wall, and into the sea.

He rushes to the ledge. Leans over. Looks down into the murky water. But it's already gone.

And as he continues on his way, head down once more, he wonders how he would cope the next time if it were to suddenly fly out of his hands and disappear all over again.

November 21st, 2007: Dinner with Leslie

We're outside the Stockpot, Leslie's nose inches from the window, a look of horror on his face.

"Oh, I couldn't possibly eat in there, dear!" he shrieks, as if it's the Auschwitz staff canteen.

I reach for his hand. "Oh, come on! You'll like it!" I drag him through the door.

Once inside, I greet Deborah, the waitress, while Leslie follows reluctantly behind—nose pointing skywards, like Queen Mary walking through a field of cow poo.

I point to an empty table at the back, take my seat, and watch as he approaches, whipping a silk hanky from his breast pocket, which he uses to dust down his chair.

"What on *earth* have you brought me to?" he hisses as

he shakes off his blazer, shimmying his shoulders as if it's a mink coat.

"What do you mean? This is a Soho institution!"

He surveys the room, taking in tables of ageing Goths, "backpack" tourists, and a smattering of gay men in various stages of beardom. "It's an institution, all right!" he sniffs, causing a woman at the next table to stop eating and look over.

"Sssshhh!"

Leslie immediately swivels round in his seat, throws the woman a withering stare. "Don't you 'Sssshhh' me!" Leslie reproves. "Who do you think you are? The bleedin' dinner lady?"

"Leslie! Keep your voice down!"

"Well! Honestly!" he huffs, brushing an imaginary lock of hair from his face and throwing back his head as if mortally offended. "It's like eatin' in a benefit office!"

I point at the menu. Try to lighten the mood. "The spaghetti Bolognese here is really nice. Do you fancy that?"

He looks down suspiciously, eyebrow arched like a chicken bone. "Ohh, I can't eat foreign muck," he says with a frown. "I'll have the tomato salad."

I catch Deborah's eye as she walks past. "Can we have one spaghetti Bolognese and a tomato salad, please?"

Leslie taps her on the arm. "And I'd like the lettuce washed, if you don't mind. Not just waved under a tap!"

"Er, yes...umm, of course," Deborah stammers, looking at me out the corner of her eye. "Drinks?"

"I'll have a Coke with ice," I say.

Leslie examines the menu. "Does this establishment have a wine list, *per chance*?"

Deborah smiles, turns over the menu Leslie is squinting at and holding at arm's length.

"House white?" he asks incredulously. "Which house? Council?"

I kick him under the table.

Moments later, Deborah's back with the drinks. I reach for my Coke and glance in Leslie's direction, wondering how today's conversation will flow.

"So, umm, how was the break?"

"Oh fine, dear. Fine," he replies, pinching his nose as he takes his first sip of wine. "I needed a bit of sea air. Me nerves were all a-jangle."

"So, er, you had time to think, then?"

"Think, dear?"

He swills his drink from cheek to cheek, screwing up his face as if about to spit it back out.

"You know… About Charlie."

He gulps. Glares at me. "What did you bring his name up for?" he snaps.

"He called."

As he contemplates his answer Deborah appears again with the food. We eat in silence, not speaking again until I've almost finished my meal. I wait for Leslie to start us off.

"S-o-o-o-o…:" he says, disinterestedly, pushing a tomato around his plate. "What did *he* have to say?"

"He wanted to know if I'd seen you."

"Hmmmm."

I put my cutlery down, wondering how he'll take the next question. "Leslie… Do you mind if I ask you something?"

He flutters his eyelashes, which I take as a "yes."

"I assumed that you'd be pleased that Charlie's back on the scene."

"Oh, you did, did you?"

He pauses. Clears his throat. Licks a finger, running it delicately along an eyebrow like an ancient drag act preparing for the stage. Then he says, "There's something you don't know about Charlie."

I lean forward, listening intently.

"Remember, I told you why he left."

"Yes. Because he got married."

He pauses again. "Well, he was *already* married."

The sentence lingers in the air.

"What?" I gasp.

"Charlie was leading a double life."

I dig a fingernail into a cuticle. "Wow! How...how did you find out?"

"His wife," he replies calmly.

"His wife?"

"Mm-hmmm... She called me at work one day, completely out of the blue."

I touch his hand. "That must have been a shock."

"I'll say, ducky!"

He looks down at his fingers, strokes a silver ring that I didn't notice before. I wait for him to elaborate.

"We arranged to meet at your shop, of course. And I was early. Well, you know me, dear, I can't abide lateness." He drums his fingers on the table. "So there I was, smoking the fag, when in she waltzed. Common as muck, I might add. 'I've given Charlie an ultimatum!' she screeched. 'End it now or I'll tell your bosses everythin'!' " He crosses his legs, looks down at his shoes. "What he saw in a loudmouthed battle axe like her I'll never know."

I smirk. He catches my eye. Raises an eyebrow. Continues.

"Anyway, the next day I got this letter from Charlie tellin' me he'd just got married—when in actual fact, dear, he was married all the way along!"

He reaches for his fork, then changes his mind, placing it back on his plate. Seconds pass. No one speaks. The mood gradually changes from reflective to sad. Leslie stares at his glass. Stripped of bravado, the haughty, confident character I came in with only minutes before transforms into a fragile, vulnerable old man.

"I did a lot of thinking when I was at Dolly's... Stupid, romantic thoughts..." He sniffs, reaching into his pocket for his hanky and dabbing at his watering eyes. "Excuse me, dear. I need to use the bathroom." He grips the edge of the table, rises slowly. "They do have a bathroom here, I take it—or is it just a hole in the floor?"

I smile, reach for his hand. "Leslie..." He stops. "Not everyone's as fearless as you."

His eyes meet mine, then he brushes past and walks slowly down the stairway.

Five minutes pass.

When he returns, Deborah walks over with the bill.

"This is mine, ducky," Leslie says quietly, taking a £20 note from his wallet and leaving it on the saucer.

I reach into my pocket. Remove a crumpled piece of paper covered in Sellotape. Hesitate. Then place it on the table in front of him.

"So is this."

He looks down at the paper, back at me.

Silence.

I pick up my jacket. Kiss him on the cheek, leave.

November 25th, 2007: I Called Him

The phone rings.

"Hello, Dirty White Boy!"

"Hello, ducky! It's moi!"

"Leslie! How're you?"

"Still alive," he sighs. "Clinging on by me false nails. How 'bout you? How's the rag trade?"

"Not good. It's really slow."

"That bad?"

"Mm-hmmm. The Inland Revenue tried to close us down last week."

"Oh, you poor luv."

"No one's buying! If we can just get through Christmas..."

"You will, dear. You will. You're a survivor. I said to Dolly, I said, 'Dolly, dear! You should see 'er! Works 'er little fingers to the bone, she does!'"

"Not that it's doing much good."

"Well, maybe this'll cheer you up." He pauses. "I called him."

"Oh, you did? That's FANTASTIC!"

"We didn't talk for long. Less than a minute, actually. Then I made some excuse about me pots needed rinsing. Well, what do you say after forty years? How's the wife?"

"You never said that!"

"No, of course I didn't! I don't even know if he's still got a wife. But—we did arrange to meet."

"Really? When?"

"Next Friday," he replies casually.

"Whereabouts?"

"Where do you think?"

"Not here?"

"Of course, dear! Where else? Look, you got me into this bleedin' mess! And besides—it'll give you something to write about!"

"It's all I have been writing about!"

"What do you mean?"

"I can't seem to write about anything else! Not until I know how this all ends."

"Well, don't blame me for bringing a bit of glamour into your dull life!" He giggles. "You wanted a story!"

"I suppose you're right... Anyway, what was it like, hearing his voice after all this time? It must've been really weird."

"Oh, it was very strange, ducky," he says excitedly. "It was like I was back in me thirties. You know, arranging to meet in Soho n'all that."

I smile. "You must be really nervous."

"Nervous? I'm like a schoolgirl in a padded bra!"

I laugh. "What're you gonna wear?"

"Oh, don't talk to me about the drag, dear! I've been in

a tizz all weekend just thinking about it. It's been a terrible state of affairs. It really has. I've been dusting knickknacks all morning to calm meself!"

I laugh again. "I don't think I've ever heard you this happy."

He gasps. "You cheeky little minx! I'm a joy to behold an' a joy to be with!"

"Leslie, I've got another call coming through. I'll have to—"

"Don't worry, dear. I'll see you next Friday. I just wanted you to be the first to know."

"Listen, it's really good news. I'm really pleased for you."

"Thank you dear. I'll troll over to yours about eight."

"Okay. Bye, Leslie!"

"Ciao for now, dear!"

November 28th, 2007: Charlie Calls Again

9:30 A.M. The phone rings.

"Hello, Dirty White Boy!"

"Is that Clayton?"

"Yes, it is!"

"Clayton—it's Charlie."

"I heard the news. How exciting!"

"Ummm… That's what I'm calling about."

He pauses.

"Charlie, is everything okay?"

He clears his throat. "I wondered if you could pass a message on to Leslie when he comes in on Friday."

"Sure. What's wrong?"

"I'm in hospital."

"Oh, no!"

"It's nothing serious," he says, reassuringly. "Just a few tests. I was meant to be out today but now they want to keep me in 'til the weekend."

"Oh, dear."

"And I don't have Leslie's number. You don't have it, do you?"

"No. No, I don't. I thought you spoke—"

"We did. But it was all so quick…"

"So…" I sigh. "You want me to tell him?"

"Clayton, I'm so sorry to impose on you like this again. But if you could just pass these details on."

"Charlie, it's no problem. It's not your fault. It's just that I know he'll—"

"Yes, I know. He's going to think I've backed out. But he can call me here at the hospital."

"Okay. Let me just get a pen… Okay. Got it!"

"It's the Chelsea and Westminster."

"On Fulham Road."

"That's the one."

He tells me the name of the ward. I stop writing.

"You know it?" he asks, hesitantly.

"Yes, yes I do…" I reply, thinking back. "I used to visit a friend of mine there."

There's a pause.

"Clayton, thank you for doing this."

"You don't have to thank me, Charlie. I'm only passing a message on. It's no big deal."

"I know, but still—"

"It's no problem. Honestly."

"So could you tell him to please call me here, or he can call me at home at the weekend."

"I'll tell him as soon as he comes in."

"Ummm…goodbye, Clayton."

"Bye, Charlie."

I put the phone back on the stand, wondering how Leslie's going to react to this.

November 30th, 2007: The Meeting

Friday. 7:30 P.M.

I'm sitting by the window. Waiting.

The street's busy despite the rain. Couples, gay, straight, young, and old, tuk-tuks threatened with overload, a posse of pimps, the Chinese woman with the limp, and the Westminster rubbish van on its nightly patrol.

Then, amid the throng, a flash of colour; a vision at odds with its surroundings; a green umbrella, a fawn suit, a crimson shirt adorned with a yellow cravat.

I watch as the vision walks carefully and magnificently through the masses, like the Virgin Queen gliding past cheering subjects; then the flicker of a smile and a little wave of a perfumed hand as he spots me while crossing the street.

"I'm here, ducky!" he announces with aplomb as he steps into the shop, holding on to the doorframe for support. "After forty years—I'm back!"

I close down my laptop. Stand. "Leslie, there's been a slight change of plan."

He looks at me quizzically, patting down his already perfectly groomed hair, waiting for me to continue.

"It's Charlie. He... He..."

"Well, spit it out, then!"

I clear my throat. "It's Charlie. He's in hospital. It's nothing serious," I add quickly. "Just tests. But he won't be out until the weekend."

Silence.

I watch him, waiting for him to erupt. The calm before the storm. But—nothing.

I move closer, cautiously. "He gave me his details, so you can call."

I hand him the piece of paper, which he holds at arm's length, squinting as he reads. "Mm-hmmm. Mm-hmmm."

"Do you know it?"

"Of course I know it!" he snaps, putting the paper in his jacket pocket. "You think I was raised in a convent?"

"No, it's just that—"

"Listen, ducky, I was visiting friends in that place there when you were sproutin' your first pubic hair! Now go and get yer coat!"

"What?"

"Well, I can't go on me own, can I?" he shrieks, hand on hip. "I might end up strangling him with his drip!"

"Leslie, you can't just turn up."

"And why not?" he sings. "Look... I've had the face done, the nails, three days of picking drag, and enough talcum powder down me pants to sink a battleship. So if you think I'm going through all that again..."

"I can't go with you," I say flatly. "We don't close 'til nine o'clock. And anyway—it wouldn't be right."

He glares at me. Takes a deep breath. His nostrils flaring, wider and wider. Uh-oh.

"Okay! Okay!" I say, backtracking quickly. "I'll ask Jorge if he can cover."

Five minutes later we're in a black cab, hurtling along Brompton Road.

We sit in silence, holding on to the door handles, looking out the window as first Harrods, then the Victoria and Albert museum whiz past.

Leslie reaches for my hand. I look down. He squeezes. His hand is red, the grip is so tight. I look out the window again. In our own worlds.

Minutes later, the driver pulls up outside the Chelsea and Westminster hospital. He switches off the engine. Turns round in his seat. "Visitin' a sick friend, are ya?" he says cheerfully.

Leslie opens the door. "Of course we're visiting a sick friend! What do you think we're doin' here? Donating kidneys?"

274

The entrance to the hospital is quiet. The reception desk empty except for a solitary guard who doesn't even look up as we pass.

We walk silently, silently except for our shoes, which click-click-clack on the polished wooden floor; past shops, artwork hanging from the ceiling, until we reach the lifts.

We enter. I press the button for the second floor.

Now we're outside the ward. We stop. Leslie turns to face me.

"Well, I suppose this is the moment when I should ask you how I look," he says with a smirk.

"You look great. You always look great."

"I look like an old queen! That's what I look like!"

I smile.

"And if he looks younger than me there's gonna be trouble. You 'ear me?"

I laugh. "I hear you."

A few seconds tick by.

"Okay," he says, pensively. "Here goes."

He reaches for my hand again, pushes open the swing doors, and we walk silently down the ward corridor.

Déjà vu.

The TV room. The videos on the shelves. *All About Eve.* *Ab Fab.* The little kitchen. The blackboard with the nurse's rota. The long reception desk. The armchair I used to sleep in. Even the way the beds are laid out. Two sections. Six to a section. And there's the bed. Number 9. The bed my first boyfriend lay in.

"Can I help you?" says the duty sister briskly, looking up from her notes.

Leslie steps forward, rests his hands on the reception counter. "I'm here to see Charlie."

"You mean Charles?"

"Yes."

She tilts her head to one side. "Are you family?"

"Of course I'm bleedin' family!"

"Could you keep your voice down, please," she says, raising an eyebrow. She pauses. "You're his partner, I take it?"

Leslie raises one back, even higher. "Yes. I am. We've been partners for—" He looks back at me. Bites his lip. "For more than forty years."

"Okay, he's over there," the nurse replies, pointing to the section in front. "The end bed, by the window. Oh, and it's lights-out in an hour."

We look toward the bed. A figure. Asleep. Leslie reaches for my hand again. Squeezes it once more. His hand trembles.

Then he walks over, slowly. Stands at the foot of the bed. Takes a seat on the bedside chair.

"Bed number 9…" I murmur.

The nurse looks up from her paperwork, puzzled. "Yes. It is. Have you been here before?"

I watch as Leslie taps the sleeping figure on the arm, looking back in my direction. I watch as the figure wakes, they speak, they hug, they hold each other—once again.

"Yes… A few years ago."

I walk back down the corridor.

The taxi stops on the opposite side of the road. I run over. Open the door. Step inside.

"Old Compton Street in Soho, please!"

The driver turns round. Pulls open the sliding hatch. It's the same driver.

"Your mate's a bit abrupt, isn't he?"

"He can be."

He turns back. Signals. Pulls out. "So, you havin' a night out, are ya?"

"Nah. I've got a shop there."

"It's a funny area, is Soho," he says with a laugh. "You must get some real interestin' characters comin' into your shop."

I look out the back window, watch the lights of the hospital gradually fade away.

Smile.

"Yeah... Yeah, we do get quite a few."

Acknowledgments

I would like to give a big wet kiss to my editor, Rupert Smith; my publisher, Frédérique Delacoste; Mark Rhynsburger and all at Cleis. Without you...

A huge thank you also to: Mum, Dad, Jay, Sara, and Tori for always being there. Miss "Josie" Joe Pearson for cover design. Paul "Sniff Sniff" Edmond, Kate Friend, and David "Lola" for photos. Elton Uliana (we'd be gone without you, honey!). My all-star cast, Pam, Sue, Charlie, and Leslie, for magical stories. David Benson for bringing them to life. Chico for staying strong. My neighbours from Hell: Sebastian "Crisp" Horsley; the best beards in Soho, the Rubbishmen; the best legs on the street, Angie; the barmaid with the mostest, Hilary Penn. James "Lloyd Webber" Seabright. Jonathan Kemp for taking me down new avenues. Patrick "Mr. Moneybags" Kocks, our saviour. Raqib Shaw and Yoko for champers and beautiful art. For all things musical, Martin Watkins. Anouk "Noopie" Cruttenden. Maria "Pippa" Jarvis. Gus and Ian. Jacques "Co Co" Humpich. Juliette for gay books galore.

Maggie Mighty K for spiritual encouragement. Dr VD for Stockpot dinners. DJ HaLo-iS for keeping the husband chilled. Arthur Wooten for support from across the pond. Stevan "BBC" Bennett (Take me back!). David Parker (I love my Marmite). Stewart Who? Fred "Bearlesque" Bear. Agents to the stars, Rob Kraitt and Juliet Pickering. Jen (my cosmic friend) Filmtopia. Ansley "what's your real name" Vaughan and all my MySpace support. You know who you are. Thank you for encouraging me.

A Note on Language

"Two countries divided by a common language," as Oscar Wilde put it—or was it George Bernard Shaw? Nobody seems to know. "I'm not Wilde about Shaw and I'm not Shaw about Wilde. But you've got to admit they had a point," added Mr. Sebastian Horsley recently.

So, with this in mind, I have decided to include a small glossary. Please thumb your way back here when you come across a term you don't understand. There are only a few, but they may be crucial in turning this book into an American classic.

Big Issue is a magazine sold by homeless people to make money.

Bollocks is a word of Anglo-Saxon origin meaning "testicles."

Caravan is a mobile home.

Chariots is a gay sauna in South London.

Chav is a common English expression meaning an uneducated delinquent identified by a certain style of dress—gold jewellery, clothes in fashionable brands (often fake) with very prominent logos, and baseball caps, frequently in Burberry check, a favourite style. The female equivalent is **chavette** (think homeboys and girls).

Cottaging means cruising for sex in public lavatories ("cottages").

Crombie is a menswear designer label, although the word often refers to the style of coat.

Cum towels are towels used to wipe off err...sperm.

"Doing a Raleigh" in this instance refers to the gentlemanly act supposedly performed by Sir Walter Raleigh when he removed his cloak and placed it over a puddle for Queen Elizabeth I to step on.

Ena Sharples was one of the original characters of the long-running British soap opera, *Coronation Street*, and her name has become a byword for a "battle axe" woman.

Fiver is a five-pound note.

Gaydar is a UK gay online dating site.

Hen night is a party held for a woman who is about to be married.

Lucozade is an energy drink.

Luvvies are actors or actresses (or other artistically minded people) who are effusive, affected, or camp.

MOT is an acronym for the Ministry of Transport, used to describe the annual test a car has to take to certify its road-worthiness. It's also used to refer to a personal health check.

NHS stands for the National Health Service.

Queue is a line of waiting people or vehicles. The British stand in queues (and have been since at least since 1837 when this word was first recorded in English).

Rough sleeping means to sleep on the street or outdoors (associated with the homeless).

Shell suit is a lightweight nylon tracksuit, often in large patterns and bold colours (sometimes worn by chavs).

TK Maxx is known as TJ Maxx in the US.

Tosser is someone who "tosses off"—another name for a wanker (one who suffers from chronic masturbation).

VAT or Value Added Tax is a tax that applies to most business transactions that involve the transfer of goods or services.

WAG is an acronym for the Wives and Girlfriends of the English national football team. Victoria Beckham, wife of former England captain David Beckham, has been described by the *New Yorker* as the "Queen of the WAGs."

You will also come across gay slang language called Polari. Popularised in the 1950s and 1960s by camp comedy characters Julian and Sandy in the popular BBC radio show

Round the Horne, Polari's origins can be traced back to at least the 19th century. It has now almost died out. Here are a few key phrases:

basket	the bulge of male genitals through clothes
bona	good
eke	face
lallies	legs
naff	bad, drab
omi	man
riah	hair
trade	sex
troll	to walk about (especially looking for trade)
vada	see